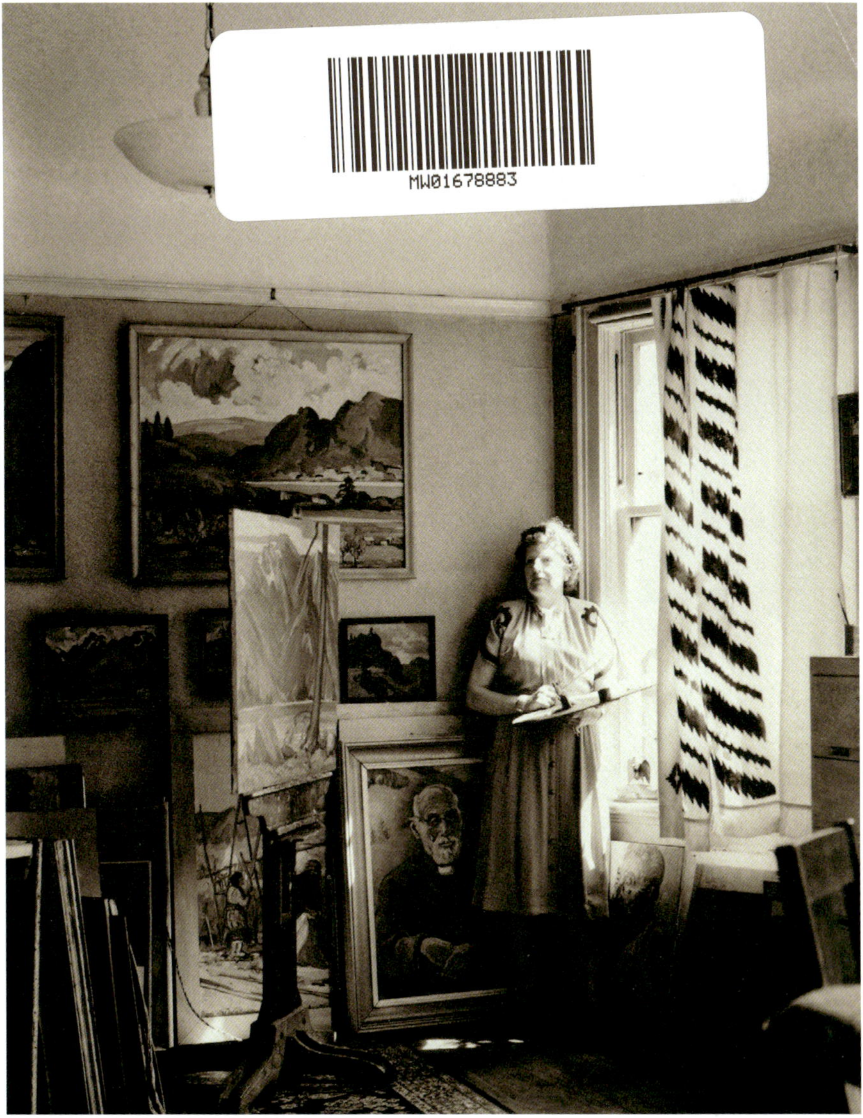

Mildred Valley Thornton in her Vancouver studio, 1771 Comox Street, circa 1944

THORNTON FAMILY COLLECTION, PHOTOGRAPHER UNKNOWN

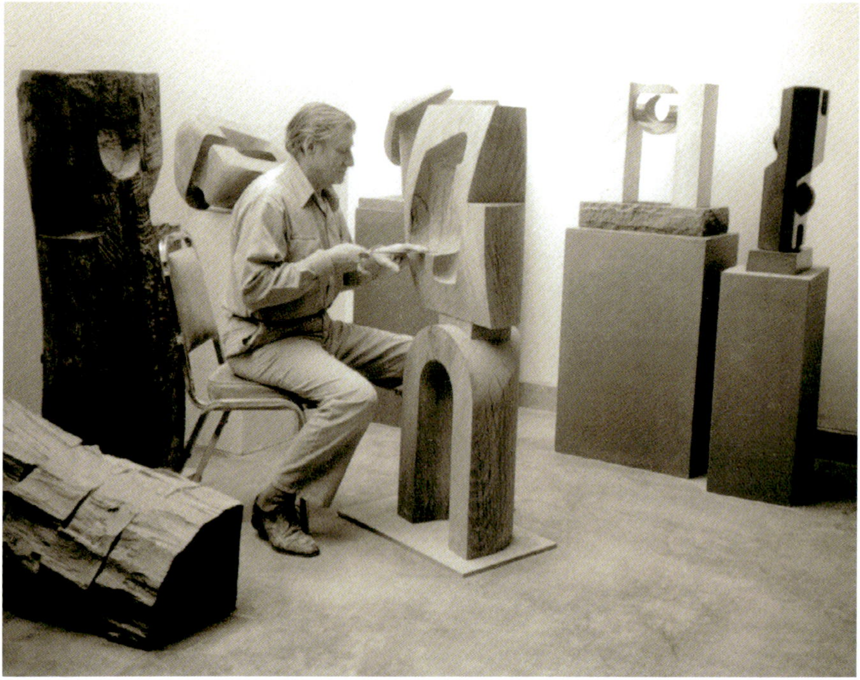

David Marshall carving in his Vancouver studio, circa 1970s

PHOTO COURTESY OF CAREL MARSHALL

A POCKET GUIDE TO

THE UNHERALDED ARTISTS OF BC SERIES

UNHERALDED ARTISTS OF BC

For further information—
All ten books in the Unheralded Artists of BC series feature over 100 colour plates, well-researched biographies, exhibition lists, detailed endnotes and indexes.
8" x 9.5"| Trade paper with flaps | 130-180 pages.

#1 **The Life & Art of David Marshall** by Monika Ullmann
Introduction by J. Brooks Joyner 978-1-896949-44-4

#2 **The Life & Art of Frank Molnar, Jack Hardman, LeRoy Jensen** by Eve Lazarus, Claudia Cornwall, Wendy Newbold Patterson
Introduction by Max Wyman 978-1-896949-02-4
Prefaces by Charles van Sandwyk, Jean François Guimond, Roy Patterson

#3 **The Life And Art of George Fertig** by Mona Fertig
Introduction by Peter Such 978-1-896949-06-2

#4 **The Life and Art of Mildred Valley Thornton** by Sheryl Salloum
Foreword by Sherrill Grace 978-1-896949-05-5

#5 **The Life and Art of Ina D.D. Uhthoff** by Christina Johnson Dean
Introduction by Pat Martin Bates 978-1-896949-13-0

#6 **The Life and Art of Edythe Hembroff-Schleicher** by Christina Johnson-Dean
Introduction by Kerry Mason 978-1-896949-27-7

#7 **The Life and Art of Harry and Jessie Webb** by Adrienne Brown
Introduction by Robert R. Reid 978-1-896949-41-3

#8 **The Life and Art of Jack Akroyd** by Peter Busby
Introduction by Paul Wolf 978-1-896949-43-7

#9 **The Life and Art of Mary Filer** by Christina Johnson-Dean
Introduction by Robert Held 978-1-896949-55-0

#10 **The Life and Art of Arthur Pitts** by Kerry Mason
Foreword by Daniel Francis 978-1-896949-62-8

Order from the publisher, bookstores or on-line.

A POCKET GUIDE TO THE UNHERALDED ARTISTS OF BC SERIES

INTRODUCTION BY MARSHA LEDERMAN

MOTHER TONGUE PUBLISHING LIMITED
Salt Spring Island B.C.
Canada

MOTHER TONGUE PUBLISHING LIMITED
290 Fulford-Ganges Road, Salt Spring Island, B.C. V8K 2K6 Canada
www.mothertonguepublishing.com
Represented in North America by Heritage Group Distribution.

Book Design by Mark Hand.
Editor: Mona Fertig.
Photos: All photos and artwork are from the ten books in the complete Unheralded Artists of BC series.
Printed on Euroart Plus Silk, FSC-Recycled.
Printed and bound in Canada.
All efforts have been made to locate copyright holders of source material wherever possible.

Thank-you to the all the writers, editors, designers, photographers, collectors, artists, galleries, museums, art lovers, researchers, friends and family of artists, special collections, libraries and art history buffs who have contributed to The Unheralded Artists of BC Series.

Mother Tongue Publishing acknowledges the assistance of the Province of British Columbia through the B.C. Arts Council. We acknowledge the support of the Canada Council for the Arts. Nous remercions le Conseil des arts du Canada de son soutien.

Library and Archives Canada Cataloguing in Publication
Title: The pocket guide to the Unheralded artists of BC / introduction by Marsha Lederman.
Names: Lederman, Marsha (Western arts correspondent), writer of introduction.
Identifiers: Canadiana (print) 20200304976 | Canadiana (ebook) 20200305050 | ISBN 9781896949826 (softcover) | ISBN 9781896949833 (PDF)
Subjects: LCSH: Artists—British Columbia—History. | LCSH: Artists—British Columbia—Biography. | LCSH: Art, Canadian—British Columbia—20th century.
Classification: LCC N6546.B7 P63 2020 | DDC 700.92/2711—dc23

Canada Council for the Arts Conseil des arts du Canada

MIX
Paper from responsible sources
FSC www.fsc.org FSC® C103567

Contents

INTRODUCTION

On my first trip to Salt Spring Island, a woman approached me after an event at ArtSpring, and handed me a stack of books. The woman was Mona Fertig, and the books were part of a series she was publishing about British Columbia artists.

The books were beautiful, but I realized, with some embarrassment, that I had not heard of even one of the artists. It must be, I thought, because I was still fairly new to the province. These were not the artists I grew up with.

Not having heard of them, of course, was the point. The series—it was right on the cover—was about the unheralded artists of B.C.

Fertig's passion project has had me thinking a lot about the art that we are exposed to—in public galleries and the school curriculum and the Zeitgeist—and how it gets there. Merit, certainly. You can't argue with the talent of Emily Carr or Lawren Harris. But what is missing from the canon, and why?

Countless artists toil away in obscurity, making magnificent work nobody will exhibit or buy or give them a grant for. And they keep going. Their passion cannot be quelled by the lack of a paycheque or published review. Long after they give up on any possibility of fortune or fame, they are driven by something more authentic.

This is the experience Mona Fertig grew up witnessing in a childhood that smelled of oil paint and rejection. Her father, the artist George Fertig, was a technical master—just look at his paintings. Look at the light! They are incandescent. And yet, the Moon Man, as he was called because of the orbs he painted, never achieved the recognition his work suggests he deserved. The family was uprooted repeatedly, they survived on welfare at times, and George remained an outsider in the Vancouver art scene.

Other artists in this series acquired jobs mowing lawns or serving burgers at White Spot, whatever it took to pay the rent so they could keep making art. "No moolah since last October," Jack Akroyd reported in his journal in February, 1983.

The series was born as Fertig began investigating her father's life as an artist, long after his death in 1983.

"I had his paintings; they were in the closet; everything was in the closet," she told me. Her sister had some others. "And I just thought they deserved to see the light of day, even if it's just a book. A book is a door. That's how it began."

Fertig spent 14 years on this research, but couldn't find a publisher for the book she imagined. So she started her own publishing company, and turned her idea for a book about her father into a series: 10 books about 13 artists.

Jack Akroyd is one of the few artists in this series who achieved more widespread acclaim, with a solo show at the Vancouver Art Gallery in 1975, even if it was part of a small exhibition series called Alternative Space, meant to "allow younger, promising artists an opportunity to show in a public context." I fell hard for Akroyd's surreal, geometric wonders—so detailed and precise, and alive.

Mary Filer, a career nurse, was a pioneer in glass sculpture. Her sharp-edged works burst with emotion—the shards, the colours. Or the stark monochrome. She was also a painter, who created a remarkable mural for the Montreal Neurological Institute and Hospital. Still in its original location, the 1954 work serves as a historical narrative, featuring some of the pioneers of neuroscience, including Hippocrates, and other early influential figures. The patient at the centre and her nurse are both self-portraits—Filer herself.

Jack Hardman made modern sculptures and prints. He was also a charismatic and influential art teacher with an impressive work ethic, waking at 5 AM to make art, before heading to his day job. He once told a reporter that teaching was his hobby, sculpture his profession. I love his 1964 ceramic grouping *Watcha Doin' Mister?* I like to imagine the question coming from a student who grew up to genuinely appreciate art—or perhaps even make it.

There is one painting of Edythe Hembroff-Schleicher's that was instantly recognizable to me: a 1932 oil of Emily Carr, which is in the Vancouver Art Gallery collection. The two women were friends and artistic associates in Victoria; both had gone to Europe to study art (but only met afterward). Hembroff-Schleicher, was an enthusiastic Carr promoter and wrote the book *M.E.: A Portrayal of Emily Carr*. Worthy pursuits, especially when you consider the trouble Carr had earning recognition for much of her life. But it is nice to see Hembroff-Schleicher get some recognition of her own.

"All that I have to say is in my work," LeRoy Jensen once wrote in an artist statement. His work has a lot to say. His paintings, mostly oils, are layered studies in rhythm; so alive they almost seem to move. He returned to the subject matter of mother and child repeatedly, but his later paintings of women suggest a darkness along with an appreciation. I became quite enamoured with his *Copenhagen self portrait*—so different from the work that would come to define him. In the 1948 painting, he is bright and serious, a scarf around his neck and a trench coat tossed over his shoulder. Here was a man who was going places.

David Marshall, the subject of the first book in the series, made large-scale, expressive modernist sculptures that beckon, almost like friends. They look like they would be fun to hang out with. He also made huge inroads in bringing sculpture to the outdoors in the Pacific Northwest. His works are now in a permanent gallery—not in Canada, though, but at Big Rock Garden Park in Bellingham, Washington, just over the B.C. border.

The connection to Europe feels palpable in photographs taken of Hungarian-born Frank Molnar at his Kitsilano apartment, where his paintings are installed, salon style. They are beautiful, but also challenging: the paintings of his wife and muse Sylvia, the vivid landscapes, the blooming flowers, the sensual nudes—which some local audiences were not quite ready for. He still lives surrounded by his work, in his Point Grey house, the world having caught up to his vision.

Like Emily Carr, Arthur Pitts and Mildred Valley Thornton applied their artistic skills to documenting the First Nations they encountered in Western Canada. Also like Carr, they were not Indigenous. Still, they approached their subjects with respect and sensitivity. Pitts's watercolour of *Tommy Paul, Hereditary Chief of Saanich First Nations*, is a fine example, bold and reverent. I feel the same about many of Thornton's portraits—she completed 300 or so, including evocative paintings of Haida, Kwakwaka'wakw and Squamish elders.

Ina D.D. Uhthoff, a key figure in establishing the Art Gallery of Greater Victoria, was a well-known art teacher, as well as an artist in her own right and a single mother. Standouts include World War II era paintings *Girl Welder at Work* and *Factory Scene*. I felt such delight in discovering the *Untitled* work, where stripped trees seem to be crying out for something.

You can imagine artistic curiosity as a magnet drawing Harry Webb and Jessie Hetherington together at the Vancouver School of Art. They married in 1950; a partnership that produced a wealth of artwork: paintings, drawings, collages, linocuts, furniture. It also produced a daughter, Adrienne Brown, who wrote the full-length publication, *The*

Life and Art of Harry and Jessie Webb. The marriage ended, but a rich legacy remains.

This series is in no way comprehensive. Fertig considered other artists, but she was hampered by a dearth of documentation, or couldn't find appropriate writers. You will probably notice the absence of non-white artists. Fertig is aware of this, but had to end the series before she would have liked; it became unsustainable. Like her artists, she had created these books in spite of financial challenges and lack of recognition. Before saying goodbye to the project, she wanted to offer one last shot at bringing these artists to a larger audience with this pocket guide.

Her main criteria included that the artists were working between the 1900s and 1960s and were dead (Frank Molnar was an exception). But there are artists all over this province, right now, producing magnificent work far from the spotlight that is worthy of our attention. Find some—even one—if you can.

MARSHA LEDERMAN
Vancouver, 2020
Western Arts Correspondent for *The Globe and Mail*

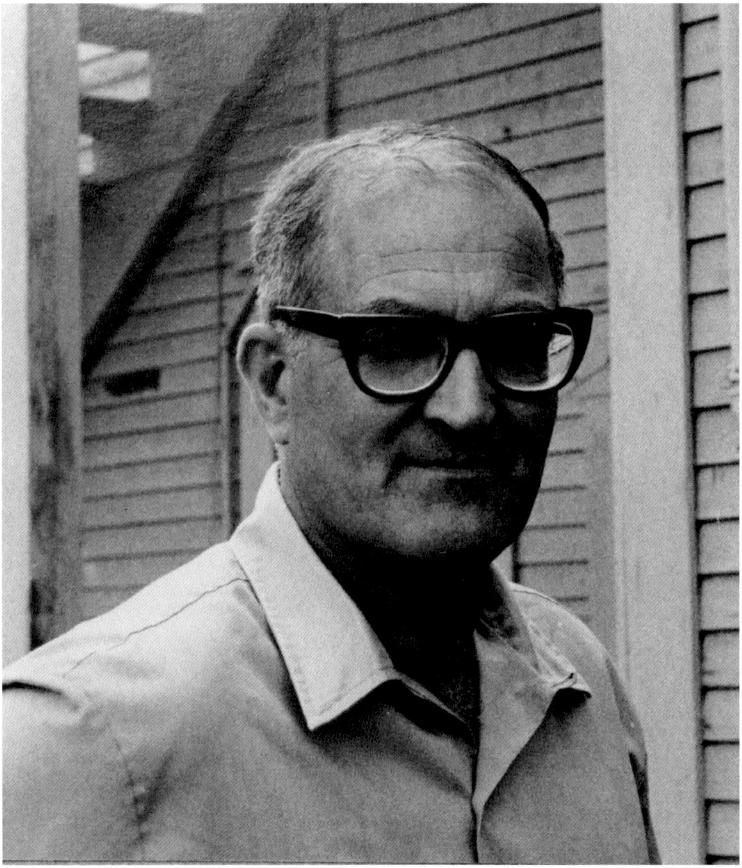

Jack Akroyd

1921-1996

"Jack Akroyd may be the most interesting Vancouver artist you've never heard of. Working during the second half of the 20th century in a mostly figurative fashion, he was a bit out of step with the times. He was neither a modernist nor a postmodernist, his illustrative imagery, precision of line and meticulously rendered detail revealing something of his background as an engineering draftsman. Although he was dedicated and prolific, he remained mostly outside the established art scene."

—ROBIN LAURENCE, ART CRITIC, THE GEORGIA STRAIGHT

Born in Halifax, Yorkshire, in 1921, Jack Akroyd (pronounced Ake-royd) was raised in Swindon, in the south of England. As a child, he was passionate about Scouting and camping and filled several books with sketches narrating and illustrating his adventures with gusto.

He attended the Commonweal, an academic school, but Jack wanted to study art. His parents were dubious and enlisted the art teacher to support them:

> My mother went to Mr. Nethercott's house to ask him about my going to an art school. "Madam," he declared. "Don't put your son into Art. Put him in an honest trade!"

So, at sixteen, he became an engineering apprentice, like his father before him. At night school, he studied the theory of steam engines, mathematics and drafting.

That was followed by five years' war service in the RAF, two of them in Canada, which inspired him to immigrate in 1948 to Toronto.

ART SCHOOL

In 1949, the Ontario College of Art (OCA) opened its doors to Jack, and he found himself amongst a vibrant group of about twenty-two talented students, including William Kurelek, Graham Coughtry, Richard

Williams and Rosemary Kilbourn. Of special interest, given the directions his life would later take, was the fact that two of Jack's classmates were Japanese Canadians born in Vancouver: Betty Mochizuki, who became a well-known painter, and Shizuye Takashima, who would later write and illustrate *A Child in Prison Camp*, about her three years in the Japanese internment camp in New Denver, B.C., during World War II.

Akroyd spent four years studying under Carl Schaefer and J.W.G. Macdonald and training in drawing and painting. Schaefer had studied under Group of Seven members Arthur Lismer and J.E.H. MacDonald, and taught egg tempera; "[he] showed us how to hold an egg and take the whiting away and roll the yolk in your hand and pop the little sack that it's contained in and how to use that alone as egg tempera, or add oil to make an oil tempera."

Jack and David Young (his roomate) did experiments together, "grinding colours on a glass plate and mortar, making linseed oil, putting it out in the sun and boiling it and doing all sorts of things." They were aware of the rich tradition of egg tempera in Renaissance art and amongst Flemish painters like Bosch.

J.W.G. (Jock) Macdonald concentrated on teaching abstraction. In 1953, he was instrumental in forming Painters Eleven. For a man of Jack Akroyd's temperament, abstraction was never an option.

THE WEST COAST

After graduating in 1953, Jack moved west, living for a short while in Nanaimo. One drawing from that time shows a man lying on a bed in a bare room, with Jack's words on the back: "What I felt like during my first winter in Nanaimo." There he met two local artists, David Denbigh and Gino Sedola, who would become lifelong friends.

In 1954, he moved to Vancouver, taking a job in the drafting office of the engineering firm Phillips, Barratt & Company. His new colleagues included a friend from art school days, Jack Dale. He collaborated on the Overlanders Bridge in Kamloops, designing the commemorative pylons at each end and making their forms. Jack continued to pursue his art and submitted work to the B.C. Artists annual exhibitions at the Vancouver Art Gallery for 1955, 1956 and 1957.

In early 1960, Phillips Barratt had to lay off some draftsmen. For Jack, this was not a disaster but an opportunity. He would travel to Japan, an experience he called "the highlight of my life."

JAPAN

Jack "had more or less made up my mind to quit and travel" even before losing his job. And it is clear he'd done his homework. He knew what he wanted to see and where and why. He knew about Japonisme, the obsession with Japanese art and culture in the late 19th century. Young people were starting to read D.T. Suzuki and Alan Watts, and Zen Buddhism was in the air. And there was David Denbigh. His son Brian recalls conversations in their Nanaimo home with Jack fascinated by Denbigh's tales of his boyhood in Japan.

That journey proved life-changing, emotionally—through an ill-fated love affair with the mysterious Emiko. He had met her in Kyoto and fell in love after several dates. He asked her to consult her parents about marrying. But her parents didn't want her marrying a foreigner and going off to live in Canada. They wanted a daughter who would look after them in old age. On Jack's 2nd trip to Japan he was all set to marry Emiko, but when the day dawned she never showed up. Her father had forbidden it, again, and proceeded to marry his daughter to someone else. Jack was devastated. He never forgot Emiko. For years after the affair, the image of a slim, dark-haired woman would appear mysteriously in his paintings, in various guises.

Akroyd travelled extensively throughout Japan and kept detailed journals. He felt a deep affinity for Japanese culture, the landscape, temples, ceramics and the art. The country profoundly affected his perspective and iconography, and he developed his signature style, a visual diary, combining detailed images of his daily life and his inner world in witty juxtaposition. Jack returned from his first trip broke but inspired.

AN ARTIST IN VANCOUVER

When he returned, Jack found an apartment at 2144 Yew Street in Kitsilano, in a row of former storefronts with high ceilings that was perfect for artists' studios. The sculptor Paul Huba, at 2146, was busy doing commissions for the new downtown post office on Homer Street: the sixteen-foot-tall *The Postman*, carved from red granite. The British art provocateur Robin Page and his wife, Cleone, lived at 2142. The sculptor Gordon Dixon and his wife, Nanon, were at 2144. His friends Jack and Greta Dale lived at 2132.

Jack ate and slept in the back and worked at the front window and began supporting himself part-time by fixing kilns for schools and potters. He also assisted sculptors by building maquettes, making decorative ceramic bricks, constructing armatures and producing sgraffito on church walls. Later he was an assistant to sculptors George Norris and Elek Imredy. His many Vancouver friends included painter George Fertig, sculptor David Marshall and newcomers to Yew Street, artist Frank Molnar and his wife, Sylvia.

In 1967, Frank and Jack started a tradition that would last for twenty years. Each spring, they set off in Frank's car, heading for Kelowna to sketch the apple, peach and plum blossoms in the orchards around the lake. Frank still cherishes the memory of these trips and recalls the pure white of the cherry blossom above the yellow-gold carpet of dandelions. "There were micro-climates," he explains. "We figured out when each was going to blossom, and get there at the right moment. The light up there is so different from the West Coast."

Egg tempera was Jack's favourite medium, especially for painting landscape. He was attracted "to its finished patina, and to its inherent beauty, durability, and historical resonance." The medium required endless patience, which Jack had, being a methodical man, with strict routines and work habits. "Jack drew and painted almost like a labourer," Frank says. "No matter whether he was inspired or not. He'd get up, work on some painting or drawing. Then lunch—cheese sandwich, no ketchup, no mayo—then back to work.

EXHIBITIONS AND LATER YEARS

When Paul Wolf and his wife moved to Ottawa, they opened Artists West, a gallery in their home, and put on a show every six months. All the participants were outsider artists from British Columbia, including David Marshall, David Denbigh, Peter Paul Ochs, George Fertig and Frank Molnar, as well as Jack. Artists West sold well in excess of 100 of Jack's paintings, drawings and *plein-air* sketches between 1969 and 1979.

In 1975, Jack had an important show at the Vancouver Art Gallery. He was fifty-four years old. It opened in March with thirty-six works that included extravagant titles: *Contrasts along the River of Life*, *don't believe in what you see on television* and *We will believe in Flying Saucers when the sky turns purple*. Jack felt it was "great to see them up on the wall, never had that many together before." Clear, dream-like, surreal: these words are a useful shorthand for much of Jack's work.

In 1976, the Burnaby Art Gallery appointed a new director, artist Jack Hardman. He came to his job with the intention of presenting B.C. artists, "especially those who hadn't had the exposure they deserved." He phoned Jack and organized a solo exhibition starting June 1, 1977. Fifty-one works in egg temperas, gouache, pen and ink, and Prismacolor. Writing to Paul Wolf afterwards, Jack admitted that "one feels very naked with one's inner feelings put up on a wall"—an interestingly candid comment given his usual public position that his paintings were "meaningless."

In February 1983, Jack reported in his journal, "No moolah since last October." Six months later, "Haven't sold anything since May." Fortunately, he still had the kiln maintenance work, which paid $5 an hour.

Five years later, he was unexpectedly invited to have three solo exhibitions in Japan, in Toyko, Fukui and Sakata. The sixty-four works he brought to Japan included examples from many eras. Jack owed his thanks to a new admirer, the Japanese art critic Toru Sunouchi. Jack's three shows were big news there.

Eventually almost a hundred works would find a home in Japan. Jack was now an international artist. He came home, and no one noticed. These three shows were to be his last major exhibitions.

In 1986, angina was diagnosed. In 1988, he moved near City Hall. He would paint on the dining table, when his health allowed. In 1996, age seventy-five, he died of a heart attack on a city bus.

Jack left no will. Brian Batsford, his good friend from Phillip, Barratt & Company days, became his artistic executor. Paintings were donated to the Vancouver Art Gallery; others were sold over time. The only asset, $20,000 from the paintings sold in Japan, was donated to the Commonweal School in England towards the Jack Akroyd Award for Artistic Excellence.

Jack Akroyd's work is held in the following public collections. Canada: Burnaby Art Gallery, Vancouver Art Gallery, Canada Council Art Bank, British Columbia Art Bank. Japan: Homma Art Museum, Sunouchi Collection at Miyagi Museum of Art. England: Richard Jeffries Museum.

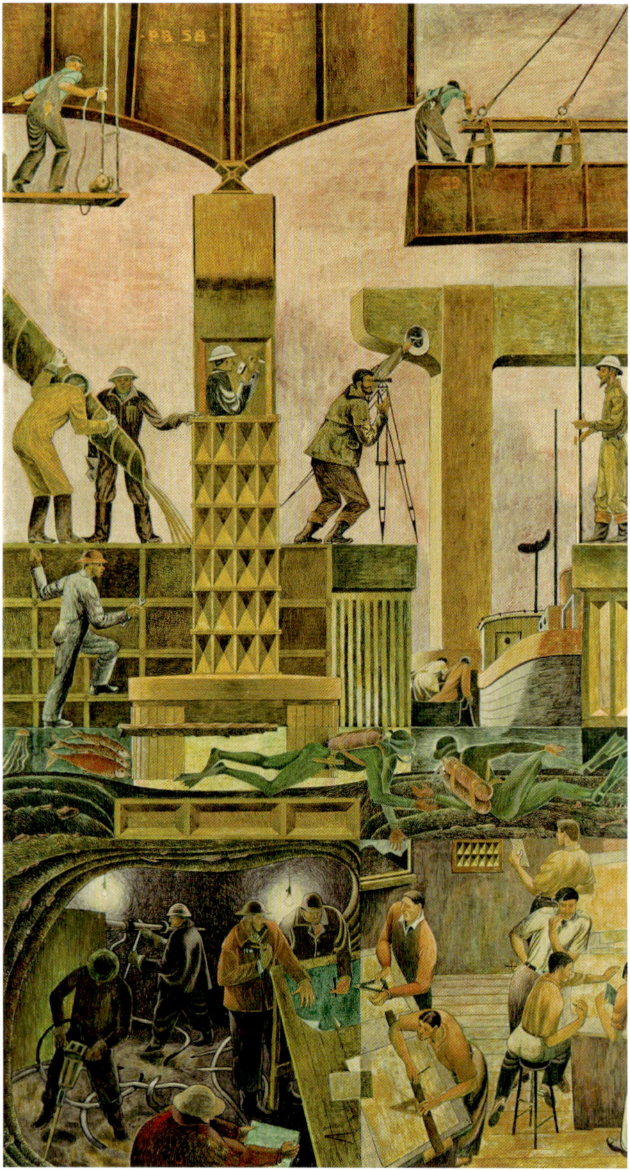

◄ Jack Akroyd, *Untitled* (Overlanders Bridge), 1958, egg tempera on board, 28" x 15"

PRIVATE COLLECTION
PHOTOGRAPHY BY
INGEBORG HARDMAN

► Jack Akroyd, *Sculptor and Assistant*, 1962, graphite on paper, 19" x 14"

PRIVATE COLLECTION,
PHOTOGRAPHY BY
FRANCIS SULLIVAN

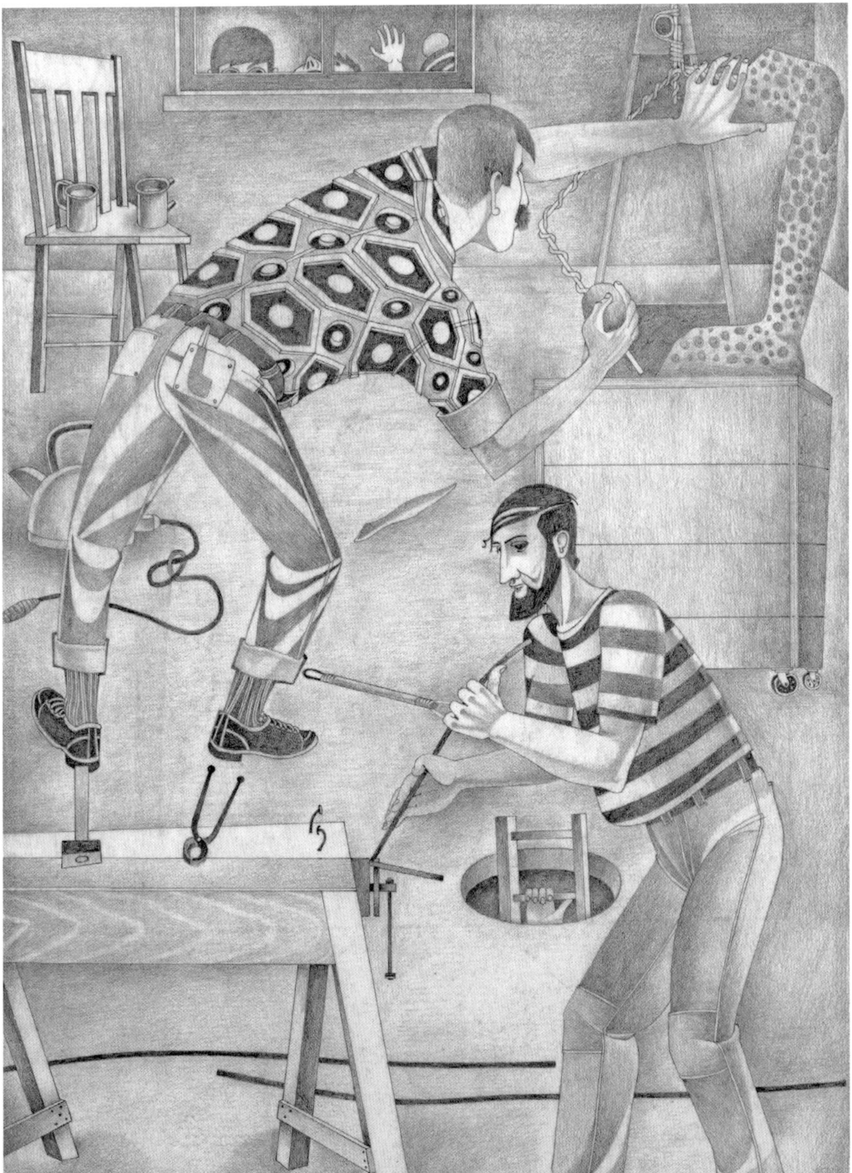

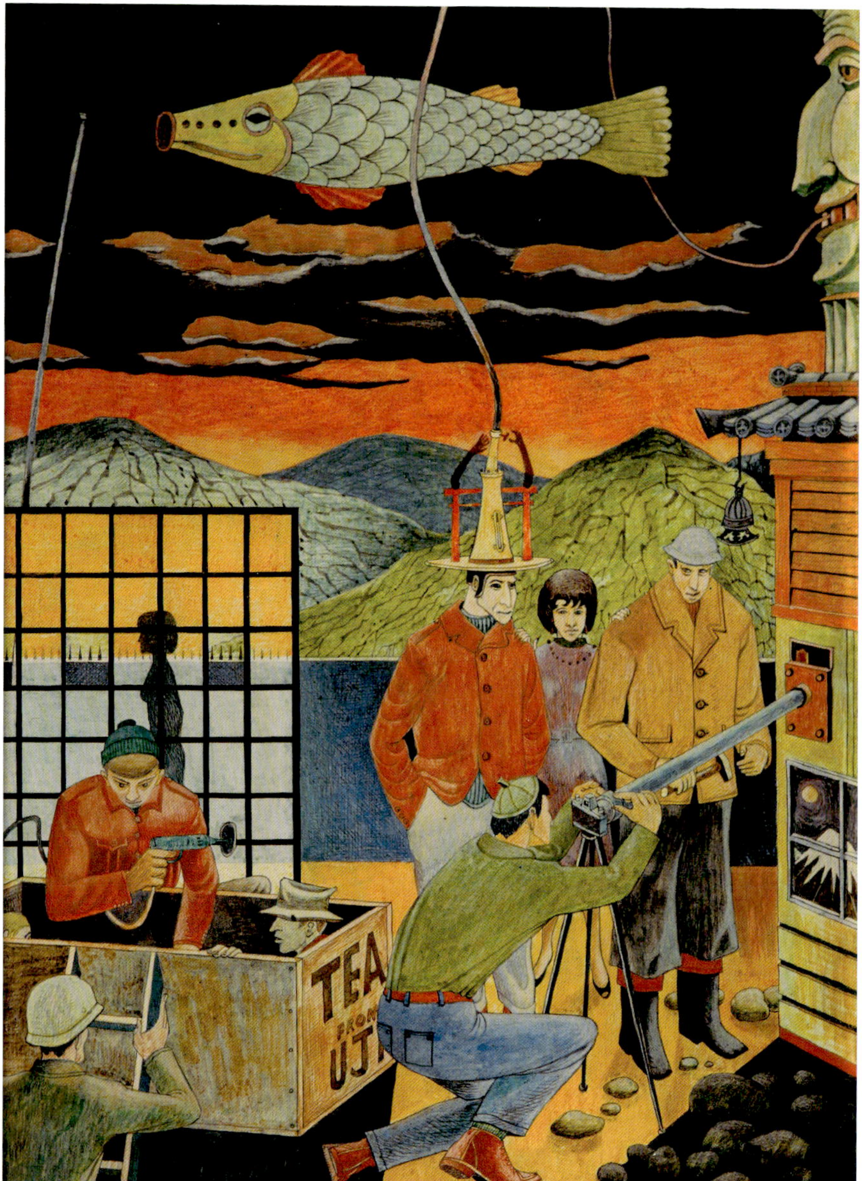
TEA

◄ Jack Akroyd *Tea from Uji*, circa 1964, egg tempera, 15" x 11"

VAUGHAN COLLECTION
PHOTOGRAPHY BY INGEBORG HARDMAN

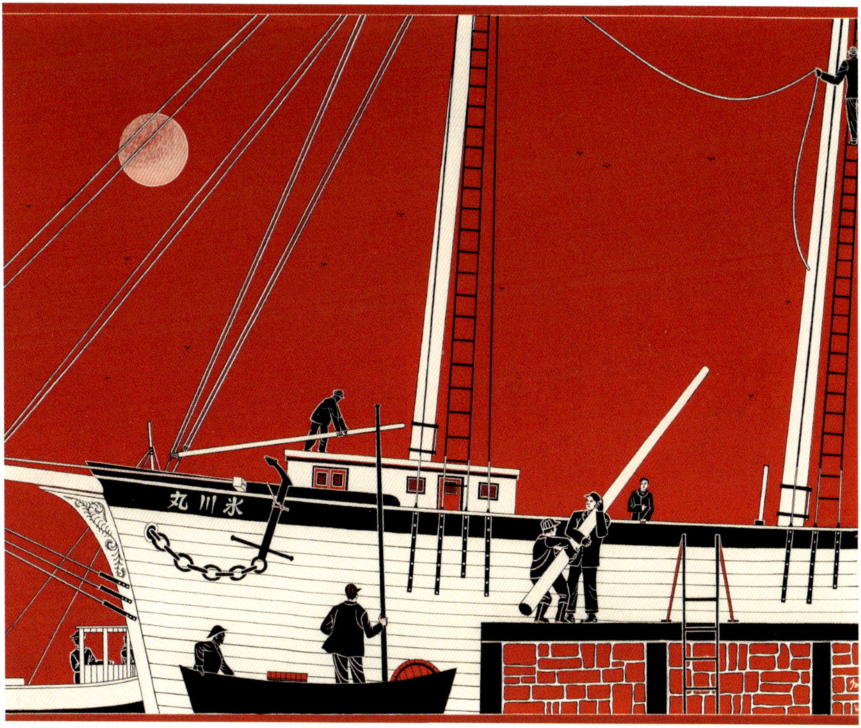

Jack Akroyd, *Red Card/Japanese Training Ship*, 1969, gouache on red card, 22" x 28"

WOLF FAMILY COLLECTION

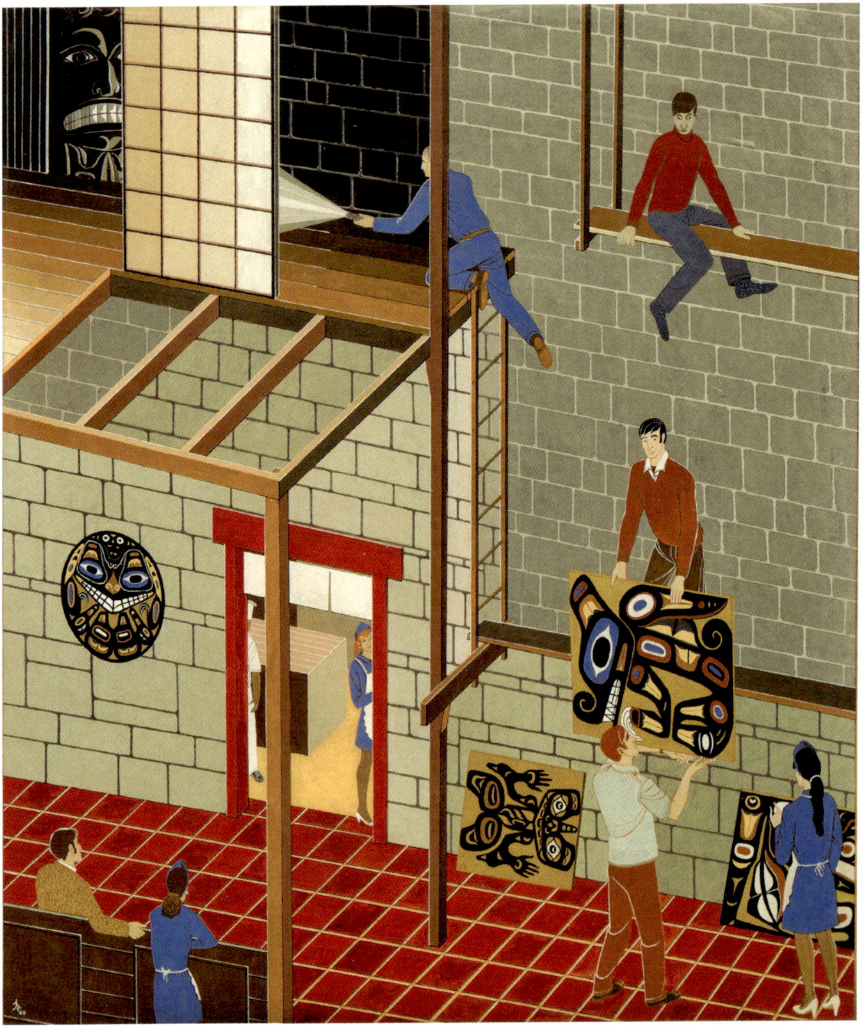

▲ Jack Akroyd, *First Nations Art Show at the Bay*, 1969, gouache, 32" x 27"

HUBA FAMILY COLLECTION,
PHOTOGRAPHY BY INGEBORG HARDMAN

► Jack Akroyd, *Life Story*, 1967, mixed media, pencil, crayon, gouache, 44" x 24"

PRIVATE COLLECTION

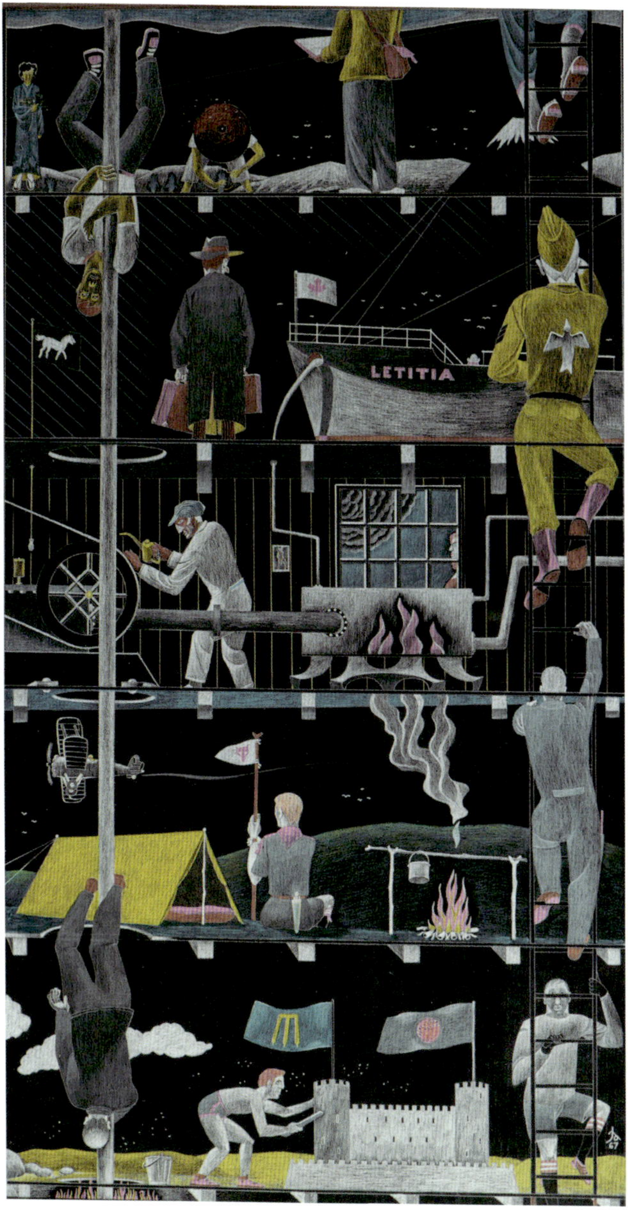
LETITIA

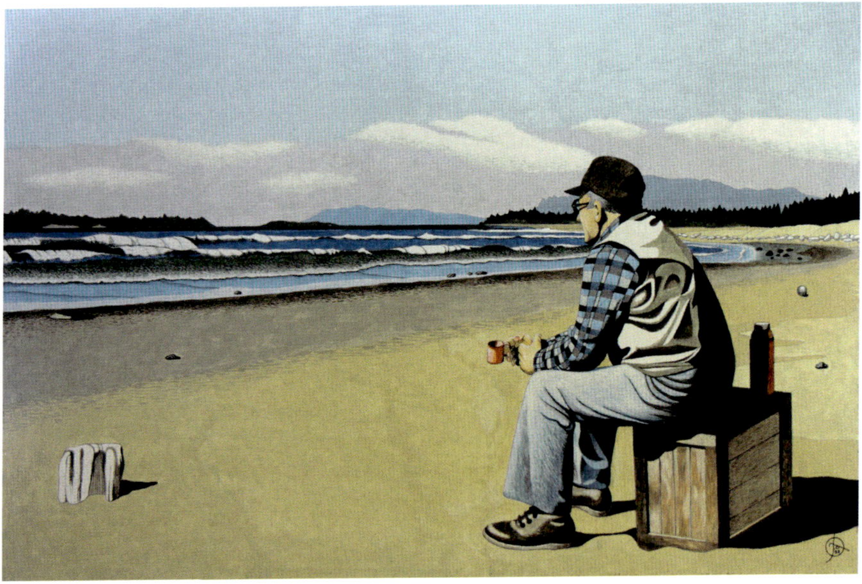

Jack Akroyd, *Florencia Bay, B.C.*, 1993, gouache, 26" x 17"

SALT FAMILY COLLECTION. PHOTOGRAPHY BY RODNEY SMITH

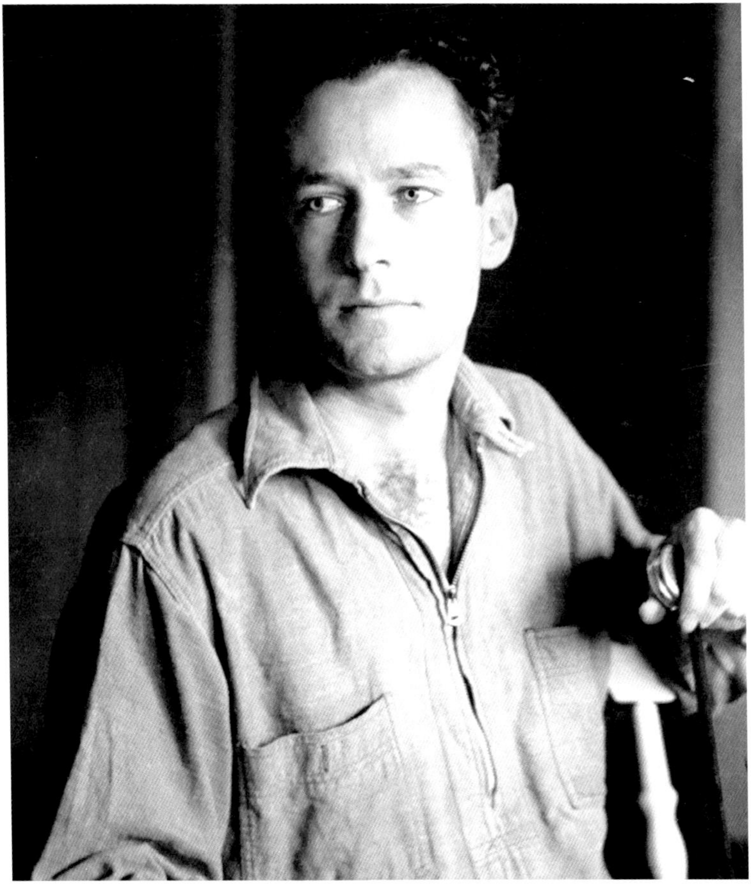

George Fertig

1915–1983

"Spiritually inspired and meticulously crafted, Fertig's paintings seek to challenge each viewer to contemplate the relationships that exist between time and space and the subjects he has chosen to represent."
—DARRIN MARTENS, FORMER DIRECTOR/CURATOR OF THE BURNABY ART GALLERY

George Thane Fertig was born in Carmangay, Alberta, on December 6, 1915. His father, George Samuel, was a horseman of German descent, and his mother, Joy Grace (nee Faulkner), was educated and from the US. When Thane was two, his father was a prisoner of war for over six months in a work camp in Banff National Park for so-called enemy aliens, and his mother moved to Edmonton with the three children. Their situation improved in the 1920s until Thane's father lost both his ranch and his Edmonton house in a poker game in 1926. Homeless, they moved to Rossland, B.C., close to work in Trail's smelter. His father hated it there, so he returned to Alberta to work as a hired hand. During the Great Depression, hundreds were laid off and bread lines were everywhere. George Samuel's sudden death in 1932 made the family destitute. Thane, a teenager, found refuge in literature and studying calculus till "he couldn't take it anymore" and suffered a nervous breakdown. Five years later, Thane and his mother returned to B.C. where he worked at the smelter. He became interested in photography then "because he still had that creativity in him."

PHOTOGRAPHY, TRAIL AND THE UNION

In 1939, Thane and his mother moved in with his sister, Bazle and her family in Fruitvale. They lived on a farm and grew wheat and oats, had cows, chickens and bees and a huge vegetable garden and apple trees. Thane loved taking pictures of the countryside with his Kodak Brownie. Photography brought him peace and hope. At twenty-four, he began to paint in oils and built a dark room.

World War II broke out in 1939. Thane, a union member and pacifist, stated "war and killing was obscene." His prior breakdown made him ineligible to fight. He continued working at the smelter, then expanding due to the war effort, which contributed to developing the atomic bomb through the Manhattan Project. In 1941, George (Thane) was fired and left Trail. As Joe Jankola said, "Boy, I tell you, they had the police hunting out these guys and anyone that was involved with the union. George was told to get out of town or else."

A NEW LIFE: VANCOUVER AND THE ART SCENE

George Fertig, at twenty-six, arrived in Vancouver and saw the ocean for the first time. It would remain a constant in his paintings. He found work at Jeffree and Jeffree's aeronautical and electrical shop on Homer Street, in military and civil projects, and attended night school at the Vancouver School of Art. George met John Ahrens, who then worked with him for six years on batteries and aircraft engine starters. John and his wife operated Ahrens' Books in the West End for thirty-six years, specializing in politics and literature.

George entered paintings in the Annual B.C. Artists Exhibitions at the Vancouver Art Gallery (VAG) in 1943, '44, '47, '48, '49 and 1950. Other exhibitors included Jane Billaux, Lawren Harris, Joe Plaskett, Mildred Valley Thornton, Charles H. Scott and hundreds more. During this era, the VAG held popular juried exhibitions that any artist could enter, budding or experienced. Its policies, egalitarian at best, supported the plethora of local artists (600 in 1949) in ways that were considered naïve and unprogressive by the 1950s.

After the war, George, interested in Mexican mural renaissance and socialism, travelled to Mexico for three months. There he met the "big three" muralists: Diego Rivera, José Clemente Orozco and José David Alfaro Siqueiros. He liked Mexico; "the people treated him well, but he saw a lot of poverty there which he didn't like." He also made a trip to New York City and Toronto to examine the art scenes there.

In 1948, George moved to a caretaker's cottage on the West Vancouver waterfront, as a gardener for a wealthy couple. There he continued painting and taking photographs, inspired by the landscape and flora. "He was a beautiful painter," stated an artist from that era. George was influenced by Fred Varley, Gauguin, Van Gogh and Cezanne. He moved back to the West End in 1949 and met and fell in love with the outgoing Evelyn Luxa, who was ten years younger. She lived at the downtown Y, worked as a receptionist and also attended night school at the Vancouver School of Art. In August 1953, they got married in Seattle and moved into a suite across from the beach in Kitsilano. In 1954, their first daughter, Mona, arrived, and in 1957, their second daughter, Moana.

THE MOON MAN AND CARL JUNG

Marriage and the birth of his daughters profoundly changed George's art. Not only did he paint *The Conception* but he began a series of huge canvases using "fabulous pinks and mauves and oranges"—moons and oceans, and depictions of the cosmos. He became deeply fascinated with Carl G. Jung, who emphasized understanding the psyche through exploring the worlds of dreams, art, mythology, religion and philosophy. Morris Graves, an American artist living in La Conner, Washington, became an important influence also. There was a strong connection between the West Coast painters and the Seattle modernists. George sought Graves out, occasionally taking the bus to visit him. As sculptor David Marshall, George's good friend, said:

> George recognized someone who had a similar kind of spiritual attitude and definite sense of connection with certain aspects of

> Chinese painting. Both were intense, serious, self-taught young men, intolerant of pretension and lovers of quiet and solitude. Both felt an affinity to Eastern philosophy and the concepts of Carl Jung.

Graves believed that one's own fulfillment derived from *not* being integrated with humanity; whereas George believed the greatest hope lay in the process "by which a person integrates unconscious contents into consciousness, thereby becoming a psychologically whole individual."

In 1956, George wrote Jung about his paintings and sent some photos of them. He received a reply:

> Thank-you for your pictures. They are quite interesting. You depict what happens when a cosmic superhuman light appears in the heavens and becomes visible to the earth. The earth bursts forth in flames, plants, arms of octopuses, serpents and the raised arms of the adorati moved by their inner passion. Good luck to you!

George was so delighted that he read the letter to his friends. LeRoy Jenson said, "It wasn't just a question of him being inspired and absorbing Jungian symbology, they had a parallel way of viewing the world. George was a person who lived completely in his inner world, and the external world was secondary to him."

In 1957, the Roman Gallery on Howe Street gave George a solo exhibition. He was now known as the "Moon Man." Painting titles included *The Moon Egg, The Pink Moon, The Blue Moon, Sea Demons, The Wave in the Trees*. This exhibit was one of the highlights of his life.

FRIENDS, POLITICS, LATER YEARS

George and other Vancouver outsider artists were no longer accepted by the VAG exhibition committee, and not many other galleries were available. George had quit work at the sawmill and was painting full-time while Evelyn worked at the *Vancouver Sun*. He hung some pictures at John Ahrens' bookshop and at the Gallery of BC Arts across from Stanley Park. They spent time with their daughters at Kitsilano Beach and knew the local artists, including Peter Paul Ochs, Jock Hearn, Jack Akroyd, Frank Molnar, Frederick House and Paul Huba.

In 1964, the family rented a house in Burnaby, and George built a pottery wheel and small one-pot kiln and made raku pottery as a relief from the intensity of oil painting. Glazes were an obsession; he loved the formulas and alchemical process. He was inspired by Wayne Ngan's early work, and pots also found their way into his paintings. He had six exhibits at the Gallery of BC Arts. In Ottawa, Fertig exhibited at Artists West, Paul Wolf's home based gallery. He did not charge the artists the usual 33% commission and would often pay for shipping. Wolf remembers, "No lightweights bought George's paintings."

Money was tight, and when Evelyn quit work after decades of supporting the family, they received social assistance. They discussed everything about art together, from the colour of paint, texture and size of canvas, shape of images, placement of signature as well as the meaning of reflected and metaphysical light and so on. Theirs was a deeply symbiotic relationship.

Bitterly disappointed that after working for years as a serious artist he still had not had any serious recognition, he burnt some large paintings. Abraham Rogatnik, co-owner of the well-known New Design Gallery in the 50s, said in 2007, "You see, I remember the artists [of that time], and those that got to show their work, they were aggressive. And obviously George was not aggressive."

George wrote a Manifesto for the Arts in 1973, titled *Proposals for a More Just Relationship Between the Establishment and the Artist*, which was sent to the Arts Access Steering Committee. David Marshall wrote a paper too. They hoped for change under the new arts policy of the NDP government. Sculptors Peter Paul Ochs and David Marshall got on the committee for purchasing a provincial art collection and kept George informed. But insularity and nepotism in the provincial art world, once again, prevailed, benefiting the usual suspects: eight works by Jack Shadbolt were purchased for $12,722, nine by Gordon Smith for $6,055, nine by Maxwell Bates for $4,360, $6,000 for Ian Baxter's plastic "joke shop"—636 works of art for $260,867. George Fertig was informed of the committtee's decision to exclude his paintings, even before the jury met.

After this last effort, at the end of 1975 he retreated into his art, struggling with depression and anxiety. Every week, he would visit David Marshall or his good friend Alan Hawthorne, and they would have in-depth discussions about art, quantum physics and alchemy, the cosmos and creativity. In 1976, George had the first of three heart attacks. The following year, Jack Hardman, invited him to participate in the Burnaby Art Gallery's 10th Anniversary Exhibition. The twenty-three exhibitors included; Alistair Bell, Molly Bobak, Frances Faminow, Lawren Harris, Jock Hearn, Vera Mortimer-Lamb, Grace Melvin, Joe Plaskett, Jack Shadbolt, Gordon Smith and Takao Tanabe. In 1977, George Fertig had his last exhibition at the Surrey Art Gallery. In 1983, he passed away suddenly in the Burnaby apartment he and Evelyn had just rented. He was sixty-eight and had completed some of his most beautiful and meditative paintings. Marshall said, "George really was a person who was very perceptive about art, and I really missed it when he wasn't here anymore looking at my work."

George Fertig's work is held in private collections and at the Burnaby Art Gallery.

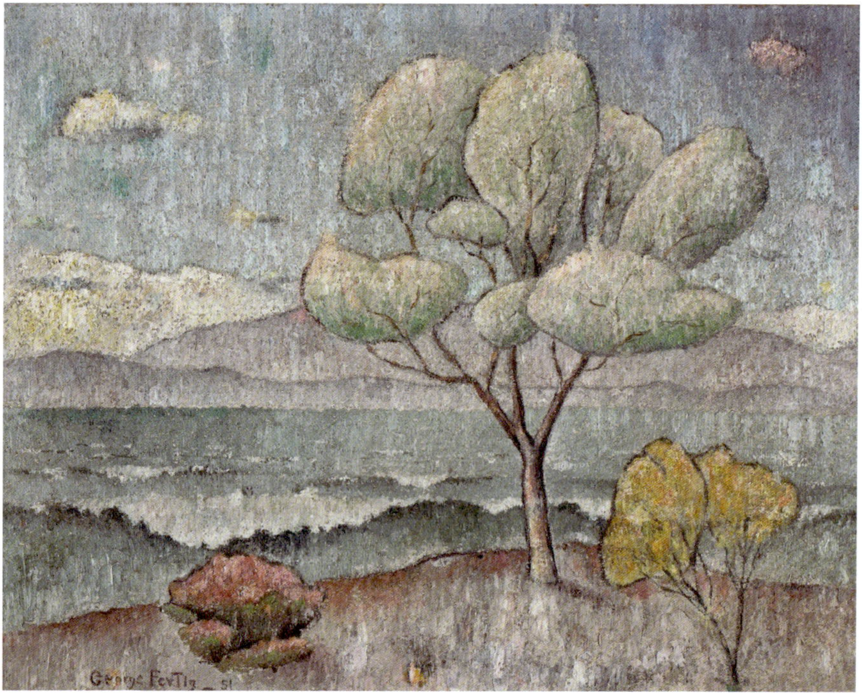

George Fertig, *Untitled*, 1953, oil on board, 20" x 9 ½"

PRIVATE COLLECTION
PHOTO BY JANET DWYER

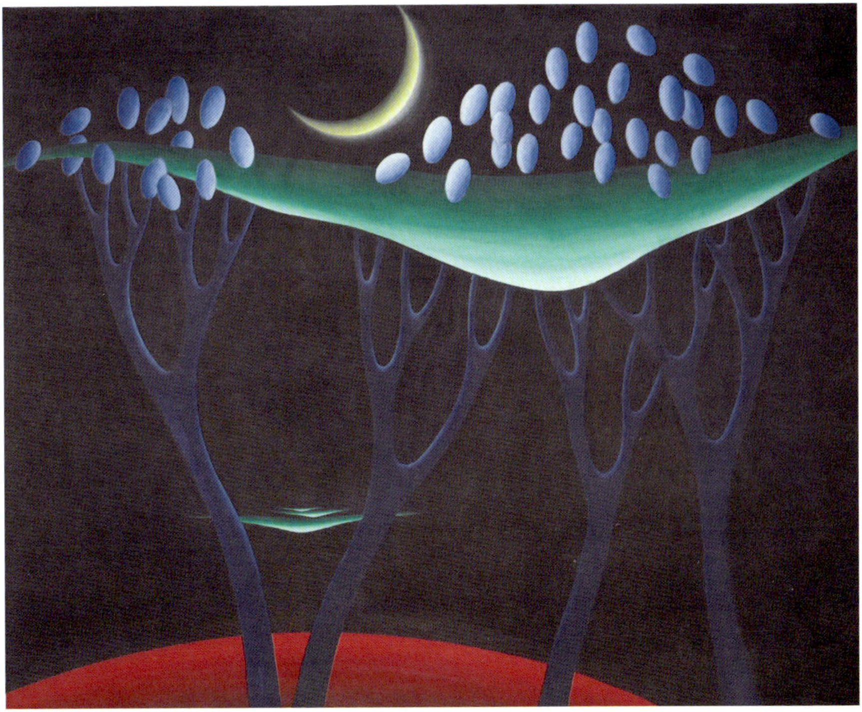

George Fertig, *The Wave in the Trees*, circa 1950s, oil on canvas, 55" x 75"

PRIVATE COLLECTION
PHOTO BY JANET DWYER

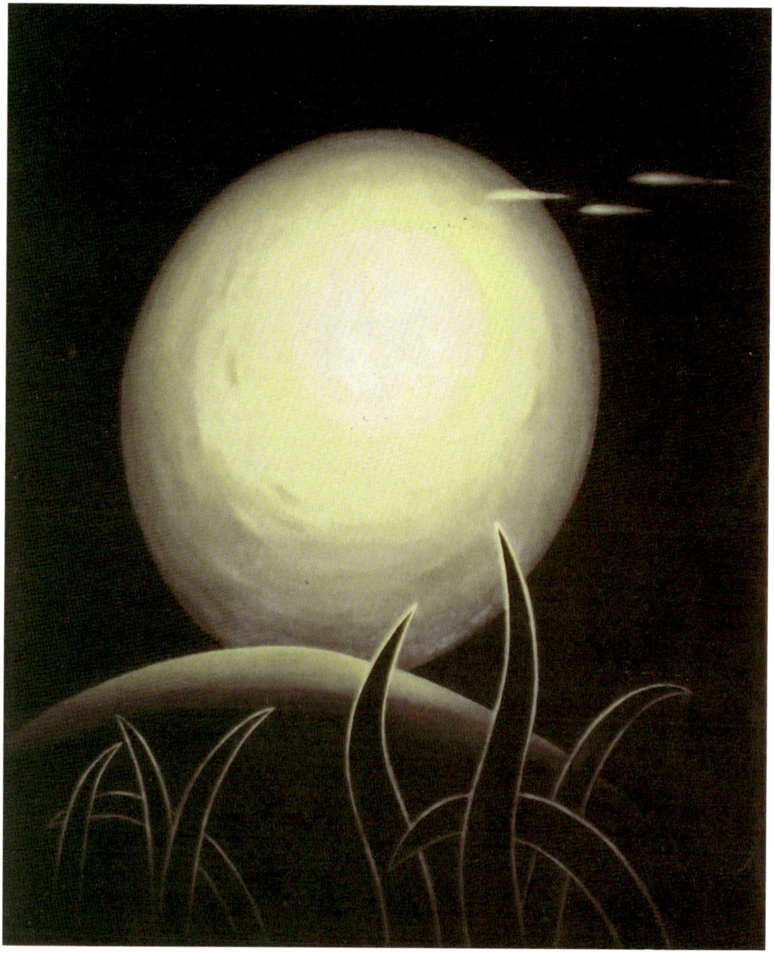

▲ George Fertig, *Moon Egg*, 1954, oil on canvas, 42 ½" x 36"

SAXBY PRIVATE COLLECTION

➤ George Fertig, *Alchemy*, 1966, oil on board. 32" x 18"

MARSHALL PRIVATE COLLECTION
DAN FAIRCHILD PHOTOGRAPHY

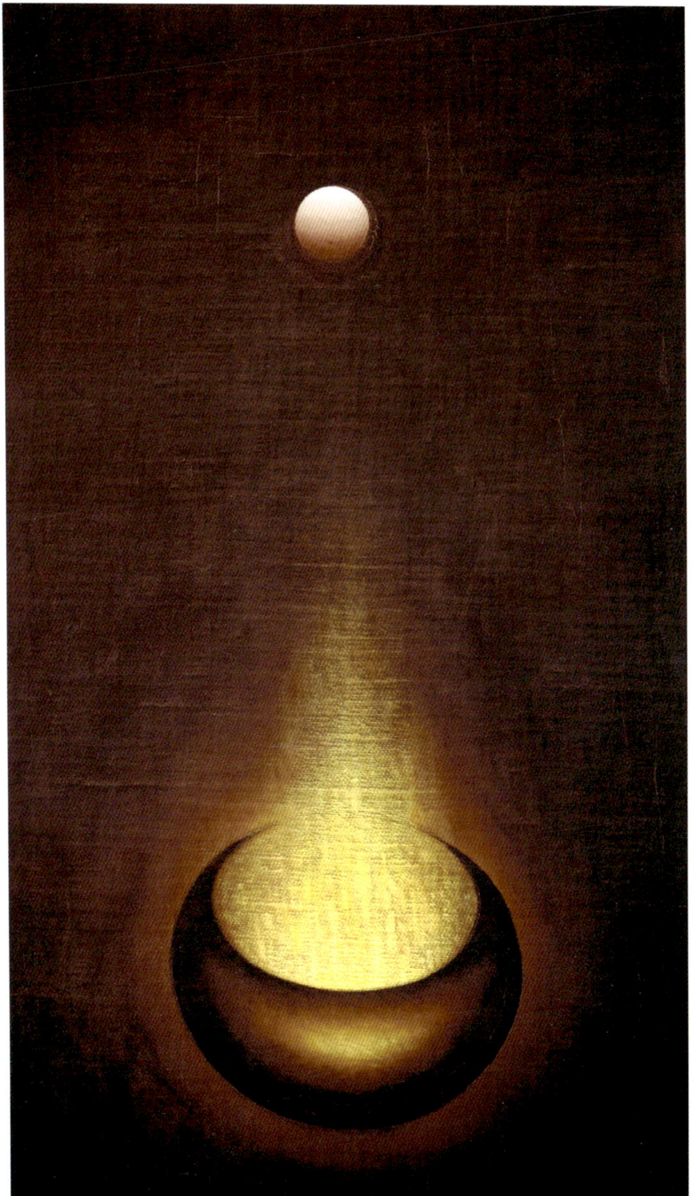

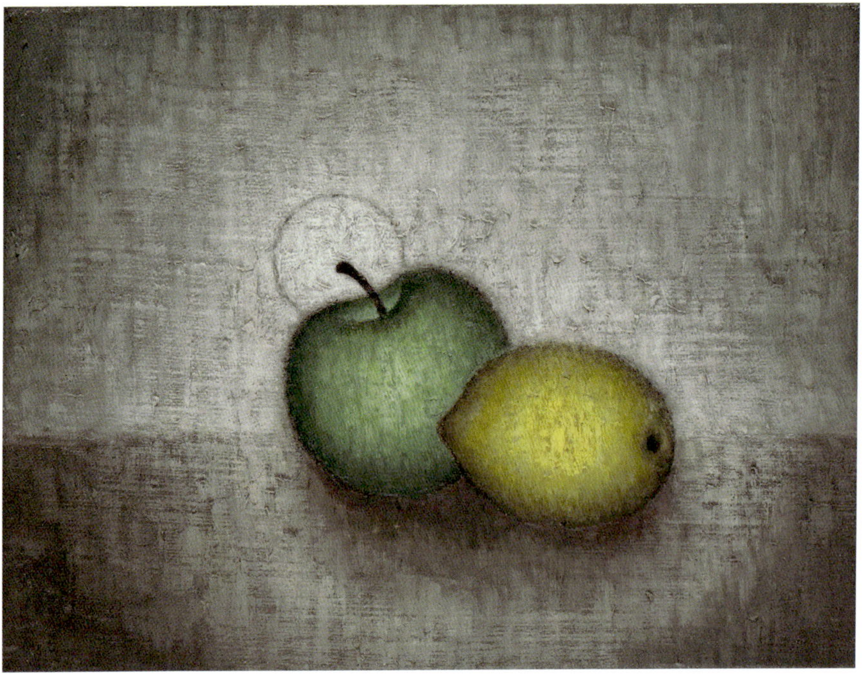

▲ George Fertig, *Untitled*, 1979, oil on board, 11" x 14"

PRIVATE COLLECTION
PHOTO BY JANET DWYER

➤ George Fertig, *Untitled*, 1982, oil on canvas, 36" x 28"

PRIVATE COLLECTION
PHOTO BY JANET DWYER

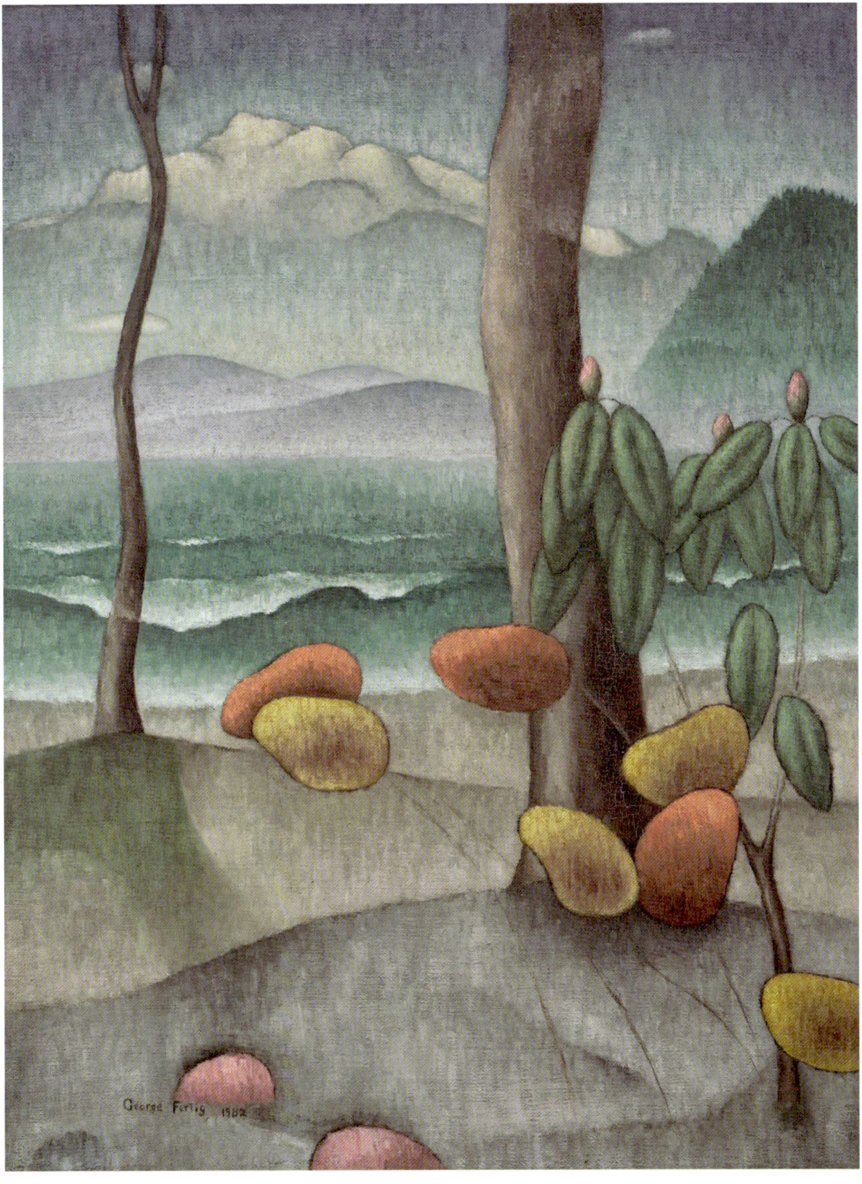
George Fertig 1982

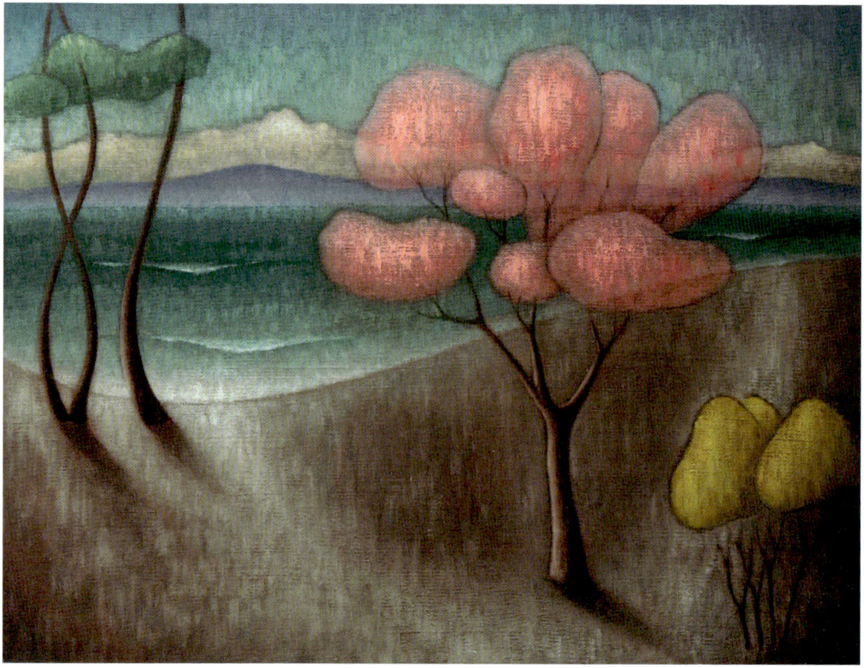

George Fertig, *Untitled*, 1982, oil on burlap, 30" x 38 ½"

PRIVATE COLLECTION OF MOANA FERTIG
DAN FAIRCHILD PHOTOGRAPH

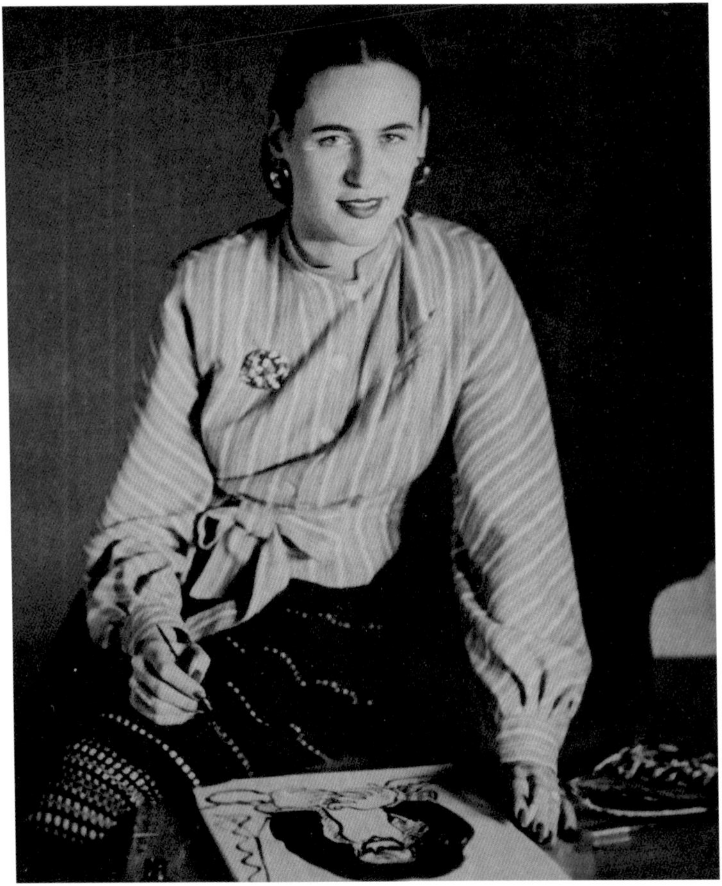

Mary Filer

1920–2016

"Over the years, I have interviewed and critiqued many women artists, mostly painters, and I don't think there is one who doesn't long for the visceral experience of wrestling plastic media: glass, metal, clay and wood, the provenance of men. For Filer, a woman with the physical and mental requisites to pin recalcitrant media to the mat, opportunity lay in her alliance with urban planner Harold Spencer-Sales, the colleague who eventually became her husband. Together they changed the conversation about public art and ensured that Filer, already a respected painter and teacher of art, had the exposure she deserved and the financial freedom to release colour that floated in real space"

—LINDA ROGERS, THE ORMSBY REVIEW

Outstanding as a youth in music, drama, visual arts and academics, Mary Filer was born in Edmonton in 1920 and grew up there and in Regina. By graduation, her gift for drawing and painting was clear, and after further studies at the Balfour Technical School, she was awarded the Special Prize in Art. However, World War II intervened, and she veered from her artistic passions to a practical career in nursing, training at the Regina General Hospital. At her 1944 graduation, she received the Dr. David Low Memorial Medal for General Proficiency, as well as the Prize for Medical Nursing. Engaged to an Air Force pilot, Mary seemed to be on track for a traditional women's career and marriage, but then life took a sharp turn.

MONTREAL: ARTIST AND EDUCATOR

Through friends, Mary was introduced to Albert Gillson, thirty years her senior, who shared an interest in art, and with his return to chair McGill University's Mathematic and Physical Sciences Department, he had connections attractive to an ambitious Mary. Inspired, she left the prairies, took a train to Montreal and soon broke off her engagement. She did post-graduate work at the Montreal Neurological Institute and Hospital

(Neuro) and nursing work with Dr. Wilder Penfield's surgical team doing pioneering epilepsy treatment. Mary also continued to draw and paint, and by 1945 she began exhibiting with the Canadian Society of Graphic Artists, the Canadian Society of Painters and the Art Association of Montreal, with Arthur Lismer of the Group of Seven informing her that she had won a scholarship for its course at the museum. She joined the Federation of Canadian Artists, exhibited frequently, most notably in the 1947 Canadian Women Painters exhibition that included Emily Carr, juried by A.Y. Jackson and Marian Scott.

Mary also began giving talks and teaching art, working under Arthur Lismer, eventually becoming teacher-in-charge at a children's art centre. She took classes at McGill, where John Lyman was another significant teacher. The university was inaugurating a degree in Fine Arts, initiated by Albert Gillson, as Dean of Arts and Sciences. In 1950 Mary received McGill's first Bachelor of Fine Arts and began teaching full-time there. Her exhibitions included a solo show at the West End Gallery and one with Ghitta Caiserman and Eldon Grier at the Montreal Museum of Fine Arts (MMFA). Despite her teaching wages and sales, all was not easy, even with her father's and Gillson's patronage. In July 1952, Mary went public about making a living as an artist: "It's almost impossible for a non-commercial artist to survive in Montreal unless he owns a magic money bag or can find a job doing something else." She emphasized the importance of her career as an artist over expectations for women: "If a woman is an artist, she [should be] an artist before she is a woman."

PENNSYLVANIA AND NEW YORK

By 1952 Mary ascertained that art education would be a more solid career and began a master's degree at Pennsylvania State College under esteemed art educator Viktor Lowenfeld. He inspired her teaching with the idea that art was not just the privilege of a gifted child but a vital means of expression, contributing to the total growth of any child. Along with teaching and researching child learning, Mary became an accomplished muralist, inspired in part by Sybil Emerson, a Penn State professor. To complete her masters, her graduate project wedded her nursing experience with her artistic skills, creating the detailed and immense mural, *The Advance of Neurology,* at the Montreal Neurological Institute. It depicted the perceptions and treatments of the brain from ancient Greek times through Western medical advances to the work at the Neuro, with a team led by Dr. Wilder Penfield operating on a patient, Mary. After teaching at Penn State for a few years, she took a more challenging job in 1955 as a professor of Art Education at New York University's School of Education, joining Howard Conant and colleagues. It was near Washington Square in a city alive with galleries and schools developing new trends—colour field, abstract expressionism, action painting, pop art, op art, constructivism, primary structure and environmental sculpture. Initially stimulated and happy with the job, exhibition opportunities, the milieu of ideas and a marriage to a Spanish graduate student at Columbia, by 1956 she struggled with overwhelming debt and a dissolving personal life.

ENGLAND AND THE ADVENT OF GLASS ART

Resigning from her job in New York, Mary escaped to the U.K. and settled near Hyde Park in London to focus on creative work and museum studies. To overcome her loneliness, she bought an apricot French miniature poodle and dyed her hair to match. By 1957 she was exhibiting with the Royal Society of Painter-Etchers and Engravers and at the National Society's annual exhibition. A solo show through the Finsbury Art Group featured elaborate woman and poodle images. With her new glamorous looks and organizational skills to invite important movers in the art world, she made quite a splash. She set up her own base, Pomona Studios, and expressed her personal take on the world with imaginative and more abstract images, emphasizing emotional and physical sensations with exaggerations in colour and proportion. Through the new Blue Cross Animal Hospital in Grimsby, she revived her skills in murals. Inspired by the new Coventry Cathedral and its baptistry windows by John Piper and Patrick Reyntiens, Mary traveled to France to learn a new medium, "crystopal," a process of fibreglass, resins and plastics incorporated with colour, which she used for windows on her first church commission at St. Luke's Anglican Church in Essex. With her brother and his family, she moved to Goldenhurst Manor in Ashford, where she had her own studio and residence and found the Kent countryside a rich source for painting and sketching, creating windows and other interior work for churches. Ever resourceful in marketing, she frequently exhibited in the U.K. as well as at a 1961 solo show at her former haunt, the MMFA.

RETURN TO CANADA: MONTREAL AND VICTORIA

Love would again steer Mary into a different direction. While in Montreal, she reconnected with Harold Spence-Sales, a professor of architecture at McGill. In 1969 she moved to Montreal and, through Harold's connections in architecture and development, was commissioned to do glass art for the Plaza Côte-des-Neiges shopping centre, as well as a Portfolio of Drawings of McGill Buildings and workshops for the Acadia Handicrafts Guild on Prince Edward Island. However, the west coast beckoned, and the couple moved to Victoria in 1970, setting up a downtown studio where Mary's cold glass work took off, including commissions for Christ Church Cathedral, Roberts House and St. Phillip's Anglican Church. Mary identified this phase of her life with "vitality." Her first Canadian solo exhibitions were held at the

Art Gallery of Greater Victoria in 1973 and at the Shaw-Rimmington Gallery in Toronto from 1975 to 1979.

VANCOUVER APEX OF GLASS ART WORK

For a highly social and creative couple, Vancouver with its vibrant arts and commercial life was an obvious magnet. After moving there in 1977, they were often the hub of many projects and social events. Mary's first solo exhibition there was at the Burnaby Art Gallery in 1979, but many of her shows were at Janak Khendry's Glass Art Gallery in Toronto. By 1982 they were in an iconic home—the old Purdy's chocolate factory—renovated with two studios and living/dining space where they traditionally served martinis and with stunning views of False Creek, downtown Vancouver, the mountains and ever-changing sky. Their home was featured in *Western Living* and was labelled, "hard-edged, urban, and highly intellectual." The couple married in 1983 and continued to travel and exhibit widely. Nationally and internationally, Mary was seen as the "godmother of the glass art scene," especially with the B.C. Glass Arts Association.

Harold and Mary collaborated on a number of commissions, notably a large glass sculpture for the entrance concourse of the Simon Fraser University Harbour Centre (1989), and in 1991 both were awarded Honorary Doctor of Law degrees. The sculpture at SFU was a visual allegory about the energy and influences of the universities upon the city's centre, with the mountains in the background, the promontory of Spanish Banks and Howe Sound balancing the horizontal and vertical grids of impact. It was 14' x 18' x 6', a triptych of multi-layered, laminated and bolted paneled glass and steel sculpture that would represent "the great primordial frontier." Art critic Robin Laurence stated it was, "a culmination, to date, of their collective wisdoms–technical, formal and philosophical. An elegant testimony to a vision that is both practical and utopian, analytical and poetic." Renowned landscape architect Cornelia Oberlander assessed it as "outstanding!" In 1992 Mary received the Royal Institute of Architects of Canada Allied Silver Medal from nominator and architect Abraham Rogatnick:

> The subject is light. Light as material. Light that is capable of being shaped, sculpted; light as an architectural material. [I spent] many enchanted hours in Mary Filer's studio, hours which have wafted me into a crystal world of glistening structures alive with light which they have snatched and gathered from the air, radiating, refracting, reflecting, dappling, glittering, glowing…

In 2005 Mary was at her apex with presentation as an Elected Academician of the Royal Canadian Academy of Arts.

Mary accumulated a lifetime of achievements and over 160 group and solo exhibitions across Canada, the U.K., Europe and elsewhere, as well as work held in leading art museums and gallery collections. Yet she has not had a major retrospective, seen by many as the crowning glory for any artist. Robin Laurence stated in the *Georgia Straight* in 2002, "[This] is a condition that seems to relate as much to the ghettoizing of glass art as to the tendency of contemporary curators to overlook senior women modernists." Mary passed away at 95 in January 2016.

Mary Filer's work is held in public collections in Canada at the Art Gallery of Greater Victoria, Art Gallery of Ontario, Burnaby Art Gallery, Confederation Art Centre, McGill University, Canadian Clay and Glass Museum, Montreal Museum of Fine Arts, Montreal Neurological Institute, National Gallery of Canada, St. Paul's Hospital, Simon Fraser University, University of Regina, Vancouver General Hospital; Gallery Oldham, Towner Art Gallery in England; Pennsylvania State University.

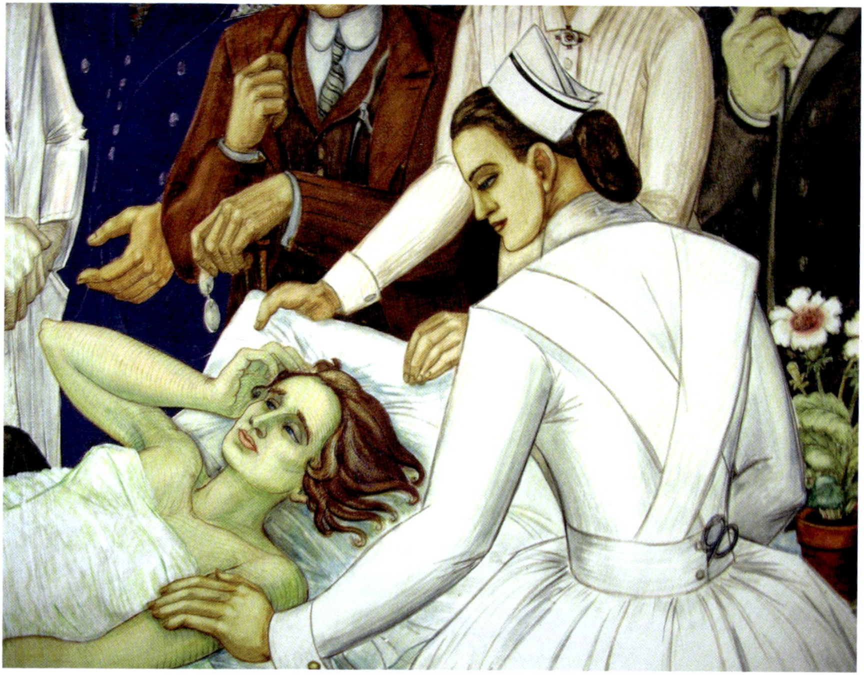

Mary Filer, Detail of *The Advance of Neurology*, mural, 1954, egg tempera on plaster, 21" x 6'7"

PHOTOGRAPHY COURTESY OF THE MONTREAL NEUROLOGY INSTITUTE AND HOSPITAL

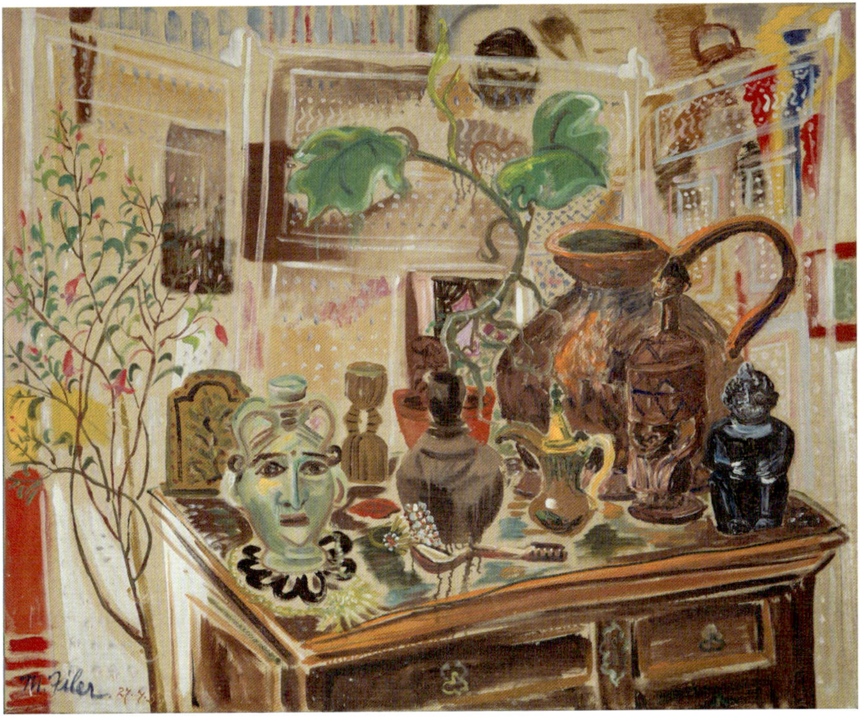

Mary Filer, *Bureau Still Life*, 1958, oil on linen, 30" x40",

GIFT OF THE ARTIST, VANCOUVER GENERAL HOSPITAL AND UNIVERSITY OF B.C. HOSPITAL FOUNDATION ART COLLECTION, PHOTOGRAPHY BY INGEBORG HARDMAN

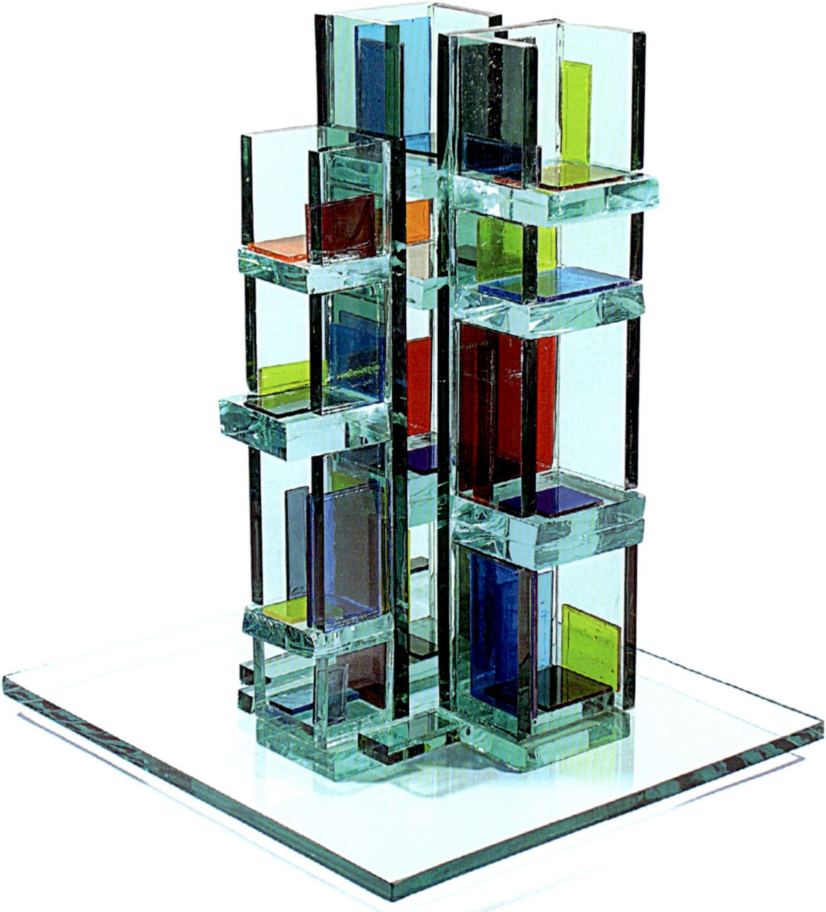

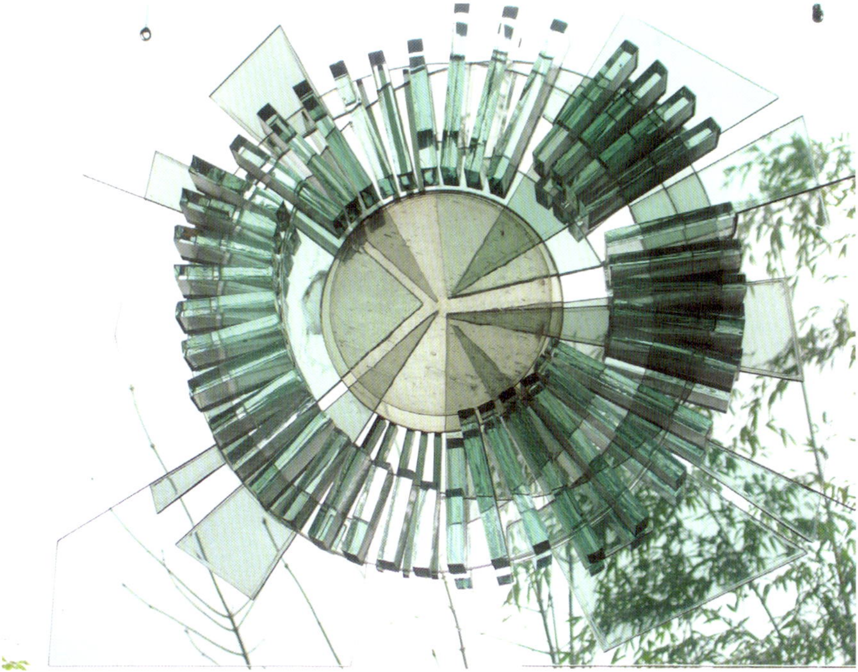

▲ Mary Filer, *Cosmos Form II*, n.d., laminated flat glass, 17 ½" x 19" x 4"

PRIVATE COLLECTION
PHOTOGRAPHY BY HAROLD SPENCE-SALES

◄ Mary Filer, From *Urban Geometry Series*, 1982, laminated float and antique glass, 15" x 13" x 12"

PRIVATE COLLECTION
PHOTOGRAPHY BY M.E. LINARDIC

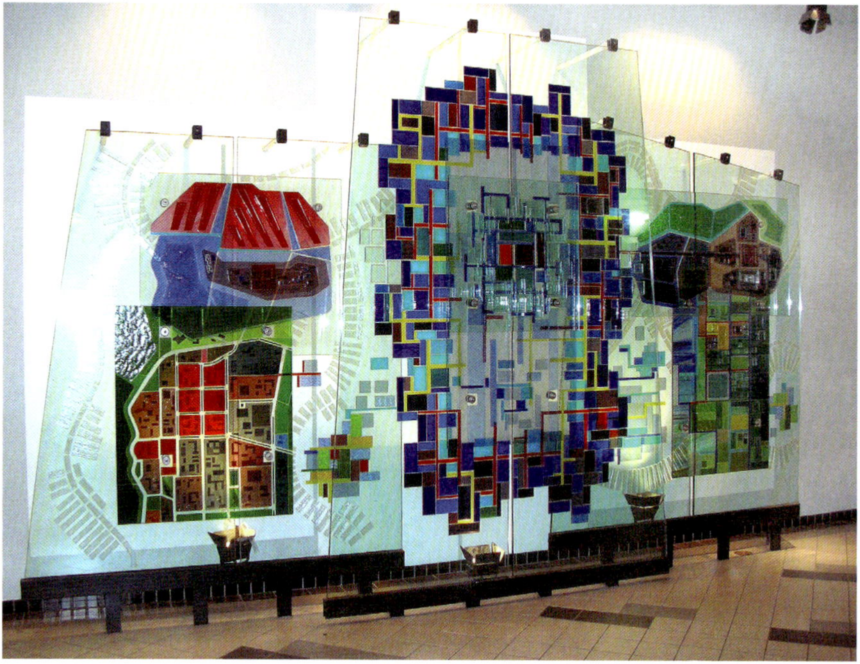

Mary Filer, *Untitled*, 1990, laminated float, coloured antique and textured glass with steel supports, 14' x 18' x 6'

GIFT OF THE ARTISTS, MARY FILER AND HAROLD SPENCE-SALES
TO SIMON FRASER UNIVERSITY (DOWNTOWN CAMPUS)
PHOTOGRAPHY BY M.E. LINARDIC

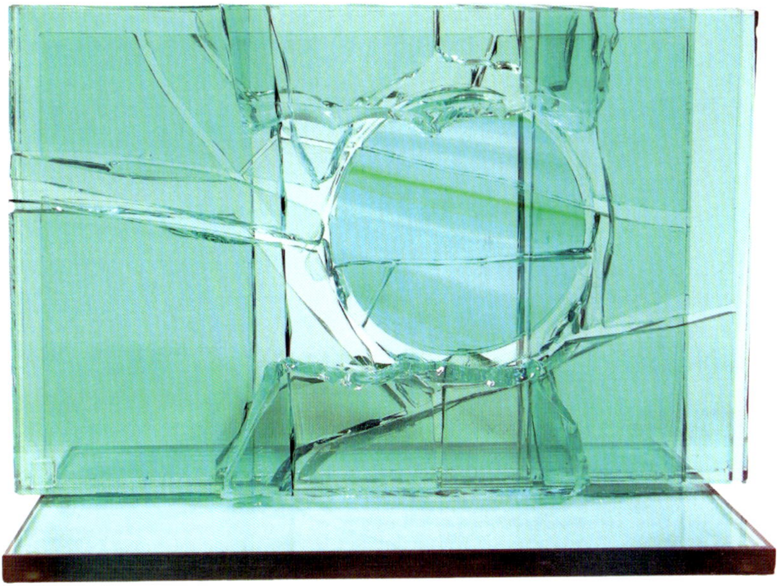

Mary Filer, *Partial Adventures in Space 1*, n.d., laminated and antique clear and shelled float glass, 14 ½" x 22" x 13 ½"

PRIVATE COLLECTION
PHOTOGRAPHY BY M.E. LINARDIC

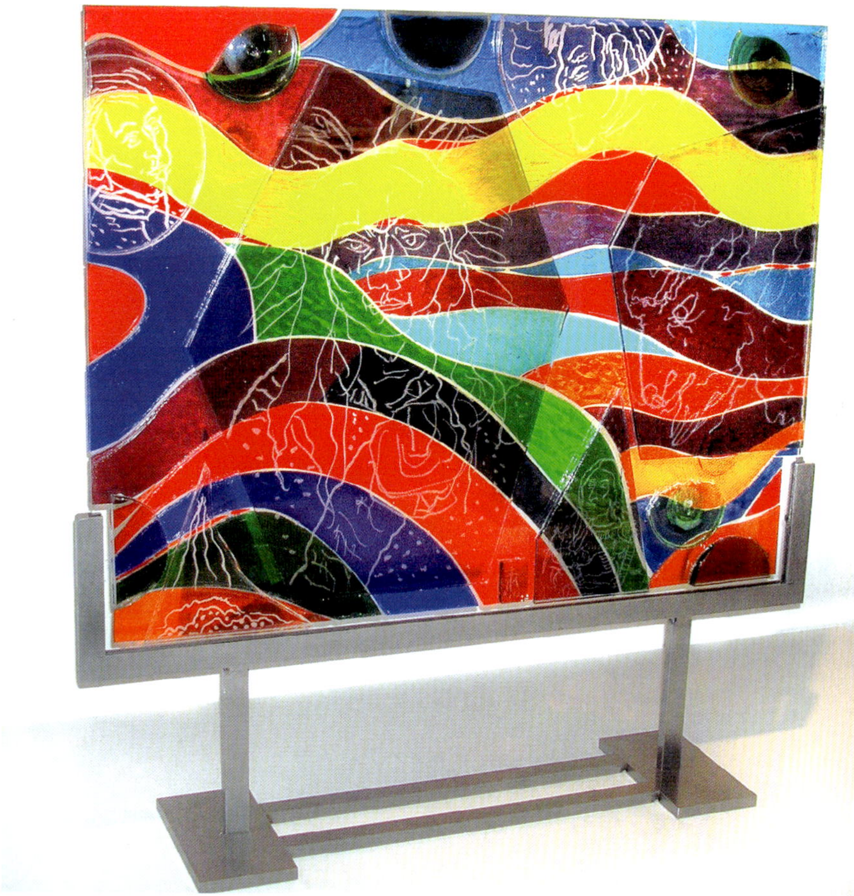

Mary Filer, *Spirits*, 2005, laminated float, coloured and etched glass, 27" x 17" x 12"

PRIVATE COLLECTION
PHOTOGRAPHY BY M.E. LINARDIC

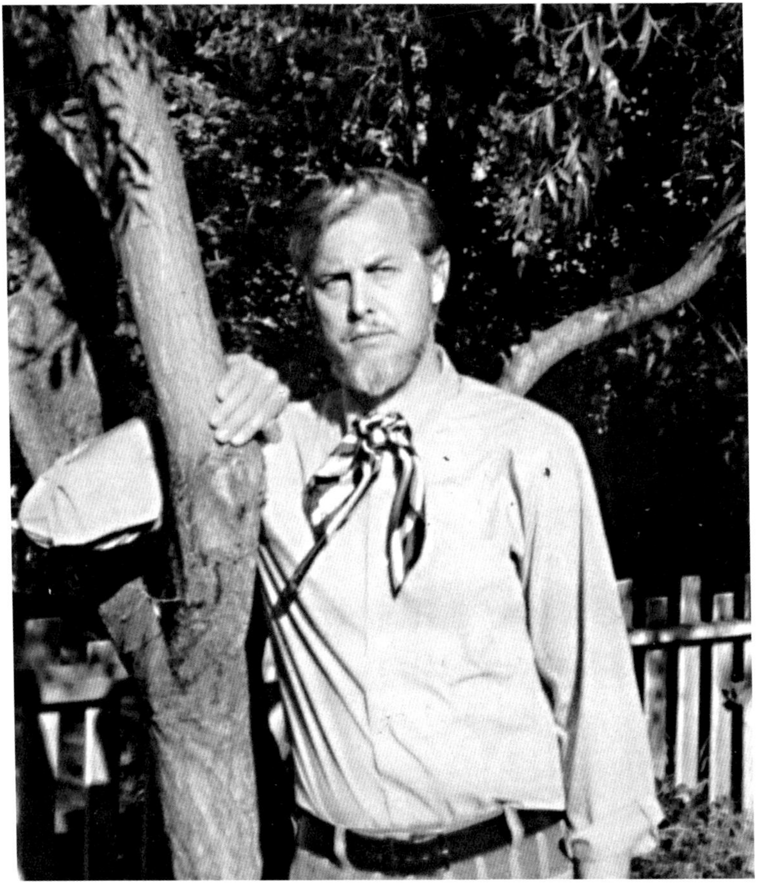

Jack Hardman

1923–1996

"I remember Jack selecting exceptional exhibitions for the Burnaby Art Gallery. Perhaps his professions of artist and art teacher groomed his curatorial acumen, enabling him to appreciate distinctive creativity. These exhibitions demonstrated that he had the courage, reflected in his own art, to stand apart from the mainstream, and expressed a singular vision. His refined eye eschewed the mundane, choosing unparalleled quality and remarkable originality over prevalent trends."

—JEAN FRANÇOIS GUIMOND,
FORMER CHIEF CURATOR OF THE BURNABY ART GALLERY

Born in 1923 to a father whose family had settled in B.C. in 1883 and a mother of Swedish heritage whose family had established a farm in Blaine, Washington, Jack Hardman and his younger sister, Elizabeth, were born and raised in New Westminster. He remembered his father for harsh and unreasonable discipline. Another misfortune was contracting tuberculosis at age twenty-two from his father and having to spend two years in Tranquille, a sanitorium near Kamloops, resulting in the loss of one lung and vulnerability to colds and sinus infections. However, while there, Jack began friendships with others interested in art, including a lifelong friend, artist Joe Plaskett. In 1947, Jack first showed his sculpture publicly at the annual B.C. Artists Exhibition at the Vancouver Art Gallery. He attended Vancouver Normal School and by 1949 was teaching at Edmonds Junior High School in Burnaby.

EUROPEAN TRAVEL AND WORK

His friend Joe introduced him to his sister's friend, Marya Fiamengo, a young poet and librarian of Croatian heritage in 1953. After two months, they were married and both taught for a year before setting off on a grand tour of Europe, first visiting Tito's Yugoslavia, which controlled the island of Vis, her mother's birthplace. They traveled for several months, and settled in London, renting a flat from Royal

Academy painter Steven Spurrier. Jack taught art at an East Ham school while Marya was a substitute teacher. Artist friends from Vancouver, Rosamund Bunting and Takao Tanabe, stayed with them on their travels. Spurrier provided perks like invitations to Royal Academy soirees, and the couple soaked up everything cultural—theatre, ballet, the National Gallery, the Tate and lectures at the Institute of Contemporary Art. On school holidays, they toured Germany and Italy and visited Joe Plaskett, who was then living in Paris, courtesy of a Canadian Council Overseas Scholarship.

TEACHING AND LIFE IN AN ARTISTS' ENCLAVE

Returning to Canada in 1955, the couple found a home on Hythe Avenue on Capital Hill in Burnaby with a view of the woods, the Ironmakers' Memorial Bridge and the sea sparkling in the background. Jack began to teach again, and in 1957, their son Matthew Dmitri Vincent Hardman was born. Capital Hill was an artists' enclave, and Jack would have afternoon tea with his neighbour, painter, art critic and collector Harold Mortimer Lamb. His wife was Vera Weatherbie, a one-time mistress of Fred Varley, and his daughter Molly Lamb Bobak was the first woman in the Canadian army to be given the title of war artist. Sculptor David Marshall (and his wife, Carel) were frequent guests for dinner; Jack valued his moral support and friendship. Doris and Jack Shadbolt lived a block away and "bestrode the artistic world in Vancouver like giants," with the power to help or deter another artist's success. Fortunately, they were remembered as being kind and supportive to Jack. Through the Shadbolts' enormous parties, Jack and his wife met Gordon Smith, Arthur Erickson, Don Jarvis, the Masseys and visiting American art critic, Clement Greenberg. By 1958, Jack was teaching at Burnaby Central when it first opened, where he was remembered as charismatic and inspiring. Ian Lidster, a student recalled, "Jack cut a considerable swath back in those days. Bearded like the bard, he was beatnik enough in ambience that he qualified as cool."

Leonard Brett, who later attended the Vancouver School of Art and became an artist, was his student in grades 11 and 12. He credits Jack with helping him to focus on art. "I did well at art but I never would have considered it a career if it weren't for him. ...He seemed like a wild man. He blew my mind."

PROFESSIONAL SCULPTOR

While teaching, Jack continued to develop his art by taking summer courses at the University of Western Washington, graduating with a BA in Fine Arts in 1960. After converting the utility room into a studio, he was up at 5 AM punching clay, sculpting, creating pottery before going to teach. Jack was influenced by cubism and English sculptors like Henry Moore and Barbara Hepworth, as well as older traditions—Mayan, Etruscan and Minoan art. His clay sculptures tended to be small so they could fit into a kiln and were semi-abstract with some visual references to the real world. Jack often portrayed family groupings or father-son pairs. In the summer of 1957, he got a job assisting Alexander Archipenko, the Ukrainian avant-garde sculptor, who was teaching through UBC extensions.

Jack was in numerous group shows in the 1950s and 1960s, starting in 1953 with a Vancouver Art Gallery show, a 1956 outdoor show organized by the Northwest Institute of Sculpture on the UBC campus and a 1958 Northwest Craftsman Exhibition in Seattle, where his piece *Eleven Saints* won the sculpture prize. Jack exhibited his sculpture while Doris Shadbolt showed her jewelry work at Alvin Balkind and Abraham Rogatnik's New Design Gallery in 1961. His *Totemic Figure*, a combination of smaller kiln-fired pieces, graced the November 1963 cover of *Ontario Homes and Living* and the pages of *Western Homes and*

Gardens, while his six-foot terra cotta sculpture was chosen to complement a building at Lethbridge Junior College. The following year, Jack's art accompanied the work of Anne Kahane and Cecil Richards in a three-person traveling Canadian sculpture exhibition. The programme accompanying the show read:

> The terra cotta (baked clay) forms by Jack Hardman… have certain literary qualities in that a number of them are witty commentaries. Others are definitely aligned to spiritual mysteries, such as are found in the totem pole or African carvings… Sometimes the forms speak of the human comedy, the solidarity of human relations or even of human panic. Hardman's work has the immediacy of today… He is using his medium in a way that suits his sharp perceptions, and his rapid translation from concept to execution successfully conveys the pulse of 20th Century proclivities.

In 1964, his *Totemic Baroque* was in the Second Canadian Sculpture Exhibition at the National Gallery in Ottawa, and other works were shown at Toronto's Dorothy Cameron Gallery and the Gallery Pascal. A reporter wrote:

> Jack Hardman, 41 and looks 31, hit Toronto Galleries last week: with the force of a six-foot-four Pacific gale—fresh, strong and lively… Vancouver's Hardman, a true westerner, is extremely frank, practical, and articulate. He fears nothing but himself. Jack told him that Teaching is my hobby. Sculpture is my profession.

The following year, his sculptures and prints were on view at the Little

Gallery in New Westminster. In 1966, Jack received a $5,000 Canada Council grant, which financed a trip to Toronto to observe new sculpture techniques. His work was included in a display of contemporary Canadian sculptures commissioned for Expo 67, while in May of that year, his one-man show, Cybernetic Sculptures, opened at the Douglas Gallery in Vancouver.

BURNABY ART GALLERY DIRECTOR

Despite these successes, Jack's mental health suffered, he had severe depressions, and he and his wife divorced in 1966. After returning from Toronto in 1969, Jack was still haunted by his own demons, and started to destroy his totemic sculptures in the garden. He could no longer see their appeal. Marya stopped him, but two pieces were lost. She said,

> He was so discouraged. George Fertig burned some of his paintings. This is what neglect drove them to do. It killed their confidence. They felt they weren't valued by their society or their contemporaries. It made them do rash and impulsive things like destroy their works.

Fortunately for Jack he took a teaching job at Centennial High School in Coquitlam, where he was enriched by other art teachers, including sculptor Peter Paul Ochs and painter Don Portelance. In 1974, he began to instruct in the teacher training programme at Simon Fraser University, but in 1976, he became Director of the Burnaby Art Gallery, a job that truly suited his experience and talent. Jack had been involved with the arts community for years—in 1958, he helped organize an invitational exhibit of B.C. artists at Burnaby City Hall, and a number of artists were inspired to form the Burnaby Art Society with Jack as the first president. He persuaded the organization to mount Canada's first open-juried print show at Centennial Pavilion on Burnaby Mountain in 1961, which became a biennial event. The City of Burnaby purchased the Ceperley Estate at Deer Lake in 1961, and it became a home to the Burnaby Art Society and an art gallery operated by the society. Married to Berenice Gilmore in 1976, Jack energetically began his job as director. By 1977, he had organized a major show marking the 10th anniversary of the Burnaby Art Gallery, attempting to recreate, as closely as possible, the first exhibition in 1958. Included were Bruno and Molly Bobak, Lawren Harris, Don Jarvis, John Koerner, Joe Plaskett, Jack Shadbolt, Gordon Smith, Tak Tanabe and lesser known artists Frances Faminow, Jock Hearn and George Fertig. His exhibitions were eclectic, comprising printmakers, sculptors, painters and artists experimenting in fabric art and film cartoons. He was keen to have Canadian artists, particularly B.C. artists, because he felt many of them did not get the exposure that they deserved. Jack expanded the print collection from 65 works by adding another 476. In one year alone (1979-1980), the gallery's diverse acquisitions included works by David Milne, Harold Towne, Lawren P. Harris, LeRoy Jensen, Jack Wise, Eric Bergman, John Esler, Laurence Hyde, Jaques Hnizdousky, Jack Shadbolt, Caroline Armington, Pablo Picasso, A.J. Casson, Ina D.D. Uhthoff and Irene Whittome. Jack loved the gallery, but in 1978, he suffered a serious stroke, which limited his mobility. Since it did not seem to affect his cognitive abilities, he carried on until the board asked for his resignation in 1981. He lived out his days actively corresponding with others before passing away in 1996.

Jack Hardman's work is held in the following public collections: Vancouver Art Gallery, National Gallery of Canada, Burnaby Art Gallery, and the University of Victoria.

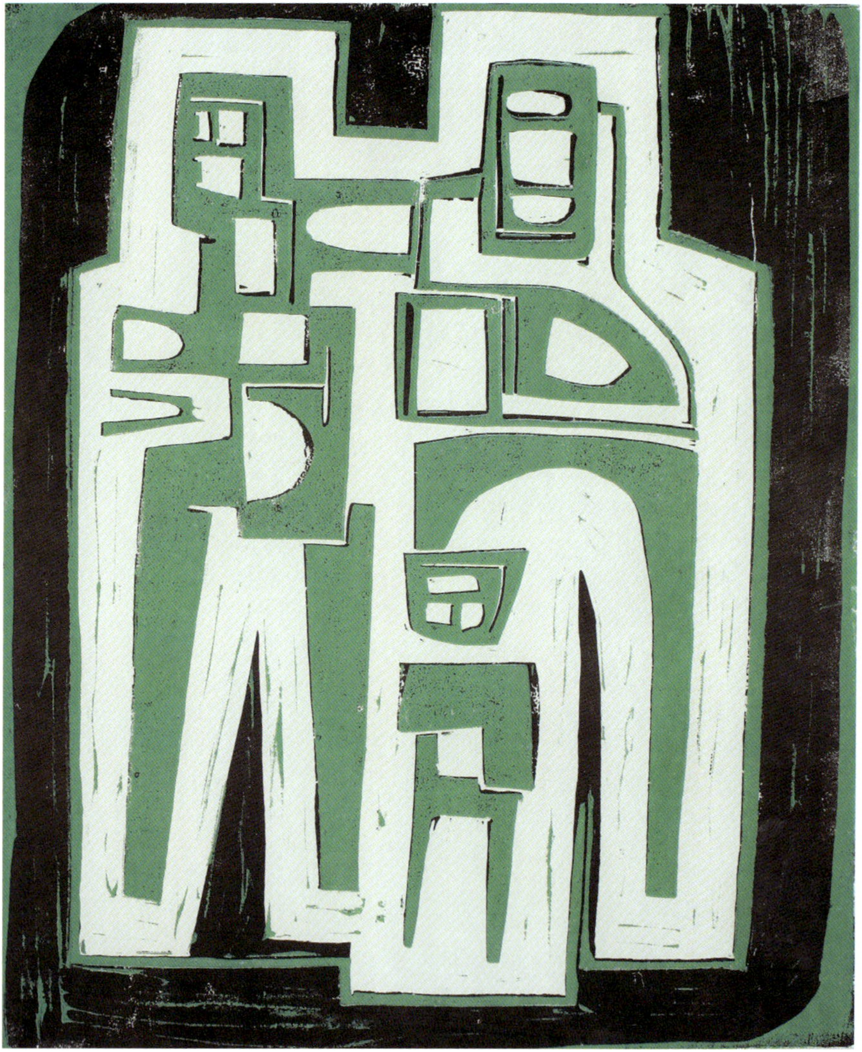

Jack Hardman, *Linocut*, early 1960s, 18" x 15"

CITY OF BURNABY PERMANENT ART COLLECTION
PHOTO BY INGEBORG HARDMAN

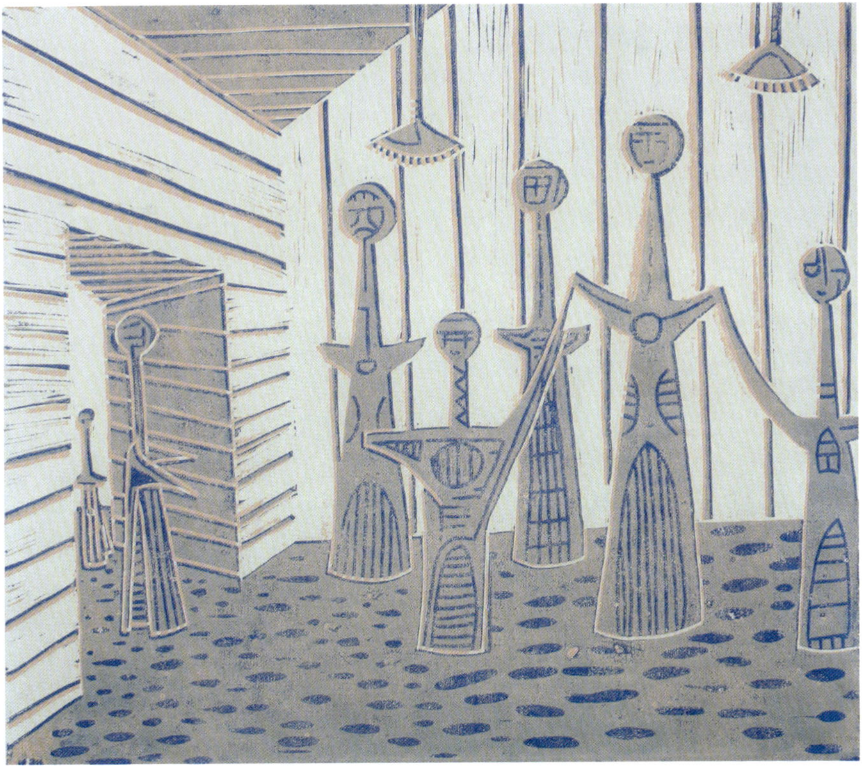

Jack Hardman, *At Home*, n.d., linocut, 20" x 18"

PRIVATE COLLECTION
PHOTO BY INGEBORG HARDMAN

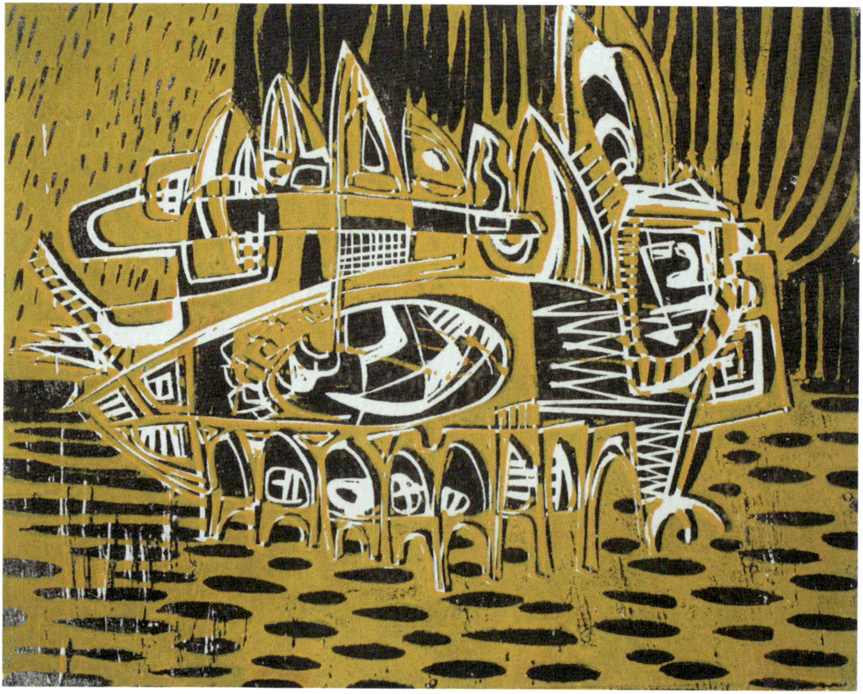

▲ Jack Hardman, *Totemic Insect*, n.d., linocut, 13" x 10"

PRIVATE COLLECTION
PHOTO BY INGEBORG HARDMAN

➤ Jack Hardman, *Totemic* #2, 1963, ceramic, 6' high,

COLLECTION OF LETHBRIDGE JUNIOR COLLEGE
PHOTO BY BASIL KING

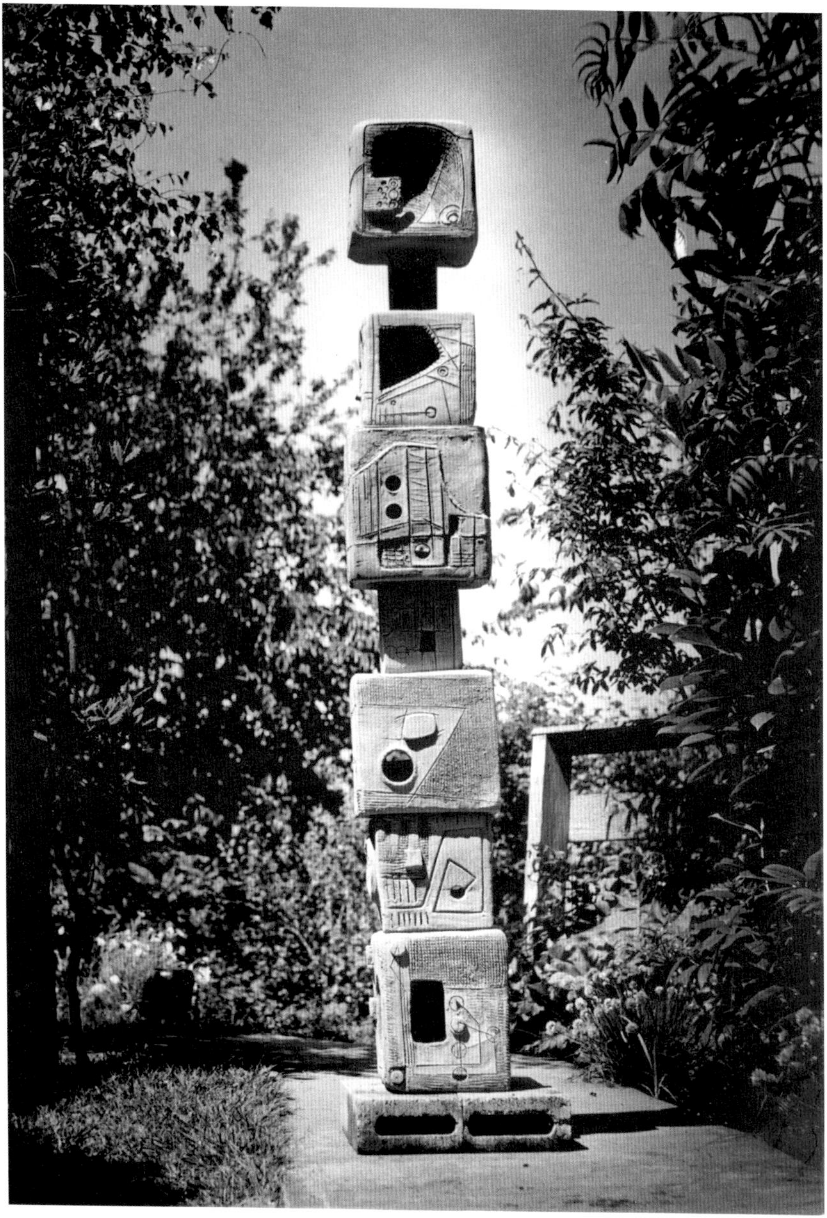

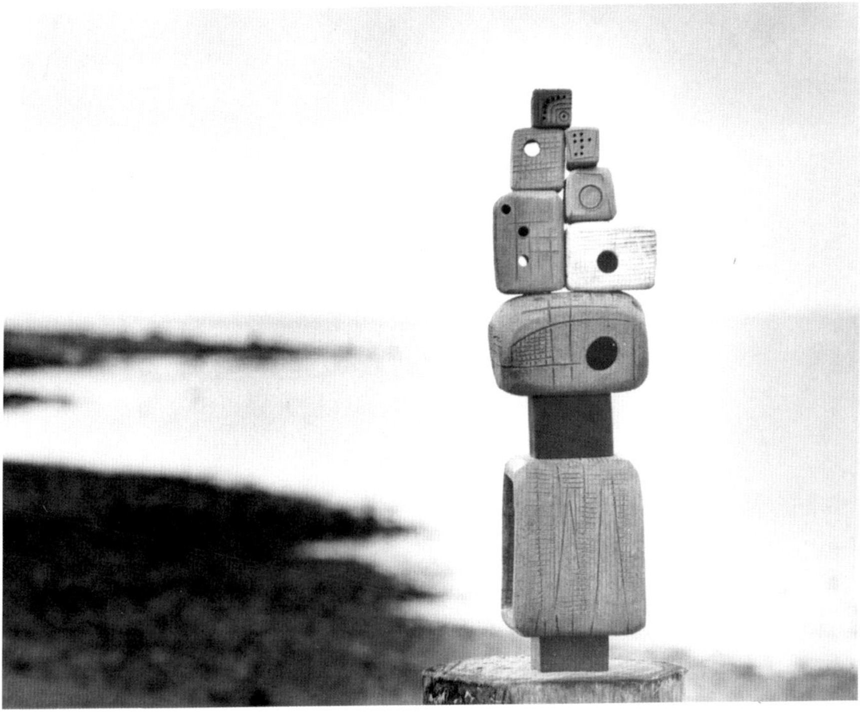

Jack Hardman, *Blocking*, mid-60s, clay, 24" x 7" x 7"

PHOTO BY JACK V. LONG

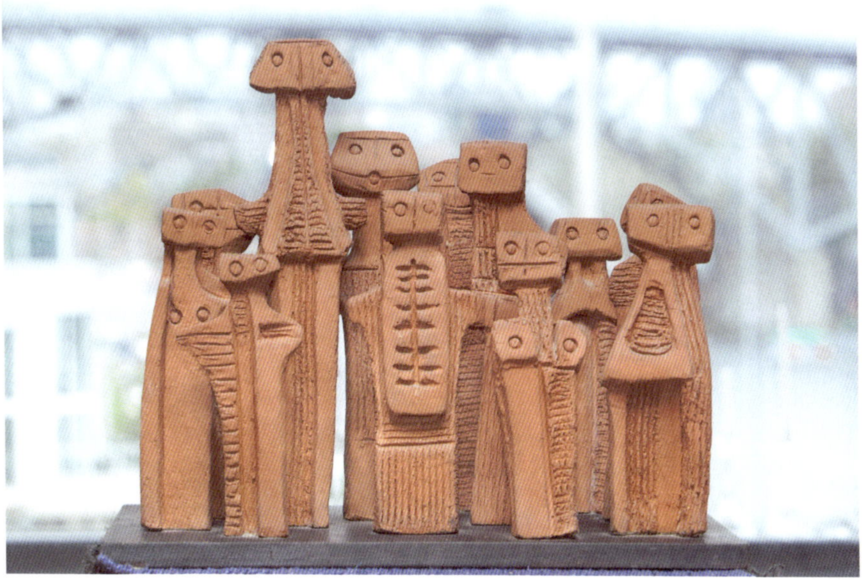

Jack Hardman, *Whatcha Doin' Mister?*, 1964, ceramic, 16" x 20" x12"

PRIVATE COLLECTION OF FRANCES LONG
PHOTO BY INGEBORG HARDMAN

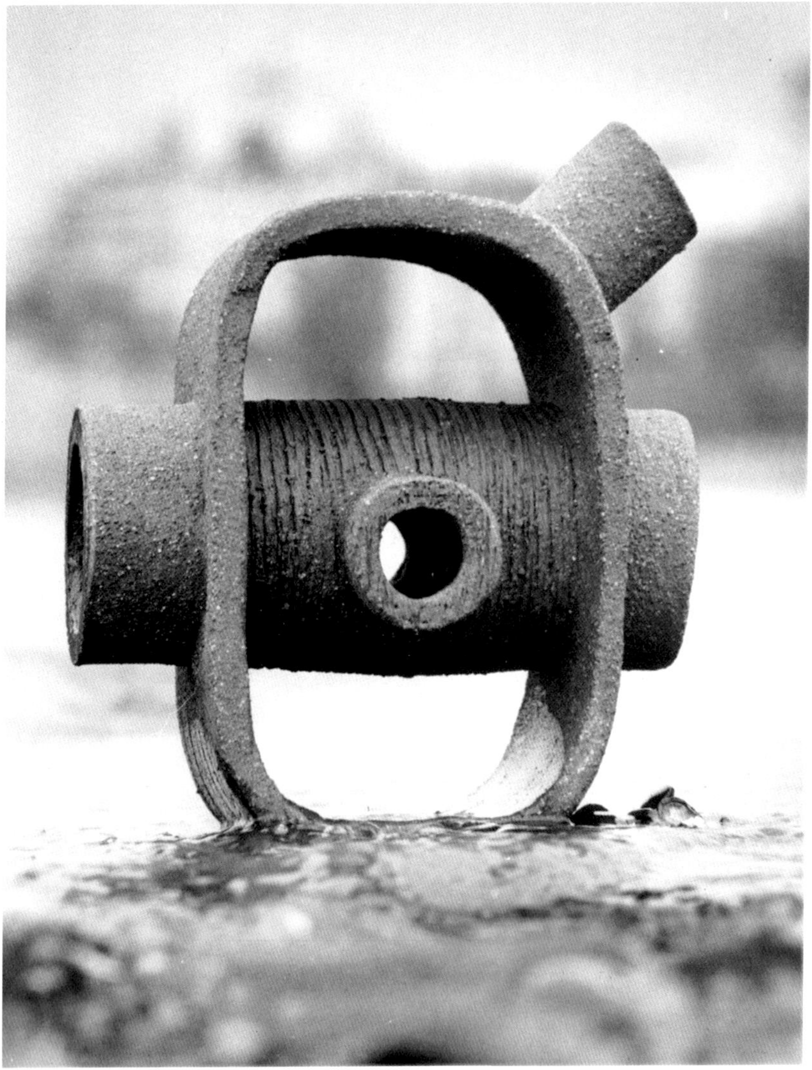

Jack Hardman, *Open and Closed Form*, mid-60s, 14" x 12", clay

PRIVATE COLLECTION
PHOTO BY JACK V. LONG

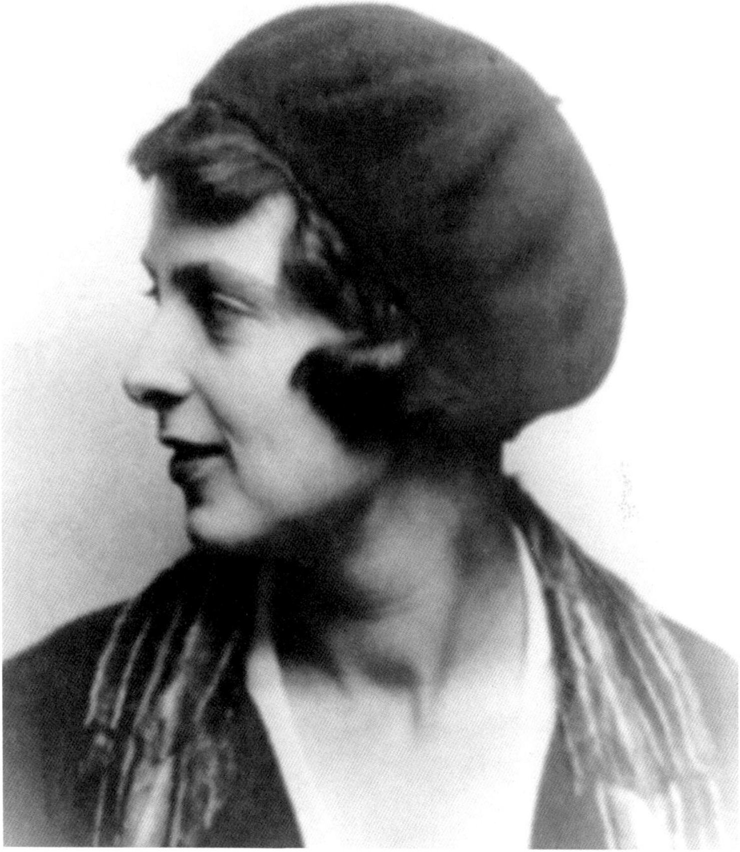

Edythe Hembroff-Schleicher

1906–1994

"Edythe Hembroff-Schleicher was part of Carr's life and also part of Carr's legacy—the first to write a book-length appreciation of her work. Yet, as revealed, [she] was also a remarkable talent in her own right. With great ingenuity she found a way to forge a career for herself as an artist, translator, and writer. Much more than a footnote in Canadian art history."
—SUSAN CREAN, AUTHOR OF *THE LAUGHING ONE: A JOURNEY TO EMILY CARR*

Raised in Victoria by a secure and prosperous family, Edythe May Hembroff, born in 1906, enjoyed a "silver spoon upbringing." There were social gatherings, holiday fun, a home next door to Craigdarroch Castle in the wealthy Rockland neighbourhood, a good education, art lessons, fine clothes, racy cars and possessions, including her own camera. Their cabin on the beach at Cordova Bay, was where Edythe would take Emily Carr on a sketching trip years later. At nineteen, she studied at the California School of Arts and Crafts and then the California School of Fine Arts in San Francisco. Not only was she exposed to courses in commercial and fine art, she experienced a broader world of art due to exhibitions of European painters such as Pablo Picasso, Henri Matisse, Wassily Kandinsky and Paul Klee. Though Edythe was a dedicated student, she was also remembered as a flashy, fashionable young woman who had a full social life.

ART SCHOOL IN PARIS AND TRAVEL IN EUROPE

In 1928, Edythe and another young woman from art school traveled by ship to France to study in Paris and develop professional careers as artists. They attended the École des Beaux-Arts, the Académie Moderne, the Académie Colarossi, and the Académie de la Grande Chaumière. Especially significant for Edythe were her studies with André Lhote.

They took full advantage of educating themselves further by visiting many museums (particularly the Louvre), a wide range of exhibitions, as well as famous historic sites and theatre. They sketched and painted regularly, lived at a pension run by a French family and fully embraced learning French language and culture. Due to their affluent parents and careful budgeting, the two young women had the funds to travel. In January 1929, they embarked on a trip through the mountains and southern coast of France, then to Genoa, Rome, Naples and eventually Sicily, before heading north through Switzerland, Germany and Holland. Along the way, they visited friends, historic sites and galleries and regularly took the time to sketch and paint, providing ample material for later work. They returned for further study in France and then traveled to Belgium and England. Edythe stayed independently in Paris, continuing her studies at Lhote's studio as well as an exciting social life and brief marriage to another art student. Her painting *Nu*, exhibited in the Salon d'Art Français Independent á Montparnasse (to which only professional artists were invited) is now in the collection of the Art Gallery of Greater Victoria.

FRIENDSHIP WITH EMILY CARR

Returning to her home province in 1930, Edythe made a splash on the society page with a hand-painted dress, which caught the eye of increasingly recognized artist Emily Carr, who invited her to tea at her home. Though they were thirty-five years apart in age, the two artists started a long-time friendship, sketching together in Carr's studio and in Beacon Hill Park, as well as on three overnight camping trips in the countryside near Victoria, and challenging each other with art and ideas. Edythe's paintings, photographs, memories and correspondence with Emily added immensely to our understanding. She recalled:

> These sketching trips were a memorable experience for me. A few bad moments were inevitable, living as I did in cramped primitive quarters with a hardy, dominating pioneer and her

> sometimes smelly animals. But those moments I scarcely remember today since harmony and humor usually prevailed. It is the hard work that comes to mind, Emily's ingenuity in making a rough camp run smoothly, the capers of wood, the gamboling of our dogs, the isolation and silence of the woods and, most of all, my contentment in the deepening friendship with a truly remarkable woman.

In 1930 and 1931, Edythe joined Emily in exhibiting in Seattle with its annual exhibition of Northwest Artists, where her painting *Nu* placed second and won the Music and Art Foundation prize. They both were also involved with the Island Arts and Crafts Society, and Emily encouraged Edythe to submit her painting of nude figures, *Quatre Nus*, in the annual exhibition because she wanted the "fun" of seeing the reaction. Edythe wrote,

> The old ladies were puffed up with indignation and the feathers flew. Emily was consulted and she said her canvases would be withdraw if mine were refused. And so, under threat, I "made" the Arts and Crafts show. We visited the gallery and Emily insisted on standing near the nudes to get the full benefit of remarks for future savouring. She chuckled all the way home. I had rarely seen her so amused.

Later Edythe joined Carr, Max Maynard, Jack Shadbolt and others in the 1932 annual exhibition which featured a Modern Room with a manifesto stating that their work was different because they were creations, rather than imitations, making a clear distinction from the traditionalist amateurs with pleasant landscape watercolours of the scenery.

After a year working as a commercial artist in New York City, Edythe married Frederick Brand, whom she had met in Victoria through her circle of friends around Emily Carr, and moved to Vancouver where he was a professor in mathematics at UBC. The couple were active in promoting the work of Emily, while Edythe worked in both commercial art and her own creations, including prints, which were easier to sell. Edythe showed her work in the British Columbia Artists Annual Exhibition at the Vancouver Art Gallery in 1935 through 1937, winning a Certificate of Merit and the Beatrice Stone Bronze Medal for Black and White for *Perugia,* based on a street scene from her travels in Italy. In 1936, they organized *Ten Artists of British Columbia* at UBC's library, featuring Edythe, Emily Carr, Frederick Varley, Charles Scott, Jock MacDonald, W.P. Weston, J. Delisle Parker, Max Maynard, Jack Shadbolt and Vera O. Weatherbie. When Carr came to Vancouver to visit, people smiled at the sight of her, "a Queen Mary hat perched on her head, sitting sandwiched into the passenger seat" of Edythe's cream-coloured MG sports car. With membership in the B.C. Society of Fine Artists, Edythe's work was exhibited from 1937 through 1939.

TRANSLATOR AND CIVIL SERVICE IN OTTAWA

With World War II, Edythe's career as an artist took a sudden turn when Frederick became a Pilot Officer (Navigation Instructor) in the Royal Canadian Air Force and the couple eventually moved to Ottawa. However, when he was overseas, the marriage dissolved. Using her skills in German, Edythe began work as an examiner and then assistant deputy supervisor for the German POW Censorship Section, Department of National War Services, where she met Julius Schleicher, a Polish immigrant and former paper manufacturer whom she married in 1951. Edythe worked as a translator in German, French and English for the Department of the Secretary of State until 1961. Though she had little time to create art, she began writing her first book, based on her experiences and letters from Emily.

RETIREMENT: PAINTING, WRITING, TRAVEL

In 1961, Edythe and her husband retired and moved to Victoria. By 1962, she was active with the art scene in Victoria, showing her work in the exhibition *100 Years of the Arts in Victoria* at the Art Gallery of Greater Victoria. In the gallery's Thirteenth Annual Jury Show the next year, she received an honourable mention for her work *Café Klatsch.*

The couple loved travel, visiting California for the sunshine in the winter and throughout Europe, especially Paris, where Edythe was able to explore her old haunts and take art classes. Back home, Edythe set up her own studio and was actively painting again. In addition, she began more intense research on Emily Carr. In 1969, *M.E.: A Portrayal of Emily Carr*, was published, which was launched at the Art Gallery of Greater Victoria, along with an exhibition of her and Emily's paintings. By 1974, the B.C. government appointed her as a Special Consultant on Emily Carr, and in 1977 the Emily Carr Gallery was opened, which exhibited works from the Provincial Archives, including *Kispiox Village*, the first Carr painting bought by the government back in 1933 at Edythe's urging. She dedicated herself to correcting dates and misconceptions in Carr's story, resulting in the 1978 publication of her second book, *Emily Carr: The Untold Story.* Edythe loved researching people and places in B.C., and backpacked at age seventy-four to Haida Gwaii, the Yukon and Alaska, retracing many of the steps taken by Emily decades earlier. In 1981, she organized and wrote the catalogue for a recreation of the 1932 Modern Room where Emily, Edythe and others had first exhibited their work to mark a difference from the traditionalists of conservative Victoria.

GOLDEN YEARS

Edythe remained active and inquiring until her death in 1994. She loved analyzing art; in the 1940s, she had written "good art without symmetry and balance is inconceivable… and there must be a strict adherence to more calculated harmonies too." In her senior years, she noted, "after the war… art had changed drastically. First came abstract expressionism, and I opted out. I hadn't spent years of my life learning to draw the figure to simply drip paint on the floor like Pollock or paint hard-edged rectangles like Hofmann." She continued painting and exhibiting in her own figurative style, as well as writing newspaper and magazine articles about other artists such as Max Maynard and Arthur Pitts as well as more about Carr—"A Queen, A Mythical Princess, and the Queen Charlotte Islands" and "Islands of Mist and Memories: How the Queen Charlotte Islands Helped Shape the Life and Work of Emily Carr." She willingly helped other researchers in their careers and set up scholarships at the University of Victoria for female undergraduates or graduates in pre-medicine disciplines. She donated her art to public institutions and saw that her letters from Emily Carr as well as her research papers, personal papers and family photographs were in the care of the Provincial Archives, paving the way for future understanding. Pat Bovey, then Director of the Art Gallery of Greater Victoria, remembered Edythe at a Memorial Exhibition as a progressive artist, writer, advocate and friend, who was "spirited, challenging and ever-questioning."

Edythe Hembroff-Schleicher's work is held in the following public collections: Art Gallery of Greater Victoria, University of Victoria Legacy Art Gallery, Vancouver Art Gallery, and the B.C. Archives.

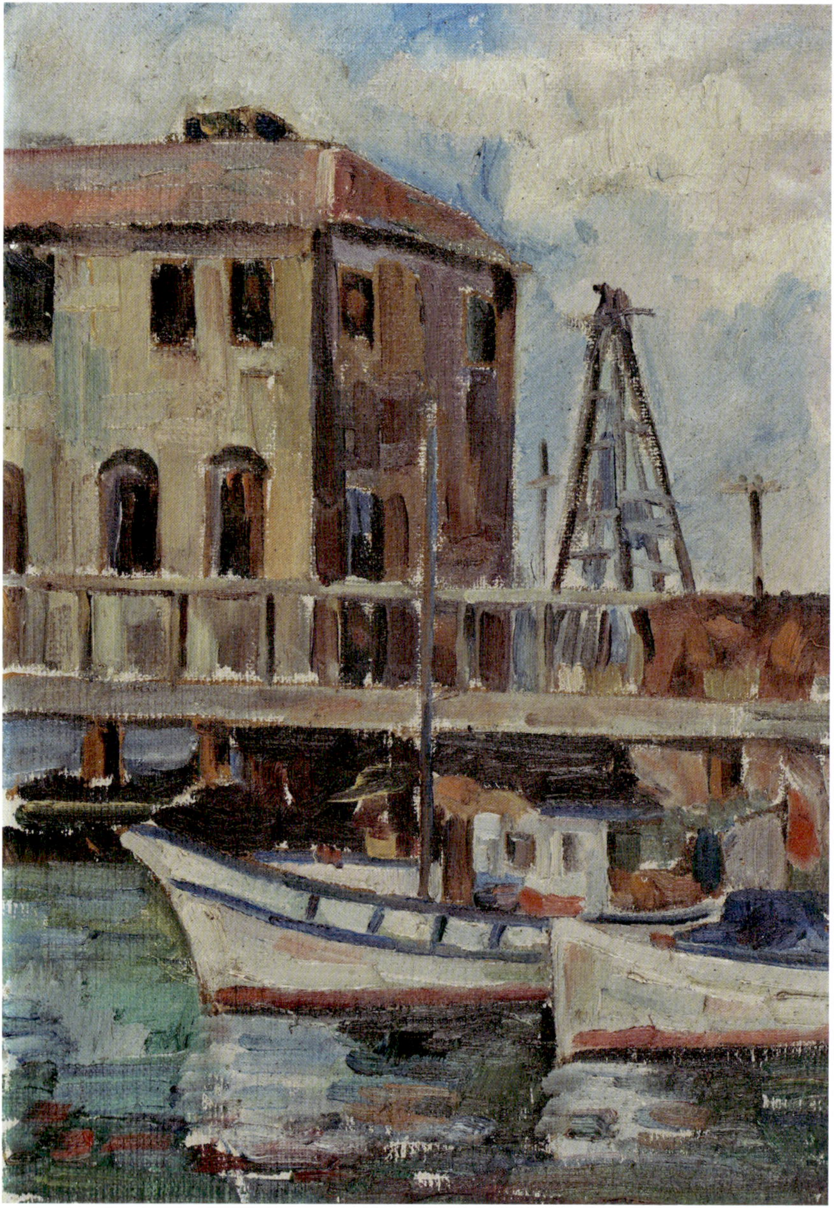

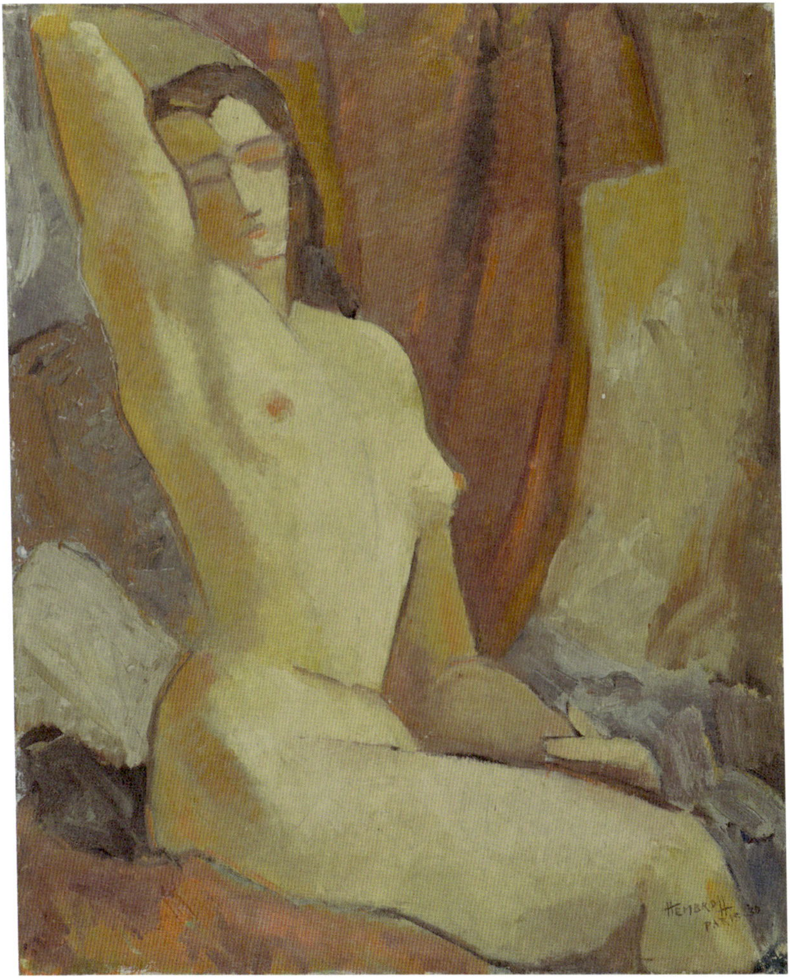

◄ Edythe Hembroff-Schleicher, *Cassis*, circa 1930, 11" x 6"

FROM THE BRENDA H. ISLE COLLECTION
PHOTO BY TIM ISLE

▲ Edythe Hembroff-Schleicher, *Nu*, 1930, oil on canvas, 24" x 20",

FROM THE ART GALLERY OF GREATER VICTORIA COLLECTION

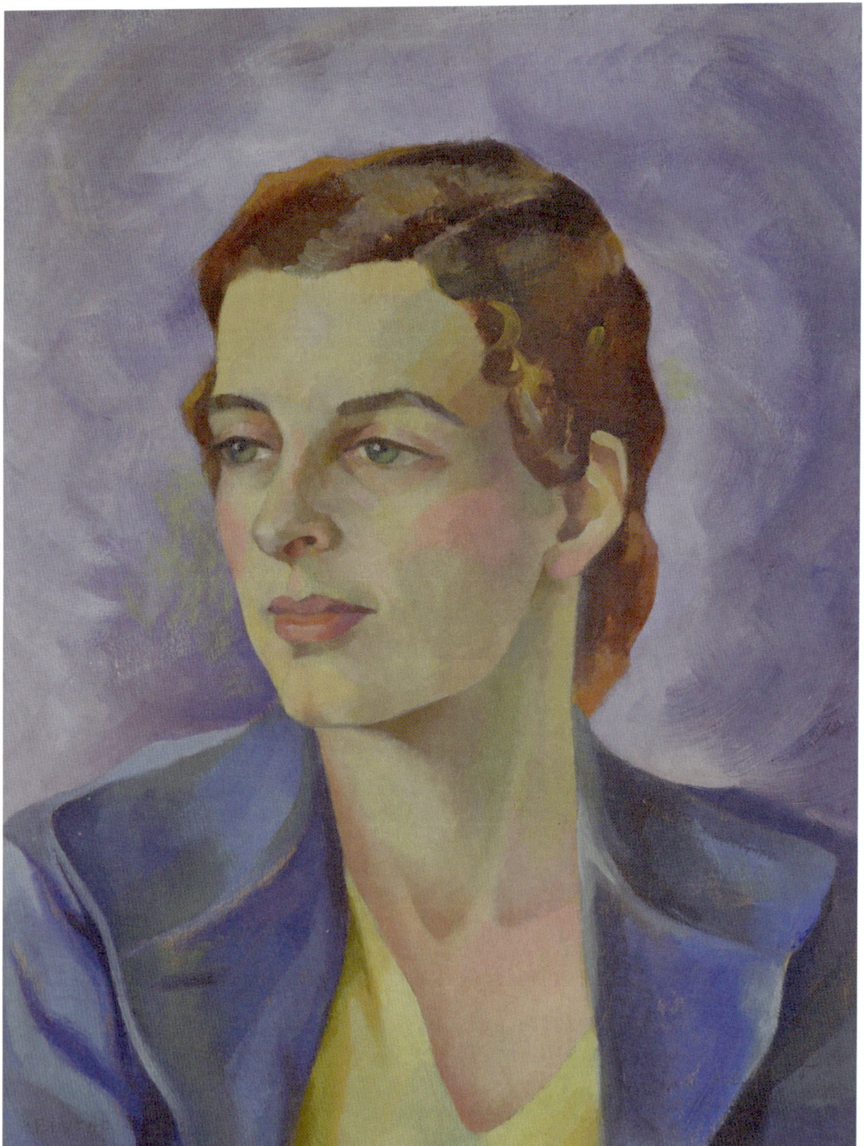

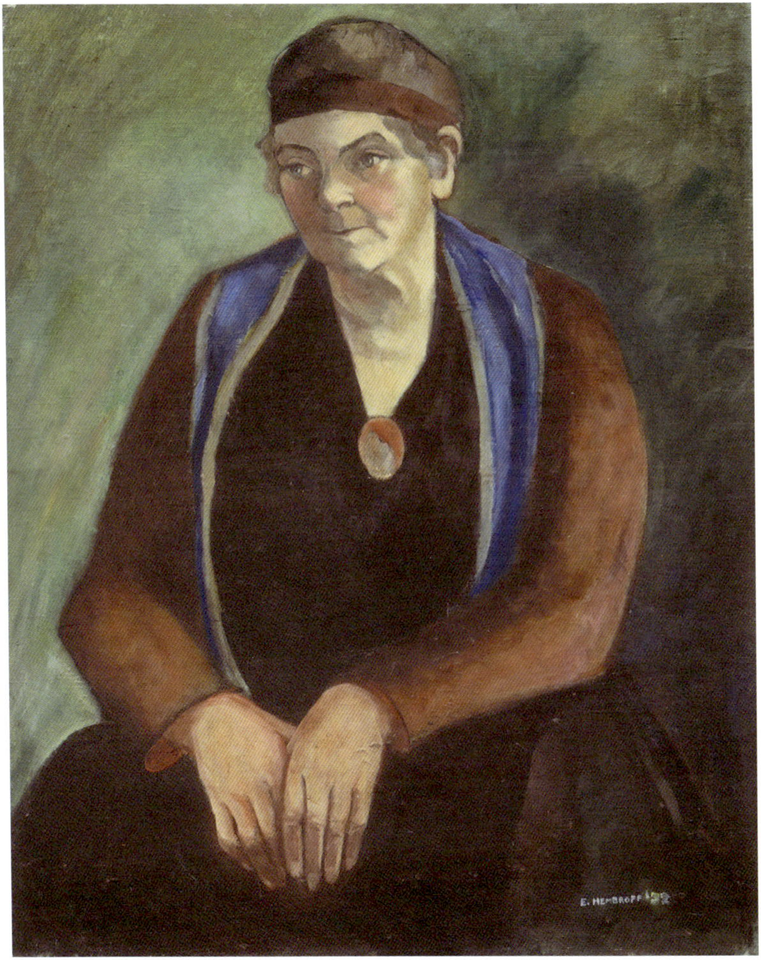

▲ Edythe Hembroff-Schleicher, *Emily Carr*, 1932, oil on canvas and hardboard, 28 ½" x 23"

COLLECTION OF THE VANCOUVER ART GALLERY, GIFT OF MISS GRACE MELVIN, VAG 41.5
PHOTO VANCOUVER ART GALLERY

◄ Edythe Hembroff-Schleicher, *Self Portrait*, 1931, oil on board, 13 ½" x 10 ½"

FROM THE ART GALLERY OF GREATER VICTORIA COLLECTION

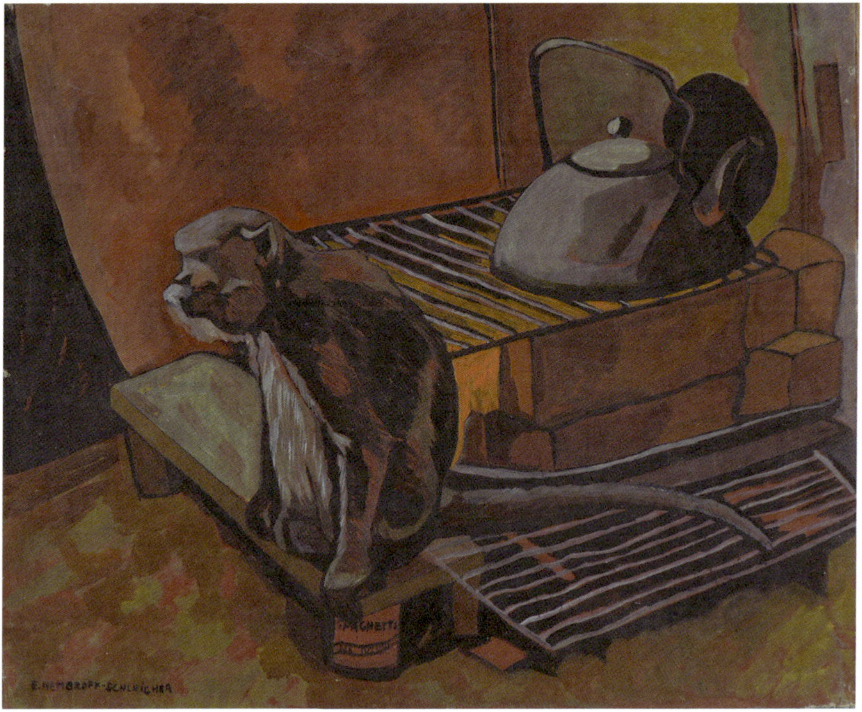

Edythe Hembroff-Schleicher, *Mrs Woo Waiting for Tea*, 1934, oil on canvas, 17" x 21"

FROM THE ART GALLERY OF GREATER VICTORIA COLLECTION

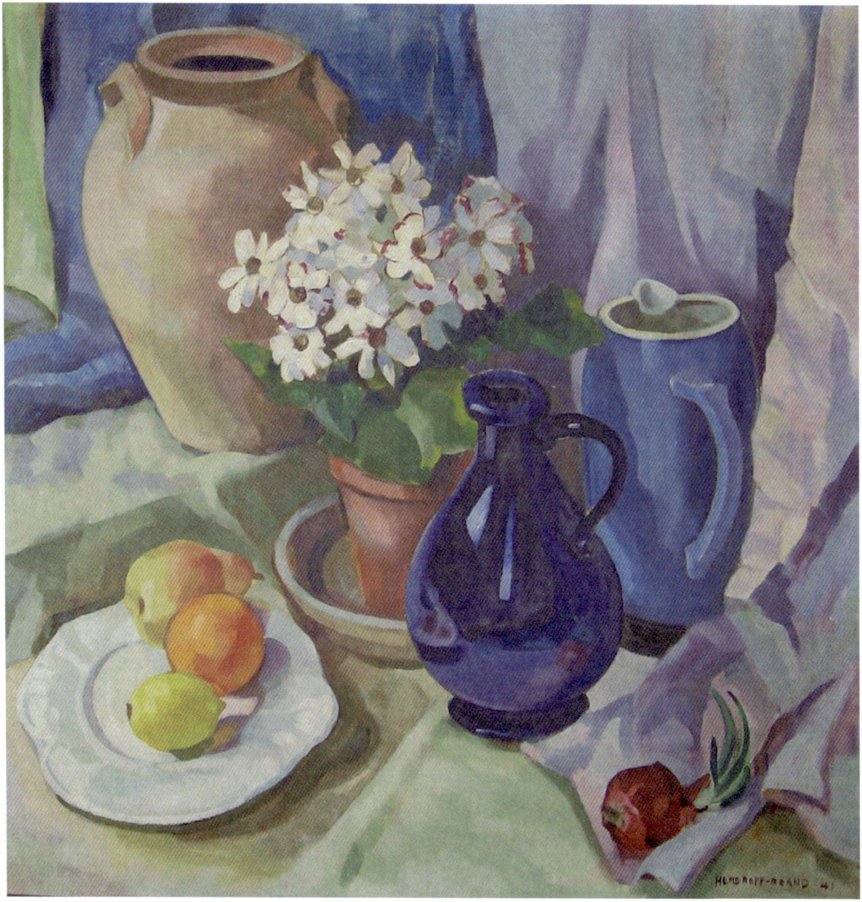

Edythe Hembroff-Schleicher, *Untitled*, 1941, oil on canvas, 27 ½" x 27 ¾"

COURTESY OF THE LIBBY O. RUCH COLLECTION

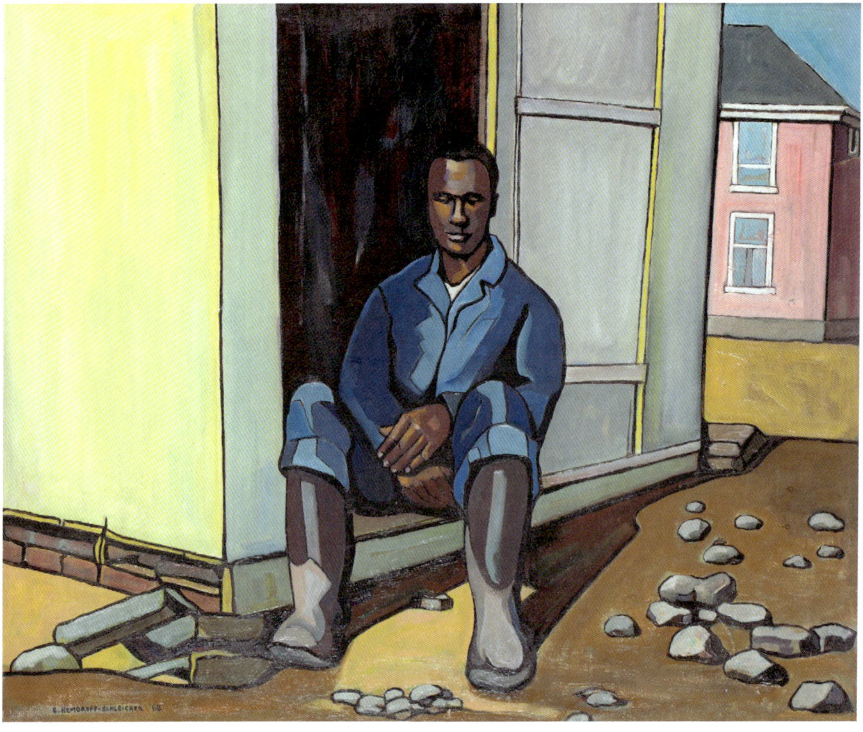

Edythe Hembroff-Schleicher, *Noon Rest* (Worker, Oakland), 1968, oil on canvas, 27 ½" x 33 ½"

FROM THE ART GALLERY OF GREATER VICTORIA COLLECTION
PHOTO BY JANET DWYER

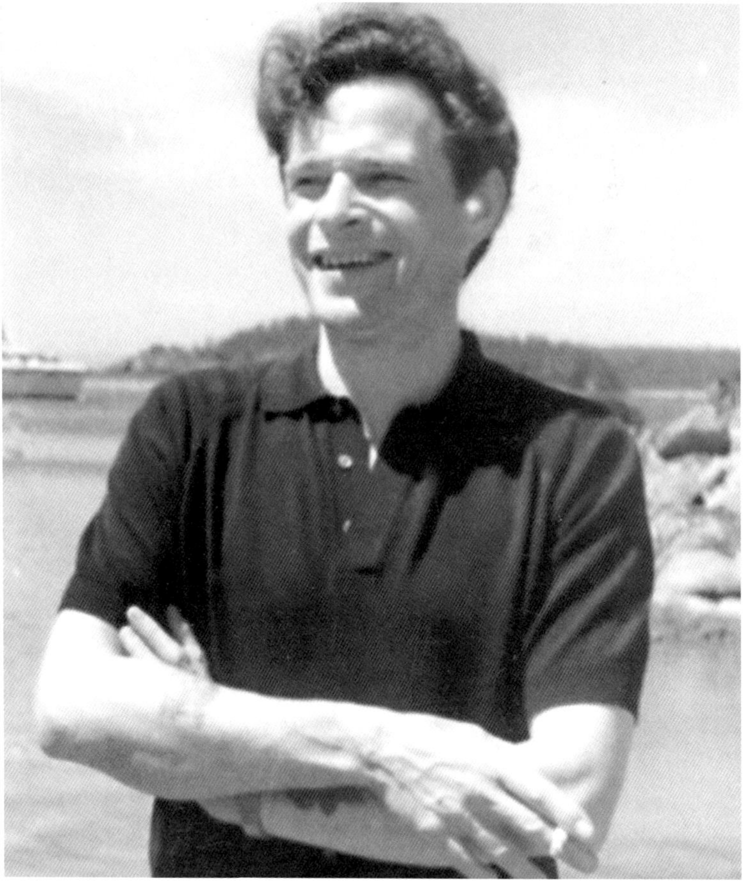

LeRoy Jensen

1927–2005

"LeRoy's robust approach to life and art was a seminal experience for his students. He gave us a solid foundation to build on and return to throughout our lives. He taught a way to begin, a way to endure and a way of life. He challenged us to live to the highest point of our present understanding, which leaves no room for self-satisfaction. LeRoy had deep respect for the masters of art throughout history. He showed us how they too were our teachers and friends. Above all LeRoy Jensen was a Master Painter."

—ROY PATTERSON, SCULPTOR, FORMER STUDENT

Though born in Vancouver in 1927, LeRoy Jensen spent his early years in Shanghai, China, with a Canadian mother and a Danish father, who worked for the Great Northern Telegraph company. When China became politically volatile, the Jensen family moved in 1933 to Nagasaki, Japan. LeRoy became seriously ill with an eye infection and his mother, who was a registered nurse, realized he had typhoid and nursed him back to health, saving his sight and his life. A Japanese gentleman taught LeRoy drawing from age six to ten. When World War II began in 1939, LeRoy and his brother, Colin, were sent to boarding school in Vancouver, which he found "a horrible place." In 1941, at fourteen, he lied about his age and began four years as a "fireman" with the merchant navy, traveling to Pacific Rim ports. Reflecting on the harsh realities of life aboard a merchant ship, LeRoy said, "I was made aware of the fact that unless I did something different there was no guarantee my life would be very long." Unsure if his parents had survived after leaving for Hong Kong, he kept in touch with his maternal grandmother in Vancouver. Fortunately, when his ship returned to that port, his mother answered the door at his grandmother's home, and he was reunited with his parents. His mother encouraged him to begin drawing again at age eighteen. In an interview later in life LeRoy said, "My art restored my sanity after those devastating years."

ART STUDENT IN DENMARK AND FRANCE

Rejuvenated by his art, he returned to Vancouver and exhibited his first painting, a portrait of his father, and another, *Early Morning Salt Spring Island,* in the 16th Annual B.C. Artists' Exhibition at the Vancouver Art Gallery. He then attended the Vancouver School of Art for a year (1948/9), but felt that their teachers gave him little direction or foundation in art. Restless and hungry to learn, he began searching for a more stimulating environment. LeRoy travelled to his father's homeland in 1949 and enrolled in the Royal Danish Academy of Fine Arts in Copenhagen. Under Axel Joergennsen, he received a vigorous art education: hours of lectures on art, art history and drawing—the model, still life, street life—as well as painting and studio work. After marriage to Nonna Bossleman, a drama student, LeRoy and his wife moved to Paris, where he studied with Andre Lhote, a Cubist painter, as well as with Ferdinand Leger, Ossip Zadkine and Jean Metsinger. Despite poverty and hunger (they lived in unheated rooms for two years), it was a time of intoxicating intellectual stimulation and creative ferment. In addition to a vibrant life in studios and cafes, LeRoy travelled, and on one trip met a painter friend of Picasso, Edouard Pignon, and studied with him.

RETURN TO VANCOUVER

In 1953, LeRoy and his wife returned to Vancouver, which seemed like a desert after living in Paris, until he met local artists Jock Hearn, Dave Marshall and George Fertig. Jensen, Hearn and Marshall formed the Pendulum Group, spending many hours discussing and gauging the depths of art, using unique pendulum symbols to identify their work in opposition to the posturing of a small clique of male artists and educators who controlled the art scene and favoured Clement Greenberg and New York abstract expressionism. Though he had a one-man show, it did not pay the bills, so LeRoy mowed lawns and painted houses to survive. A rare exhibition was the 1956 show organized by the B.C. Region of the Federation of Canadian Painters at the New Design Gallery, a private avant-garde gallery in West Vancouver started by Alan Balkind and Abraham Rogatnick. Ten artists under thirty years of age were featured—including LeRoy, Bill Mayrs, Ron Kelly, Herb Gilbert and Heather Spears. Interested in ontology, as defined by the philosopher Alexander Baumgarten, LeRoy studied and gave lectures on the subject, and was greatly influenced by French painter Georges Rouault.

By the 1960s, LeRoy, his wife and two sons, Kim and Anthony, lived in Powell River, then Argenta in the central Kootenays, and also in Kelowna. He produced art for exhibitions, shared several two-man shows with Vancouver sculptor Egon Milinkovich, and briefly taught at the Okanagan Landing School of Art. However, by 1965, he had separated from his wife. In 1967, he gave a six-month lecture series on ontology in New York, where he met actress Lynda Woolley, whom he married in 1968. Returning to Vancouver, he had a renewed commitment to his art, and in addition to oil painting and etching, he began doing frescos, stained glass and floor mosaics, exhibiting at the Gallery of B.C. Arts, across from Stanley Park. LeRoy and the Pendulum group held the view that a work had to honestly convey something legitimately felt or perceived, otherwise it did not function as art, only as decoration. They saw art as an intriguing method of self-discovery and response to the world around them.

> My only wish is for my work to be seen for what it is, not framed in clouds of publicity. Only one thing interests me, some humane expression. I believe in the individual, in his or her actual value. I believe in Revolt—primarily in relation to myself. In this I have some childish success.

TEACHING ART

LeRoy accepted teaching posts at the University of British Columbia and the Banff School of Fine Arts, but resigned after struggling with the way art schools spent time on ancillary activities—negotiating interviews, conversations with critics, press releases, catalogues and wall texts—rather than on teaching as a sacred trust with a student whose art is an internal journeying, enhanced by communication and learning from others. By the fall of 1970, he offered a class on drawing and painting through the Vancouver Free University at the Vancouver East Cultural Centre, now known as The Cultch. It proved life-changing for a core of students, including Roy Patterson, Wendy Newbold Patterson and Don Wunderlee, who valued the skills he taught as well as his philosophy of encouraging self learning. Along with drawing and practical skills, such as mixing pigments, LeRoy believed that painting and drawing were based on Four Forces: movement, luminosity, rhythm and spirit. He stated:

> All that I have to say is in my work, and it is grounded in my constant effort to find suitable language for my expression. For me, painting is movement, luminosity and a discovery of the rhythm that underlies a subject. I must find the proper blend of these forces and set them free; then the reality appears by itself.

ART, FAMILY AND ACTIVISM

In the 1970s, LeRoy and Lynda had two daughters, Amber and Gabrielle, and juggled parenting them and his two sons with his painting, teaching and work at the Vancouver Aquarium. They lived in a small two-bedroom home with a studio on French Street. LeRoy loved the sea and knew his way around ships, so he decided to build a 26-foot wooden sloop, *Friend.* The boat provided happy times for the family, as they began to spend their summers sailing around the Gulf Islands. LeRoy's powerful sense of social justice found a new outlet with Greenpeace, which was founded in Vancouver in 1971. He went with Greenpeace's second expedition on the *Edgewater Fortune* to confront U.S. Navy ships doing underwater nuclear testing near Amchitka Island, as well as another expedition to interfere with whaling ships. Later he became a supporter of the Green Party.

SALT SPRING ISLAND

In the summers, the young Jensen family moored *Friend* in Vesuvius Bay, off Salt Spring Island and visited LeRoy's parents on their nearby property. In 1982, after his father died and his mother's health declined, the family moved to his parent's small, three-bedroom home. His studio was unheated, but it was an austerity he embraced. His children were always welcome in his workplace. While living there, LeRoy's friend and fellow artist Herb Siebner invited him to join the Limners, a group of professional artists (sculptors, printmakers, potters, painters, poets and a fabric artist) mostly from Victoria. The group included Walter Dexter, Carole Sabiston, Karl Spreitz, Myfanwy Pavelic, Colin Graham, Pat Martin Bates, Jan Grove, Elza Mayhew, Robin Skelton, Roberto de Castro, Helga and Jan Grove. He exhibited his work in numerous galleries, including Winchester Gallery in Victoria and J. Mitchell Gallery on Salt Spring Island. Robin Skelton, in his review of the Winchester exhibit said:

> The [women's] bodies are sometimes at rest in a pause between demanding hours; they are sometimes thinking, perhaps meditating. They suggest not particular women, but Woman, and are made more universal by such simple titles as *Dawn* and *Winter*, as if they were not merely caught up in earth's movements but embodiments of it.

Bernie Raffo, former owner of Winchester Gallery wrote:

> I first met LeRoy at a Limner show [1986] and was immediately struck by the deep compassion LeRoy had for art. To me he was a traditionalist and a modernist painter all at the same time. I once expressed to him that I thought his figures had a landscape quality to them, which, to my surprise, he heartily agreed.

LeRoy's primary medium was oil, but he also produced etchings on a small press in his studio, gouaches, watercolours, lithographs, conte sketches, pastels and volumes of drawings, exploring the subject of "mother and child" his whole life.

He continued to be involved in issues, writing letters to the local newspapers and opposing clear-cutting of old-growth forest in B.C.'s Clayoquot Sound and Carmanah Valley. He visited the valley and contributed his art to a fundraising book, *Carmanah: Artistic Visions of an Ancient Rainforest*, which also included the work of Salt Spring artists Simon Camping, Carol Evans, Robert Bateman, Diana Dean and Diana Thompson. When Texada Land Corporation, which owned 10% of Salt Spring, clear-cut forests on the island between 1999 and 2001, LeRoy participated in protests, which saved half of the land slated for logging. However, the inclement weather during one protest precipitated a decline in his health. He continued to draw and paint, but refused open heart surgery when the doctor recommended it. LeRoy's last painting was sitting on his easel when he died in the spring of 2005.

LeRoy Jensen's work is held in public collections: Burnaby Art Gallery, Maltwood Art Museum and Gallery at the University of Victoria and the Art Gallery of Greater Victoria.

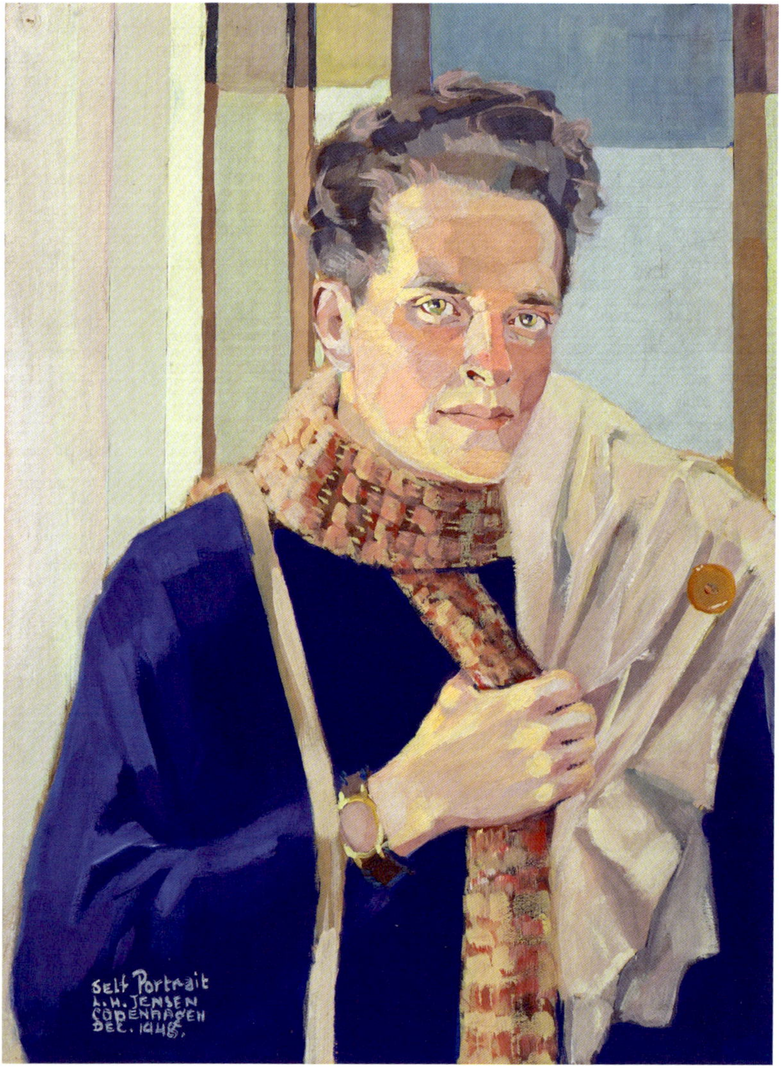

▲ LeRoy Jenson, *Copenhagen self portrait*, 1948, egg tempera on prepared paper, 17 3/4" x 23 1/2"

PRIVATE COLLECTION
PHOTO BY JANET DWYER

➤ LeRoy Jenson, *The Deep Net*, 1968, oil on canvas, 33 1/4" x 22"

PRIVATE COLLECTION
PHOTO BY JANET DWYER

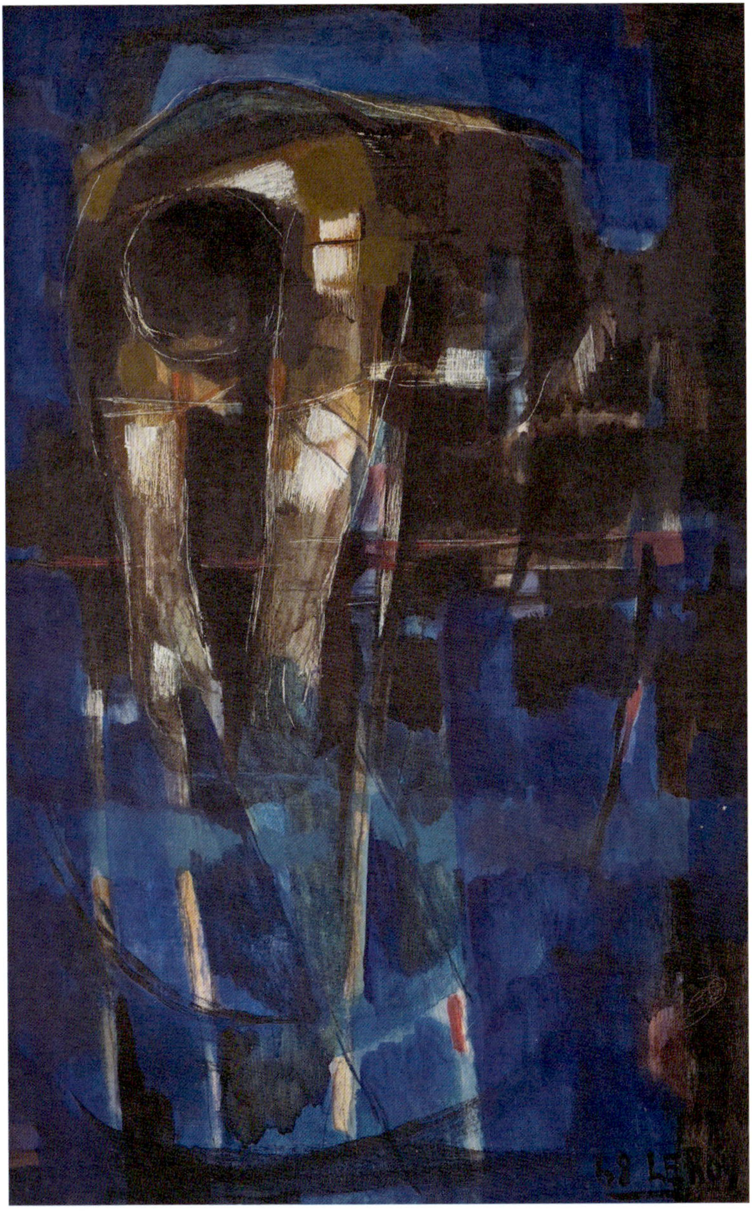

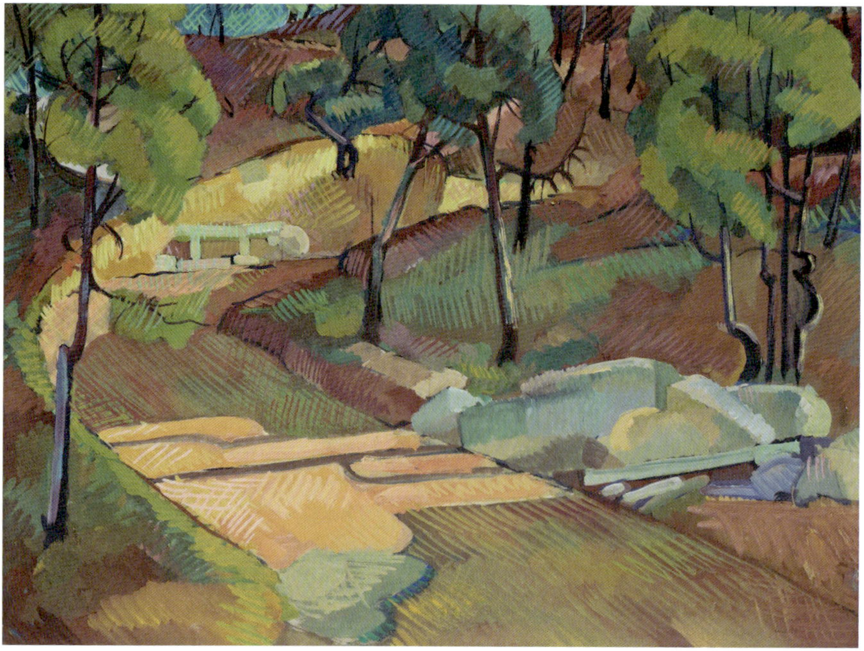

▲ LeRoy Jenson, *So, France*, circa 1950s

gum arabic, 24" x 17 1/2"

PRIVATE COLLECTION
PHOTO BY JANET DWYER

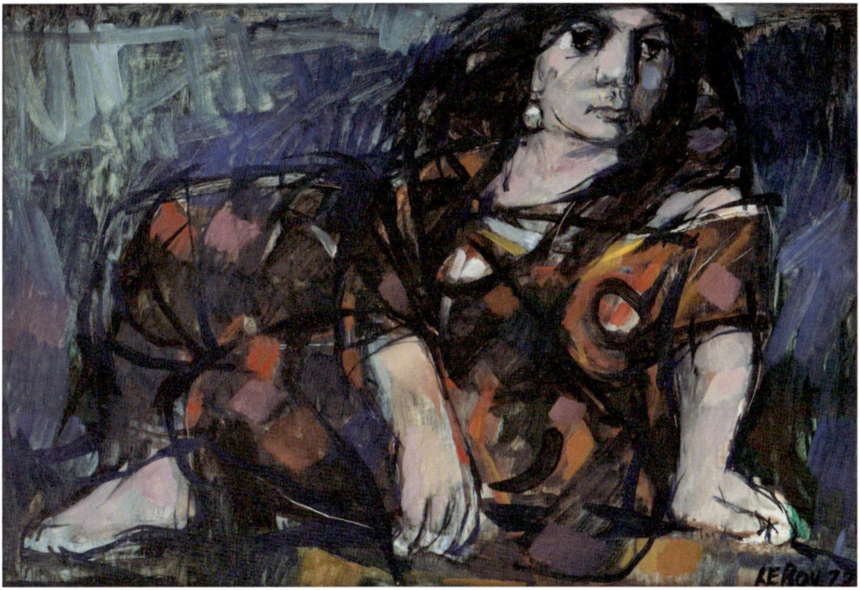

▲ LeRoy Jenson, *Untitled*, 1972, oil on board, 72" x 24"

PRIVATE COLLECTION
PHOTO BY JANET DWYER

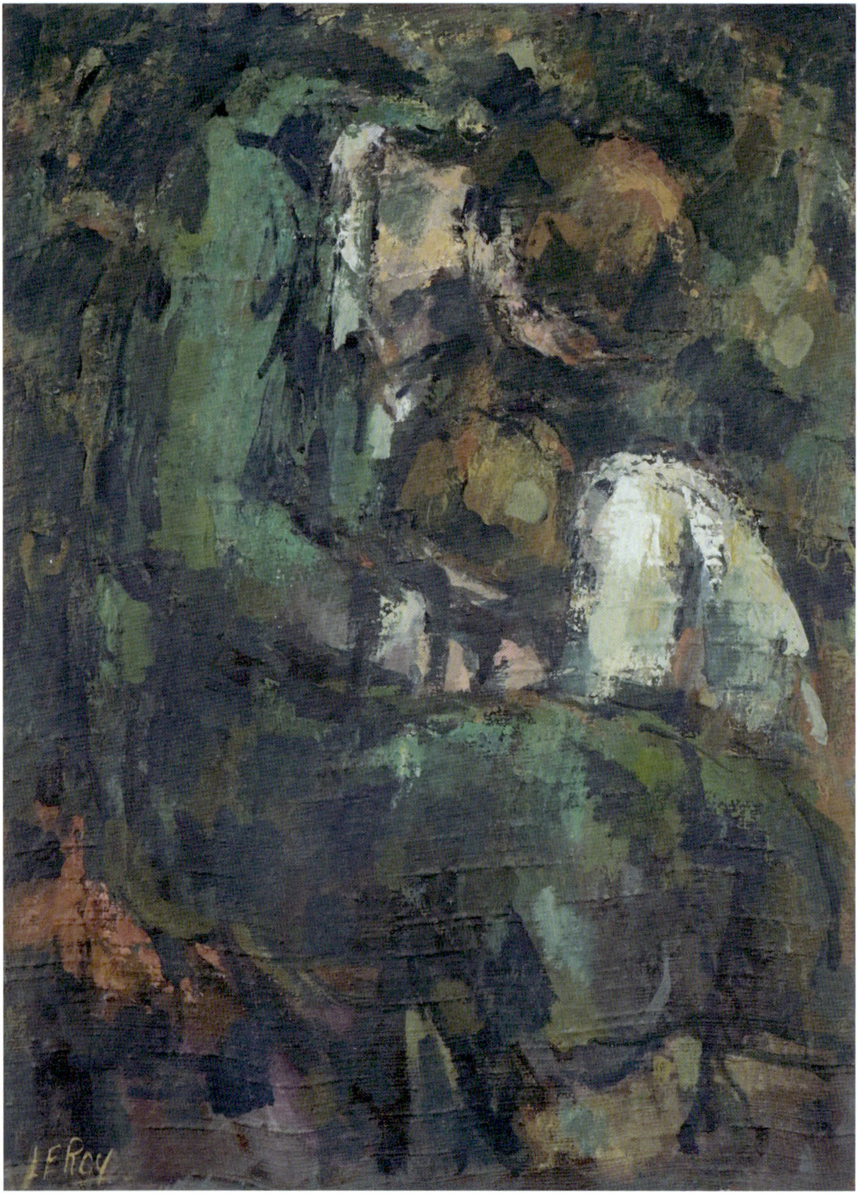
J F Roy

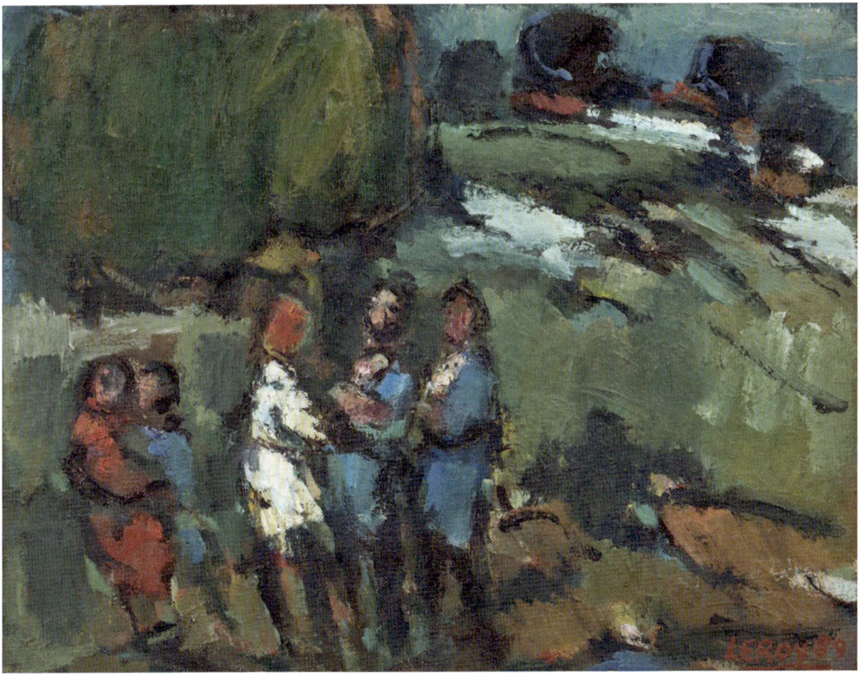

▲ LeRoy Jenson, *Little Family*, 1989, oil on canvas, 23" x 29"

PRIVATE COLLECTION
PHOTO BY JANET DWYER

◄ LeRoy Jenson, *Mother and Child*, circa 1980s, oil on linen, 29" x 24"

PRIVATE COLLECTION
PHOTO BY JANET DWYER

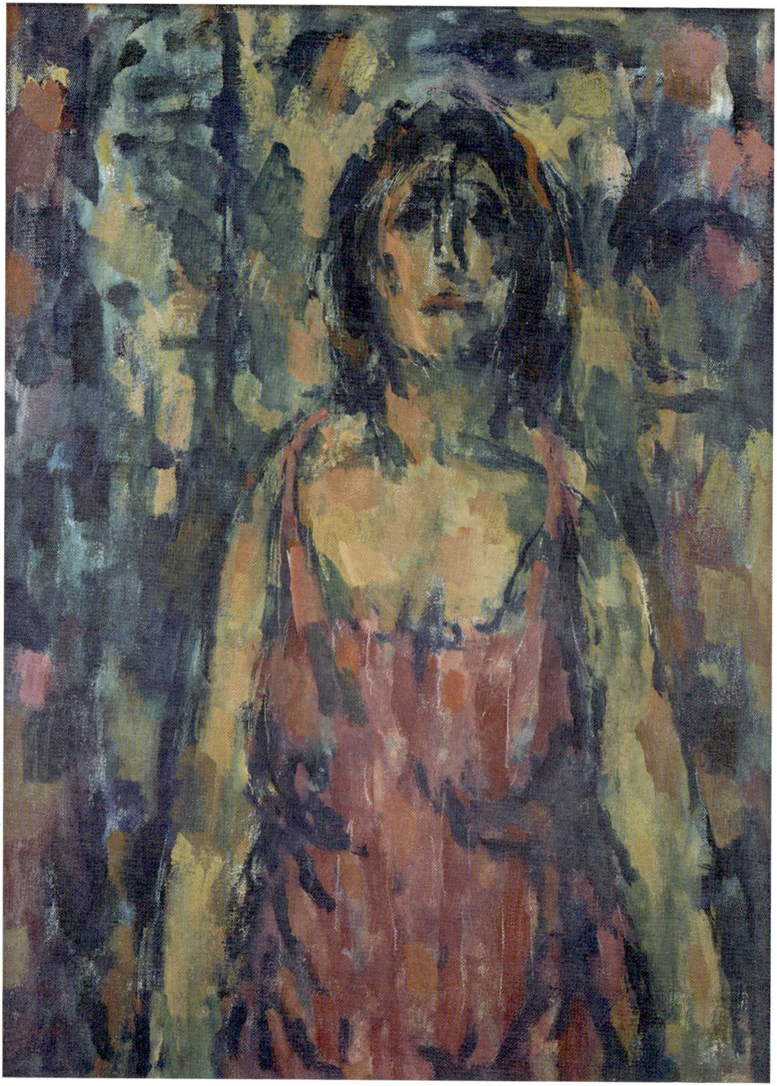

LeRoy Jenson, *The Last Painting*, 2004-5, oil on canvas, 29" x 24"

PRIVATE COLLECTION
PHOTO BY JANET DWYER

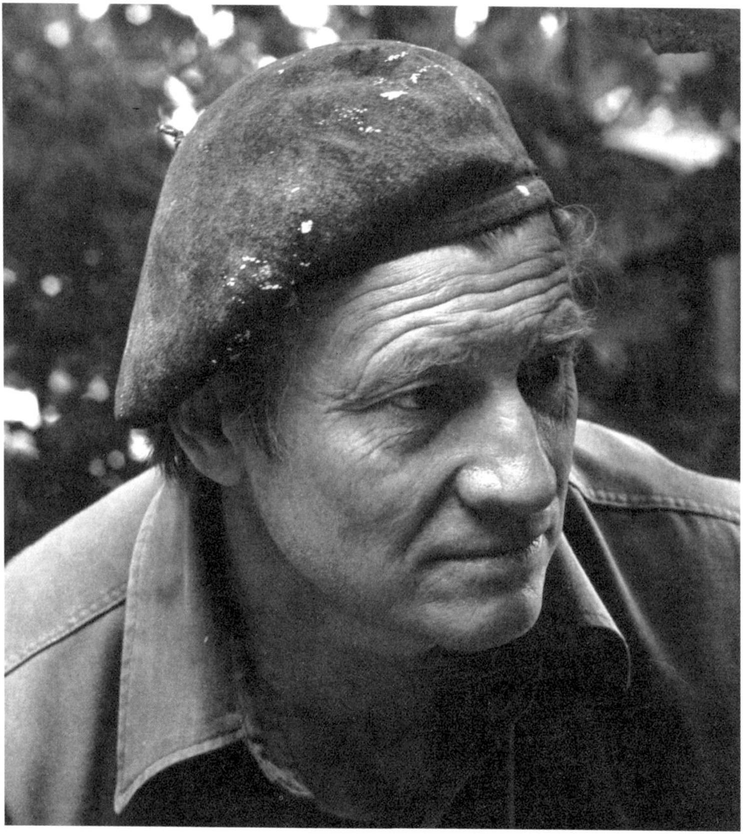

David Marshall

1928–2006

"He was the consummate artist, craftsman, teacher who embraced great art from every generation and from all civilizations. This very expansiveness of thinking and intellectual generosity made David Marshall a sleeping giant of an artist. Because of this legacy and the determination of his friends and with [The Life and Art of David Marshall] *we have a glimpse into the man and his remarkable devotion to art and creativity."*

—J. BROOKS JOYNER, FORMER DIRECTOR OF THE VANCOUVER ART GALLERY

David Marshall was born in 1928 on a horse farm in Islay, Alberta, sixteen months before Black Tuesday, the second son of Robert and Betty Marshall. His childhood and adolescence were marked by a series of family disruptions and poverty. His father simply disappeared one day, leaving his mother behind. Life on the farm without a husband was too much for her, so she departed for Toronto, leaving her two sons in the care of her parents. Marshall was six years old.

FROM FARM TO TORONTO AND VANCOUVER

When David turned twelve, he reunited with his mother and siblings in Toronto. Showing a talent for drawing portraits—he used to make his sister sit for hours—and getting good marks, he nonetheless dropped out of school at fourteen, doing odd jobs up north and in the city. His family was poor, but he pursued another, richer life at the galleries, museums and libraries of Toronto. Art was his refuge, his muse and mentor. In the quiet galleries filled with treasures from the world's great cultures, he discovered himself as an artist. He got his first exposure to sculpture through Rodin's *Adam* and a bronze head of *David* by Mestrovich.

His love for three-dimensional art was born in Vancouver, which he reached in classic Depression style by hitchhiking across the Dominion of Canada with his buddy, Ken Yeung. When they arrived penniless but hopeful in the winter of 1948, an article in *Canadian Art* proclaimed that the unique contrast of "an advanced civilization" flourishing on the edge of a spectacular rainforest wilderness was the key to the "exhilarating climate" for the arts in Vancouver during the mid-fifties.

For about a decade, Marshall was not only part of that "climate," he helped to define it as far as sculpture was concerned. Marshall organized and took part in several important art exhibitions, including his first and last one-man show in1959, at the Vancouver Art Gallery (VAG). Though never famous, he attracted and was part of a group of artists, all rebels, who considered him a master of form and technique. They included George Fertig, Peter Paul Ochs, Jock Hearn, Fred Douglas, LeRoy Jenson, Jack Hardman and Curt Lang.

TEA WITH HENRY MOORE

Buoyed by this early recognition, Marshall and his new wife, Carel, decided to make an epic voyage focused on art to London, England. They arrived on December 6, 1953, and within a month had enrolled at Heatherly's School of Fine Arts. They haunted the museums and galleries while struggling with smog and classes without instructors.

Eventually, they meet and impress one of the greatest sculptors of all time, Henry Moore himself. This was no accident; attending a large Moore exhibition, David finagles an invitation to an open house at Moore's home and studio on April 15. Over tea and crumpets, Marshall takes the opportunity to ask discerning questions, and as they leave, Moore invites them to come back for a visit to the studio.

This second visit on June 12 gives David the chance to have a sculptor-to-sculptor conversation that was to be important in his later development as an artist. They discuss the *Warrior with Shield* on view in the studio, with Moore removing the shield to discuss the space behind it. A third invitation is issued, but lack of time prevents it.

While Moore was the great humanist, Marshall was the great

analyst; he was interested in the same universal and eternal themes as Moore, and spent his entire life developing a language of form to integrate his profound knowledge of physics, mathematics, cosmology and biology into those themes.

Though he never returned to London, the powerful impressions of those nine months set Marshall firmly on the path of what is now known as mid-century modernism. He interpreted it in a way that echoes the Inuit sculptors, who carved some of their work specifically for the sense of touch; they thought the carving was revealed by touch, not by looking at it. David agreed; his work invites touch and rewards with a sensuous experience that totally bypasses the frontal lobes. When Marshall says "you can fool the eye but not the hand," he is echoing a similar statement by Jacob Bronowski who held that in the act of carving "the hand is the cutting edge of the mind."

On one of his infrequent trips to Toronto to visit his mother, they went on a pilgrimage to witness the installation of Henry Moore's *Archer* at the new City Hall in 1966. Apparently he measured it carefully and looked at it for a full eight hours before they could finally pry him away.

ART MAESTRO AT CAPILANO COLLEGE

While the fifties were a period when Marshall dared to dream of a future that allowed him to play a role in the emerging cultural life of Vancouver, the sixties ushered in a different era. As a child of the Depression and a classicist engaged in a formal quest for purity of line and form, he watched it, analyzed it and could tell you exactly where all these changes were coming from—and why they weren't for him. He was increasingly sidelined by the VAG and felt out of step with the reigning Zeitgeist.

He was also tiring of the eternal scrounging for funds. It was time to solve this problem once and for all. After acquiring a teaching certificate, he lasted all of four years teaching grade six art. But this short stint gave him the confidence and classroom experience to make the leap to teaching adults at Capilano College.

In 1973, he accepted a contract position, eventually became a permanent instructor in sculpture, teaching a studio course until 1990. Naturally, he did it his way, clashing openly with the then prominent post-modernist school.

However, his students admired his calm, well-organized classes, his knowledge of art history and his precise use of tools. He was also charismatic and made connections that were global as well as surprising. Teaching adults with a genuine interest in art suited Marshall's temperament and abilities perfectly.

A THIRST FOR INTERNATIONAL CONTACTS

Marshall was always involved in furthering the cause of sculpture and fellow sculptors, and the 1975 Vancouver International Stone Sculpture Symposium gave him a perfect opportunity. This event opened the new Van Dusen Botanical Gardens, a pivotal moment in the evolution of public sculpture in Vancouver. David carved a major piece, *Three Forms,* in Travertine marble, and his friend Gerhard Class directed the symposium. A committee consisting of local sculptors, including Marshall, selected twelve sculptors from nine countries.

After over two months of relentless work, the symposium and the Garden were formally opened on August 24, with small works exhibited at the VAG and eleven works sited permanently at the Gardens. It was regarded as a complete success by the public as well as the sculptors.

This symposium whet Marshall's appetite, and luckily during 1978, Sweden and Yugoslavia were hosting international stone carving symposia. Marshall was accepted, and so for the first time since 1954, he found himself in Europe for six months. The results can be seen to this day in the Palace Grounds of Sofiero Castle in Helsingborg, Sweden, and the Sculpture Garden of Aranjelovac in Yugoslavia. In Yugoslavia, Marshall produced a marvelous sculpture he named *Aquarius*, which later became a bronze he cast in an edition of three in Vancouver.

The next year, 1979, the Marshalls traveled to Mexico City, and Marshall made a connection to Gallerias Mer-Kup, one of its most prominent galleries. Here was a chance to arrange another symposium. He already knew the Mexican sculptor Sebastian, and they arranged an exchange of sculptors between the two countries with the help of the Sculptors' Society of British Columbia (SSBC).

Malcolm McTaggart, Zelko Kujundzic, Dwane Neuberger and David Marshall participated, working on their pieces throughout the summer in Mexico and exhibiting them at the Gallerias Mer-Kup in October. The Canadian Ambassador opened the exhibition. Marshall even sold one bronze, *Hands and Eye*.

During July and August,1980, UBC's department of continuing education, Capilano College and the SSBC hosted Mexican sculptors Sebastian, Moayo, Marta Palau and Mauricio Guerrereo in a similar workshop, focusing on bronze casting. The summer was capped by a formal dinner and reception at the Mexican Consulate. These Symposia cemented Marshall's international reputation.

FINAL YEARS AND INTERNATIONAL RECOGNITION

After "retiring" in 1990 from his position at Capilano College, he spent the next dozen years carving, casting and creating to his heart's content on the campus. Among the most important sculptures created during this period are three large standing figures carved from Carrara marble. Unlike much of Marshall's later work, which grappled with the concept of evolutionary change, these figures evoke a timeless realm of absolute values, almost like totems for the species.

David also continued to exhibit with the SSBC annually, and in 2000 he mounted his third one-man show, his first retrospective, at SFU's Teck Gallery.

His second big retrospective in 2001 happened at the Big Rock Garden Park in Bellingham, Washington, organized by one of his most fervent admirers, Professor George F. Drake. At the May 13, 2001 opening, Marshall wiped away tears. "Nobody has ever done anything like this," he said, "my work has never looked this beautiful."

When Marshall started to show signs of a serious illness in 2004, it was two years before doctors at Burnaby General Hospital finally made the diagnosis: cancer, a virulent form of leukemia. During his last week in the hospital, he was still making plans and sketches while dozens of his friends, admirers and fellow artists came to his bedside to bid him adieu. It was January 2006, and he never went home again.

He was seventy-eight, and his achievements included no less than eight one-man shows, seventy-three group shows and works in public and private collections in Canada, U.S., Mexico, Sweden, Serbia and Japan. Marshall left behind his wife, Carel, and an enormous legacy of art that is, to this day, looking for a permanent home in Canada. Alas, in 2020, not in Canada, but in Bellingham, Washington, after the persistence of George Drake, the David Marshall Sculpture Gallery at the Big Rock Garden Park was created.

David Marshall's work is held in the following public collections: Vancouver Art Gallery; VanDusen Gardens, Vancouver; Burnaby Art Gallery; James Cowen Theatre, Burnaby; David Marshall Sculpture Gallery, Bellingham; CAITAC International Inc., Okayama, Japan; Public Sculpture Garden, Aranjelovac, Serbia; Sofiero Palace, Helsingborg, Sweden.

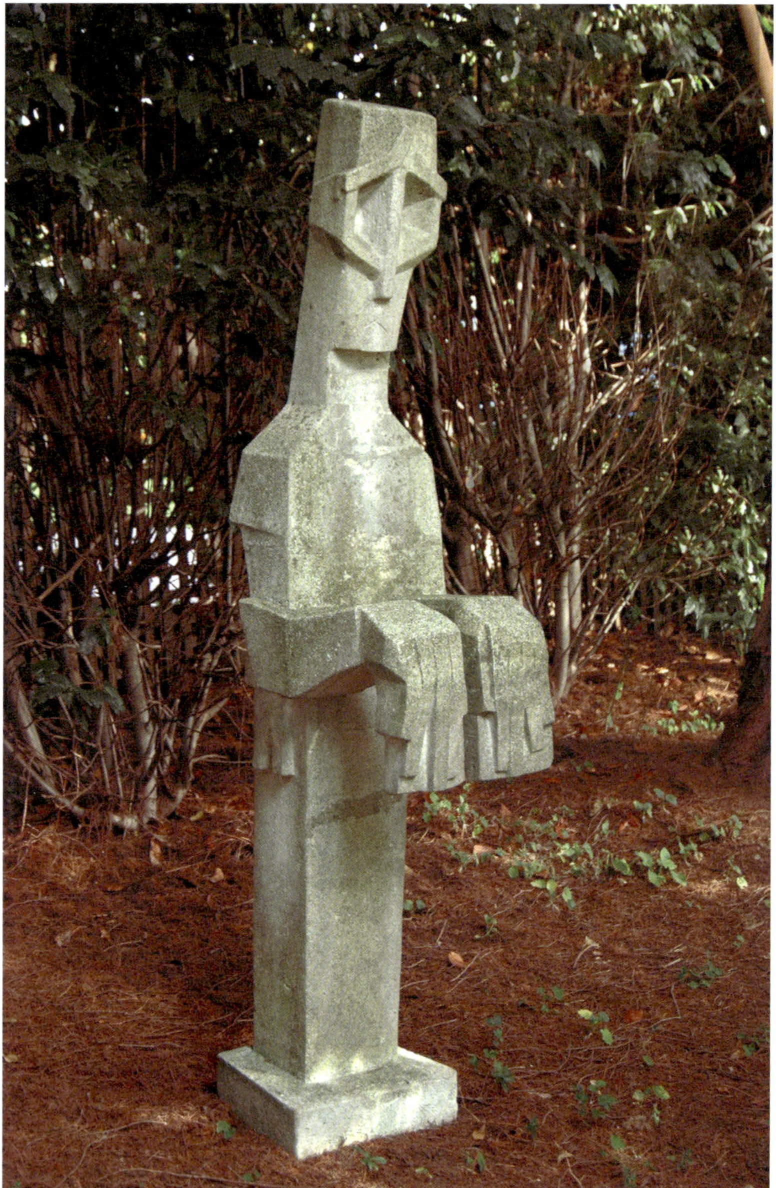

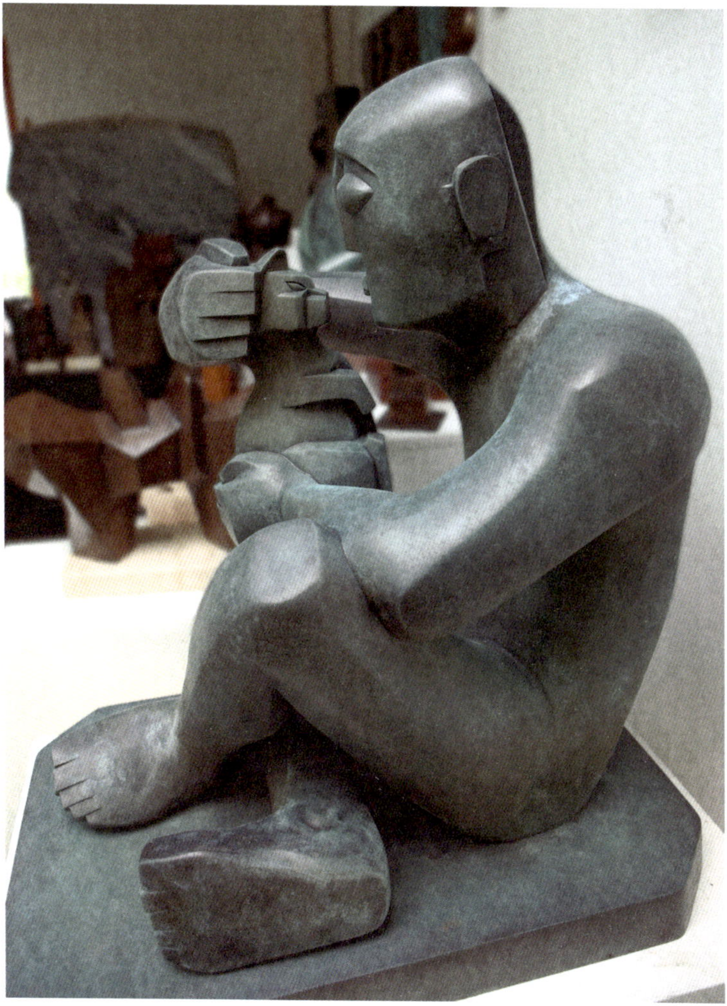

◄ David Marshall, *Injured Fireman*, 1957-8, Concrete, 80" x 18" x 22"

PRIVATE COLLECTION
PHOTO BY SUSO GYGAX

▲ David Marshall, *Boy with Cat*, 1955-1991, Bronze, 28" x 20" x 26"

PRIVATE COLLECTION
DAN FAIRCHILD PHOTOGRAPHY

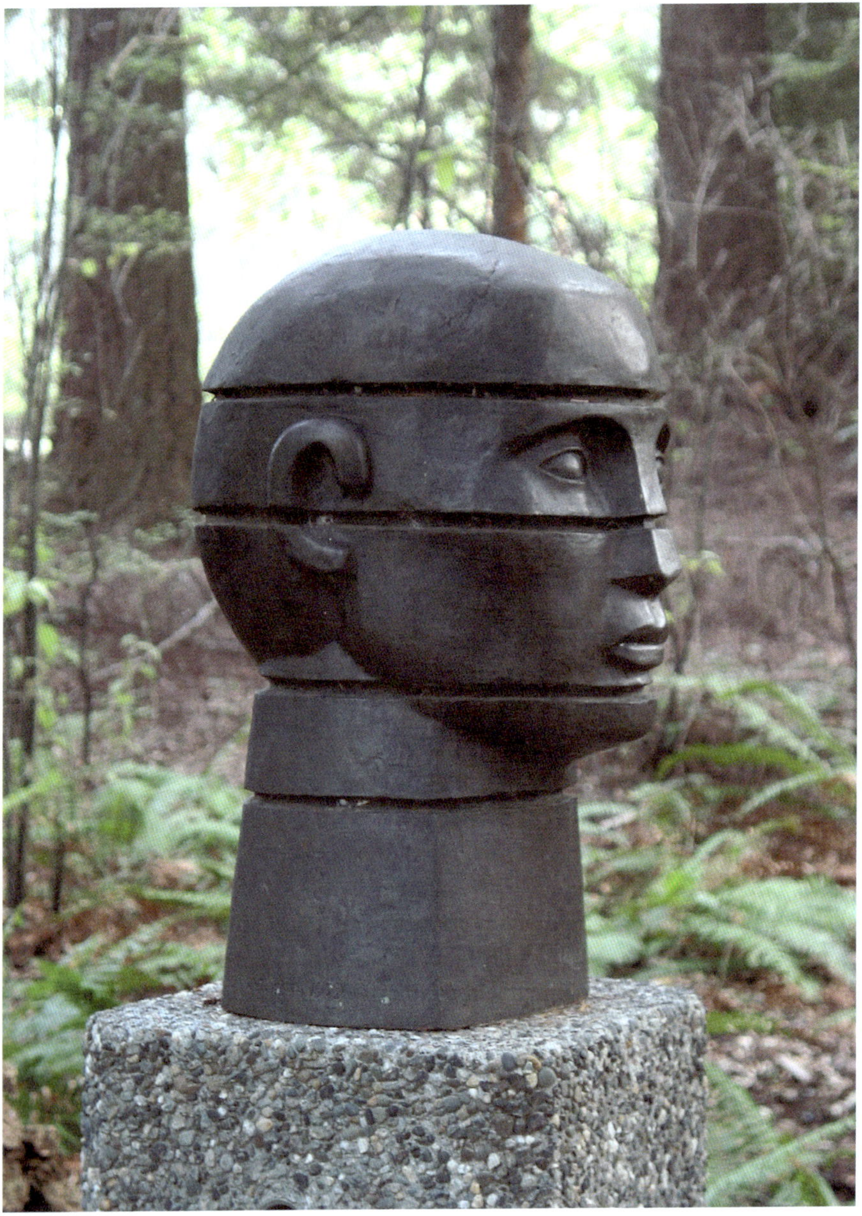

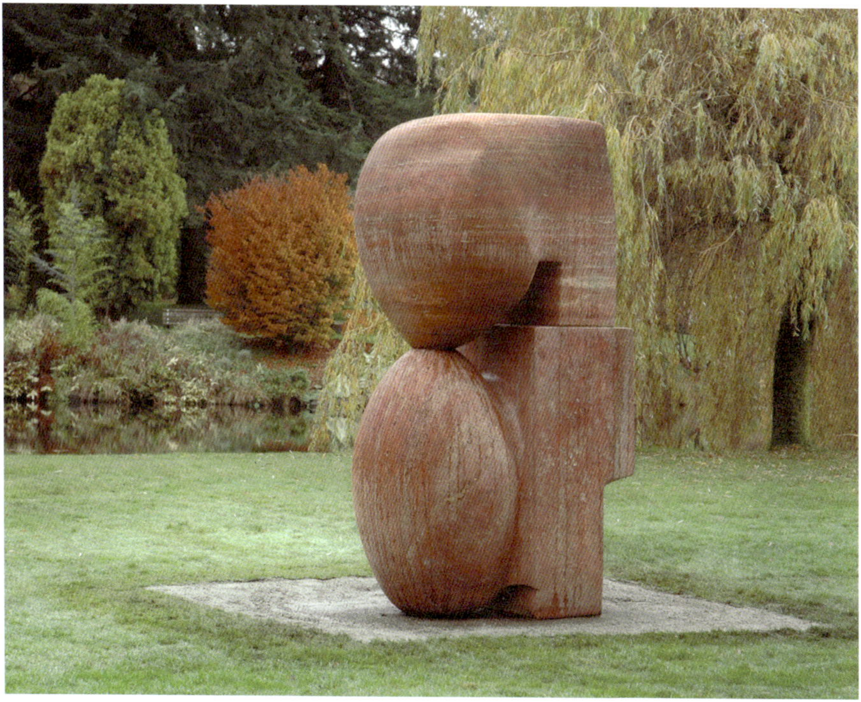

▲ David Marshall, *Three Forms*, 1975, Travertine marble, 8'

COLLECTION OF THE VANDUSEN GARDENS
PHOTO BY K.E. OHRN

◄ David Marshall, *Head*, 1978, Bronze

COLLECTION OF THE DAVID MARSHALL SCULPTURE GALLERY, BIG ROCK GARDEN PARK, BELLINGHAM, WASHINGTON, US.
PHOTO BY TORE OFTENESS

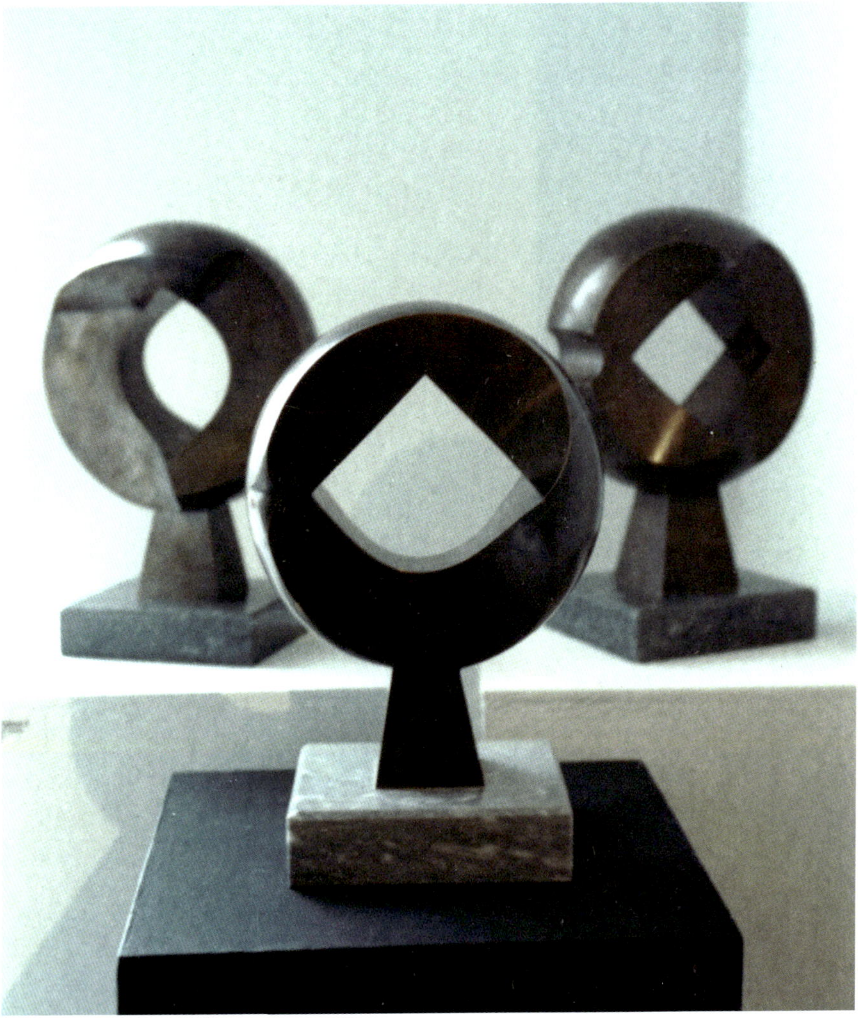

David Marshall, *Variations on a Sphere*, n.d., dimensions unknown

COLLECTION OF THE DAVID MARSHALL SCULPTURE GALLERY, BIG ROCK GARDEN PARK, BELLINGHAM, WASHINGTON.
PHOTO BY GEORGE DRAKE

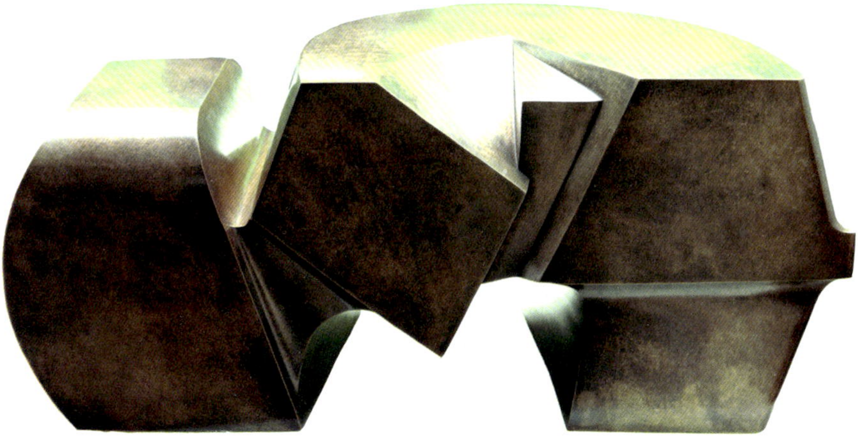

David Marshall, *Sculpture #4*, 2005-2008, Bronze
11 ¼" x 27" x 9 ½"

PRIVATE COLLECTION
DAN FAIRCHILD PHOTOGRAPHY

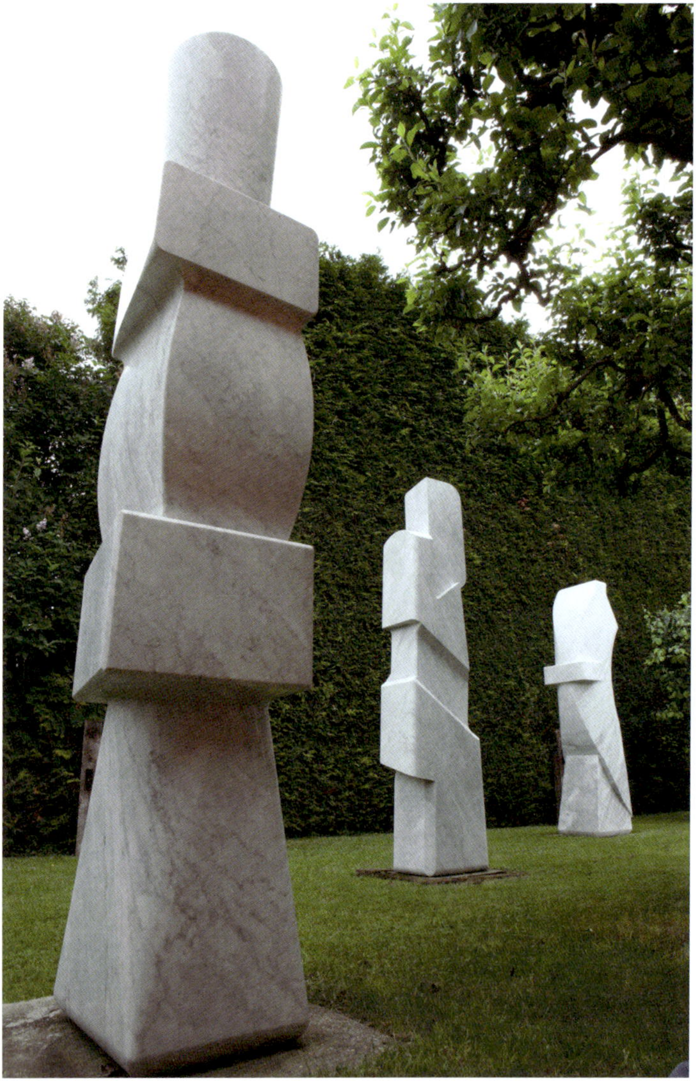

David Marshall, *Three Carrara's*, 1990s, Travertine Marble, 8'

COLLECTION OF VANDUSEN GARDEN
DAN FAIRCHILD PHOTOGRAPHY

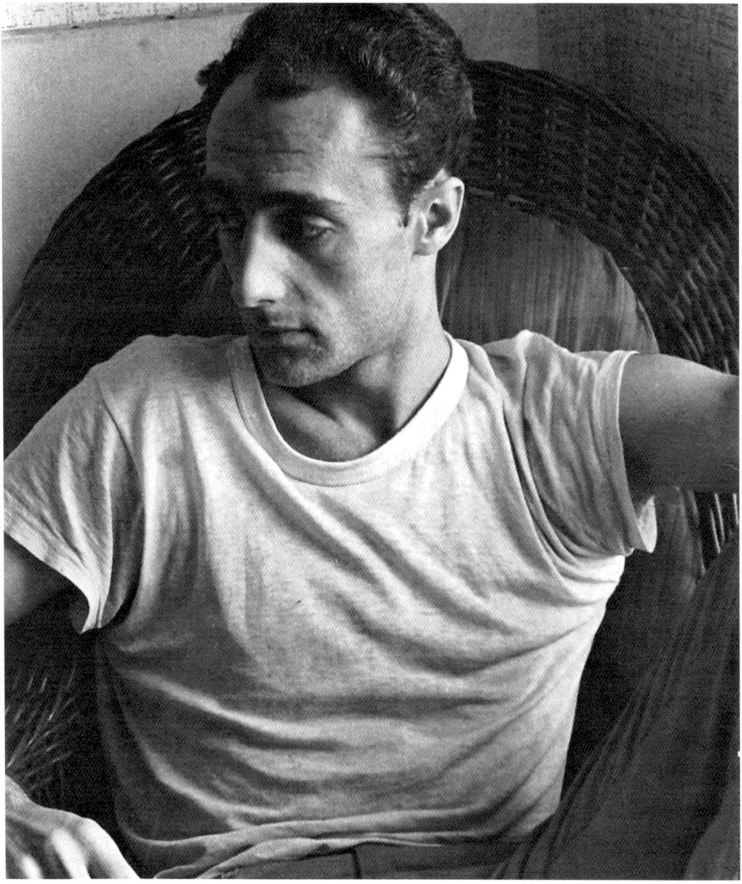

Frank Molnar

1936–

"Those great masters of the brush stroke have influenced him: the sparseness and hesitancy of Bonnard, the chiseling directness of Van Gogh, the otherworldly colouring of Gauguin. They have all come to play in the field of Frank, and then some. But by now, his style and imagery are all his own."

—CHARLES VAN SANDWYK, CANADIAN ARTIST, ILLUSTRATOR AND WRITER

Frank Stephan Molnar was born into a typical working-class home on the outskirts of Budapest in 1936. After studying agriculture and animal husbandry at a technical high school, he applied to veterinary school, but without family ties to the Communist Party, post-secondary education was impossible. Young Frank also craved the freedom to paint, an impossible dream under communist rule. "Art was out of the question," said Frank.

So, at age 20, Frank fled Budapest during the 1956 Hungarian Revolution. He and four friends found their way to refugee camps, first in Essen, Austria, then in Vienna and Munich, before heading to America.

He scored a fellowship to Saint Vincent College in Pennsylvania where he took general studies and learned English, and then went on to the Pennsylvania Academy of the Fine Arts, studying under well-known American artists, including painter Franklin Chenault Watkins. Frank learned different painting techniques, drawing, artistic anatomy, art history and perspective, all the time perfecting his figurative work. "All painting is essentially abstract if you get down to the nitty gritty, but to be non-figurative and non-representative never really interested me." As he was finishing his studies, the Vietnam War was escalating. Draft looked like a certainty. Frank took the train to Montreal and arrived in Vancouver on May 5, 1962. He quickly discovered that Eastern European immigrants were not warmly welcomed in the largely Waspish Vancouver.

THE NUDE

Frank's passion for bold dynamic nudes with provocative themes and sensuous colours immediately set him firmly apart from the artistic trends. Inspired by the romantics and the impressionists, he put his own interpretation on goddesses and Greek mythology. In 1963, he painted the first of a series of erotic canvasses depicting Leda and the Swan, as Michelangelo, Correggio, Francios Boucher, Leonardo da Vinci and other artists had also done. He worked in his studio upstairs, drew from live models and seemed to switch effortlessly from figurative work and still lifes in oil to watercolours, a softer medium better able to capture West Coast land and seascapes.

According to Frank, Canadians simply cannot handle nudes: "They think my art is disturbing for the children. They say they wouldn't have it in their living room, wouldn't have it in their home."

Frank considers himself a colourist in the same tradition as French romantic painter Eugene Delacroix, and later Georges Seurat, Paul Gauguin and Pierre Bonnard.

"I love the human figure, I love the feminine figure, I love the sensuality of it," Frank explained. "Colour to me is a manifestation of sensuous painting. You can paint an apple and make it sensuous and romantic by the use of colour; it's a much more European concept of colour." He pointed to a huge nude canvas painted in a surrealist style. In it there's a woman lying down with her arm outstretched, a child, angel trumpets and gladiolas, a hummingbird and the moon. It was Frank's valentine present to his wife Sylvia in 2000. He hired a model for the body so she would not know and painted her face from a photograph.

Frank paints on expensive Irish or Belgium linen that he sizes and stretches. Using acid-free canvasses, he applies top-quality imported paints. He finds that if he looks at something too closely, he gets carried away by the reality of it. Instead of painting from the model, he'll sketch first and paint from the sketches.

KITSILANO, OSOYOOS AND LONG BEACH

Through friends in Vancouver's Hungarian community, Frank met Sylvia Pidraziuk, a student at UBC who modeled part-time to help pay for her tuition. They married in 1966.

Frank and Sylvia moved into an apartment above a grocery store at 2205 West 6th in Vancouver's Kitsilano. They paid $65 a month for their two-bedroom apartment with a large kitchen and a fireplace in the living room.

The Molnars were surrounded by a lively artistic colony that included painters Jack Akroyd, Jock Hearn, Jack Dale, Jack Akroyd and Roy Kiyooka, poets John Newlove, Judith Copithorne and bill bissett and sculptor Elek Imredy. Poet Judith Copithorne modeled at the art school, and remembered Frank as being, like most artists in the area, "severely underemployed" but always painting.

Molnar and Akroyd shared the costs of models for weekly drawing classes in Imredy's studio. The older sculptor frequently paid both painters one dollar an hour to help with the clay and the plaster molds and other labour-intensive parts of sculpture.

Outside Frank's Kitsilano home and studio, Vancouver was a young city in constant change, and the cultural elite comprised a handful of men such as Gordon Smith, Jack Shadbolt, B.C. Binning and Toni Onley. These middle-class artists with mostly English backgrounds tapped into the Vancouver Art Gallery and taught at the Vancouver School of Art.

Serious, soft-spoken and intellectual, Frank seemed much older than his years. Growing up in the midst of war and deprivation left him no time for abstract expressionism, performance art, photography, popular culture or, by the 70s, conceptualism.

Although Frank Molnar and Jack Akroyd had vastly different personalities and painting styles, they were close friends. For years, they would hit the road in the early spring, drive to Kelowna and paint the orchards.

In the 1990s, Frank switched from painting orchards to painting seascapes at Long Beach on Vancouver Island. "On the West Coast of Vancouver Island, you have the constant rain and moisture, and in the summer, there is the fog. The fog starts to lift and the sun comes out and its unbelievably beautiful." "Most people," he said, "believe that fog is grey, but if you look at it in the changing light, it reflects every colour that you can think of because the droplets break the light into the components of the rainbow." Frank said these sensitive colour changes come through best when using watercolours. "The medium gives the painting freshness," and he enjoys the immediacy of it. Because of its delicacy, Frank's method is to sketch and take pictures of the changing scene—sometimes as much as every half-hour then go back to the studio and paint.

ART SHOWS AND SALONS

Twice a year, the Molnars held weekend salon-style art shows in their apartment. On the whole, the shows were successful, but also stressful and expensive for the couple. Sylvia would prepare the invitations, do the mailing and then cater the parties, often for up to 200 guests. "I firmly believe that we were way ahead of our times. We were doing home visits, studio visits, meet the artist, that kind of thing, and people weren't used to it," said Sylvia. "We did it with class, but we were very poor."

Frank said, "Sylvia was the moving spirit when we had exhibitions. She would give me 100 percent support every which way." For a time, she became Sylvia Molnar's Artists' Agent, representing various artist friends. Sylvia recalled, "It was very difficult, I was new on the scene, and it was hard to break through."

While today's buyers want to meet the artists and expect to see their work displayed in their own studios, bypassing the galleries was considered heresy in the '60s. It's a price Frank paid as he has rarely exhibited his work in public.

A few exceptions were the five shows he held at Peder and Anne Pedersen's Danish Art Gallery in Kitsilano, two with Akroyd. In the mid-1960s, he had a brush with the law when the police were called to the Danish Gallery over the exhibition of one of his full-frontal nudes. The gallery owner refused to take it down.

His early work showed at the Gallery of B.C. Arts across from Stanley Park, and he held joint shows with Georg Schmerholz, at the sculptor's Kitsilano studio.

In 1970, Frank was one of forty-six artists selected from over 450 entries to exhibit work at Survey 70: Sondage Realism(e)s, a co-production of the Montreal Museum of Fine Arts and the Art Gallery of Ontario. Frank exhibited three oil paintings, *View from Mission Abbey, Kalamalka Lake* and *The Slough,* alongside such well-known names as Michael Snow, Toni Onley, Tony Urquhart, Ken Danby and Joyce Wieland.

But Molnar, like other artists of the '60s and '70s, was largely ignored in the gallery rush to embrace modernity. Aiding their obscurity was the problem that there were only a handful of galleries in Vancouver and little chance for exhibitions.

TEACHING

Jack Akroyd introduced Frank to Peter Aspell, another figurative painter living in Vancouver. "Peter said, 'Frank, you and I are the only sensualists in this damn town,'" recalled Frank. At the time, Stephen Leskard was establishing a commercial art and design school at Capilano College and looking for instructors. Aspell, who taught at the Vancouver School of Art, suggested he hire Frank.

As the '60s drew to a close, Frank had no illusion that he would be a career painter. He took a teaching job at the newly formed Capilano College. Having an income freed him to continue painting exactly the way he wanted without worry of putting food on the table.

David Marshall joined the college sculpture department and foundry, and he and Frank were colleagues and friends for almost 20 years. He would often give Marshall a ride home after classes.

Frank taught artistic anatomy and life drawing. Not everyone loved his style. His insistence that students mastered the technical skills grated on those who were used to a conceptual approach where the idea is more important than the art. "I tried to teach them to be an artist, to have the eye of an artist, to look at things and see things as an artist," he said, adding that many of his students got jobs instantly and went on to be well-known illustrators and commercial artists—people such as Charles Van Sandwyk, Andrew McDermott and Cori Creed.

Van Sandwyk believes that Frank will be remembered as one of the great sensualists of this province:

> "I think he'll be remembered in the same tones as painters like Varley who were fabulous painters that did their own thing."

Frank Molnar continues to paint in his studio.

Molnar's work is held in private collections in Canada, Europe and the U.S.

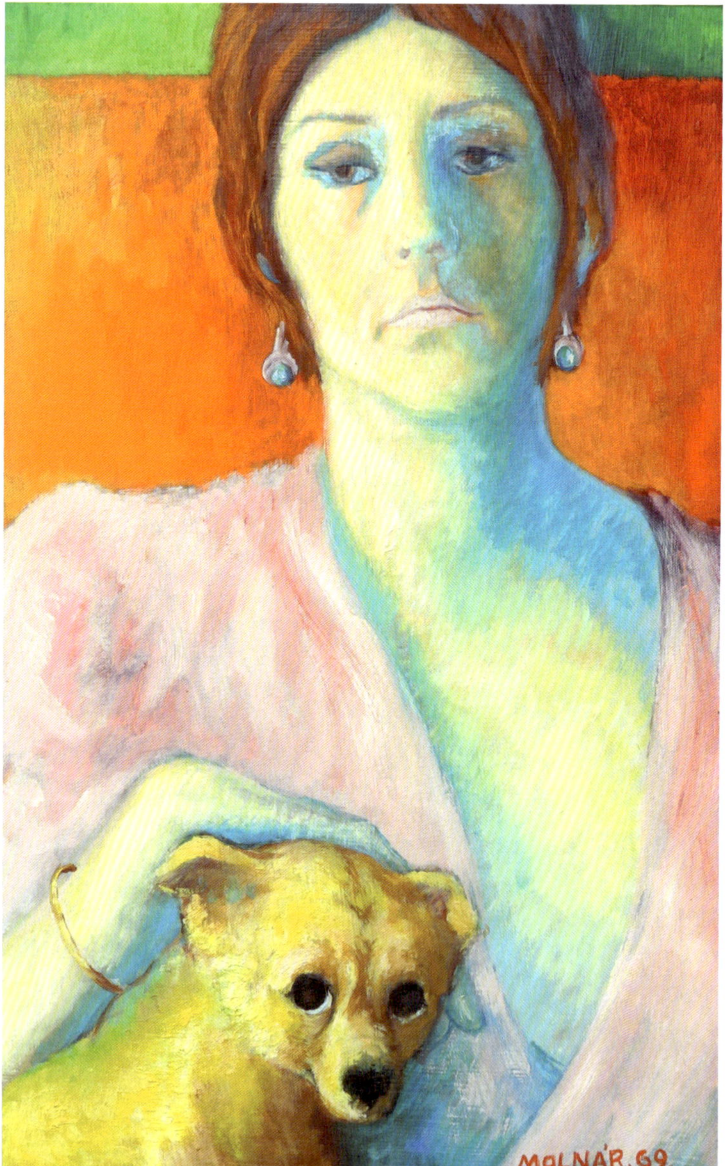
MOLNÁR.69.

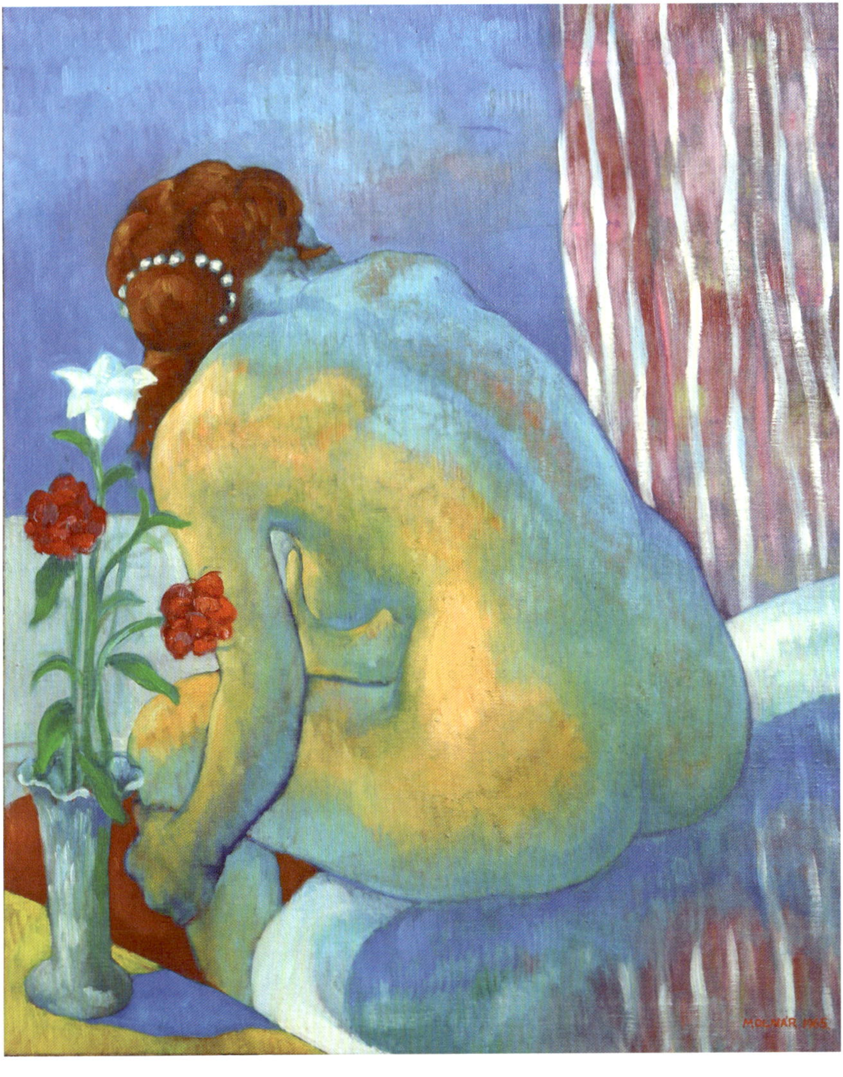

◄ Frank Molnar, *Sylvia*, 1969, oil on canvas, 18" x 12"

PRIVATE COLLECTION
DAN FAIRCHILD PHOTOGRAPHY

▲ Frank Molnar, *Untitled*, 1965, oil on canvas, 36" x 30"

PRIVATE COLLECTION
DAN FAIRCHILD PHOTOGRAPHY

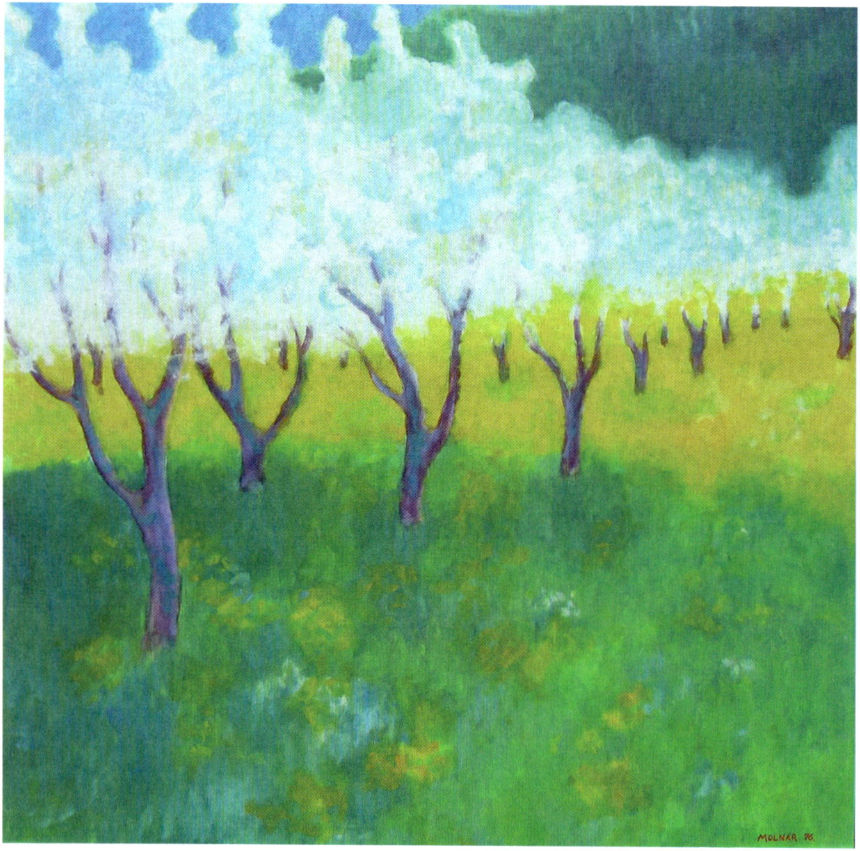

Frank Molnar, *Orchard Blossoms*, 1976, oil on canvas, 40" x 42"

PRIVATE COLLECTION
PHOTO BY NICHOLAS WESTBRIDGE

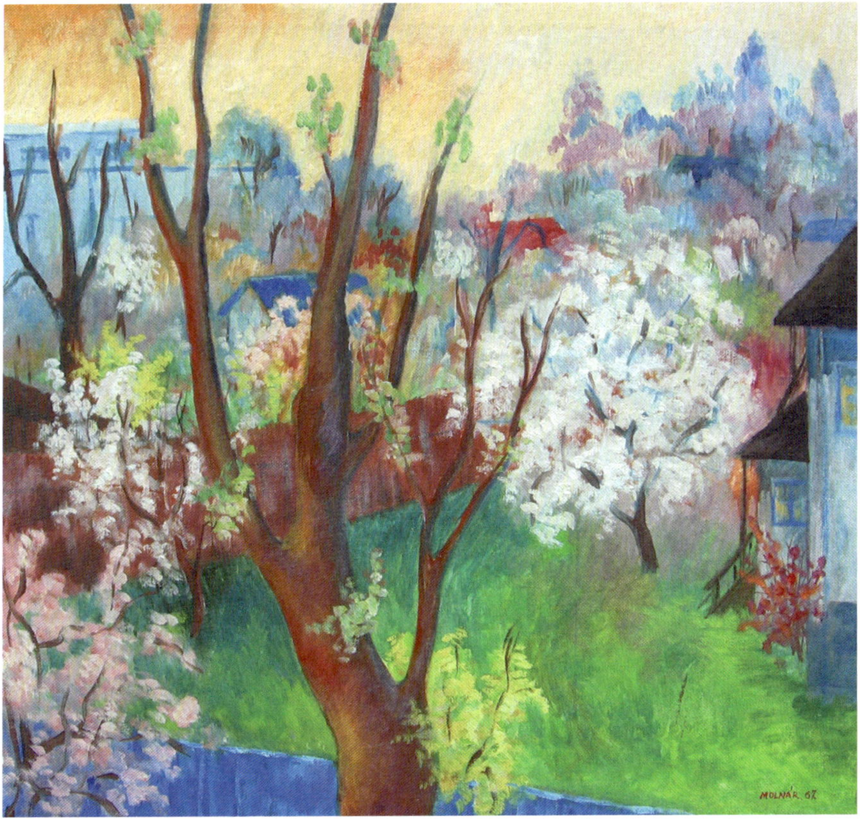

Frank Molnar, *Backyard Blossoms*, 1967, oil on canvas, 30" x 33"

PRIVATE COLLECTION
PHOTO BY NICOLAS WESTBRIDGE

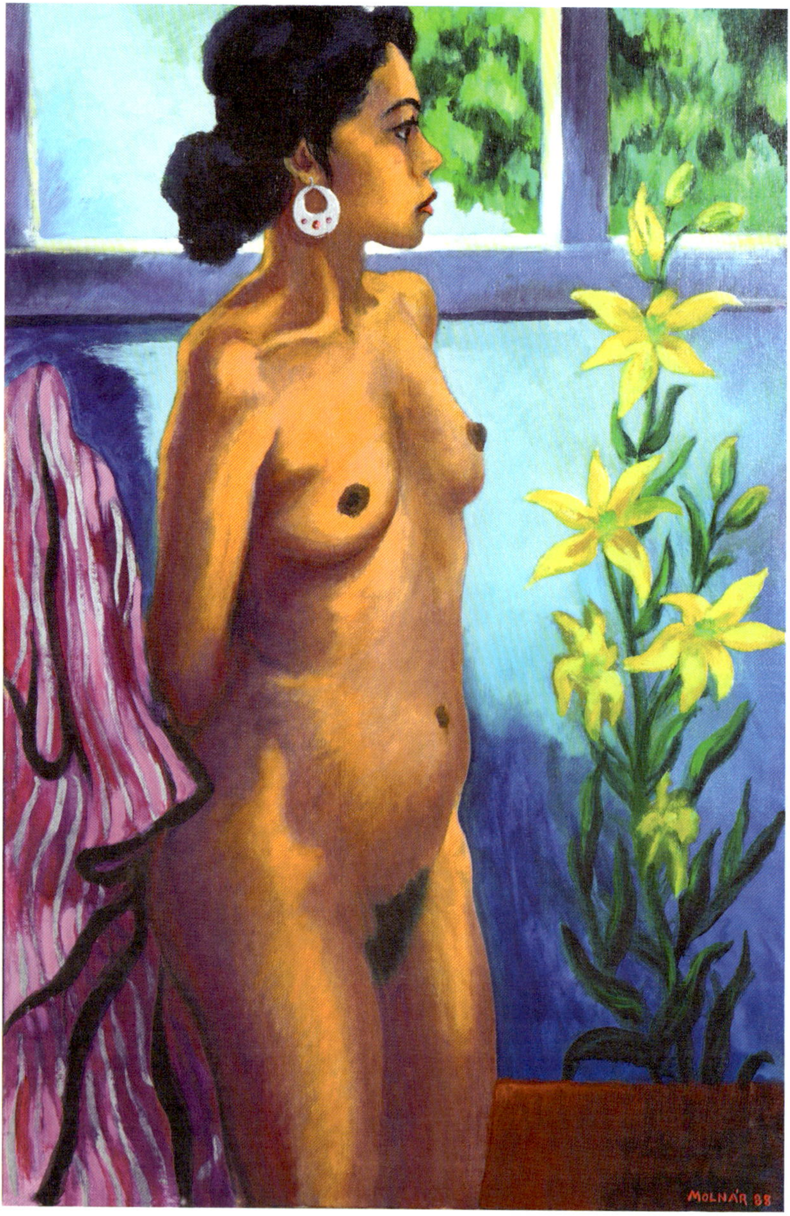
MOLNÁR 88

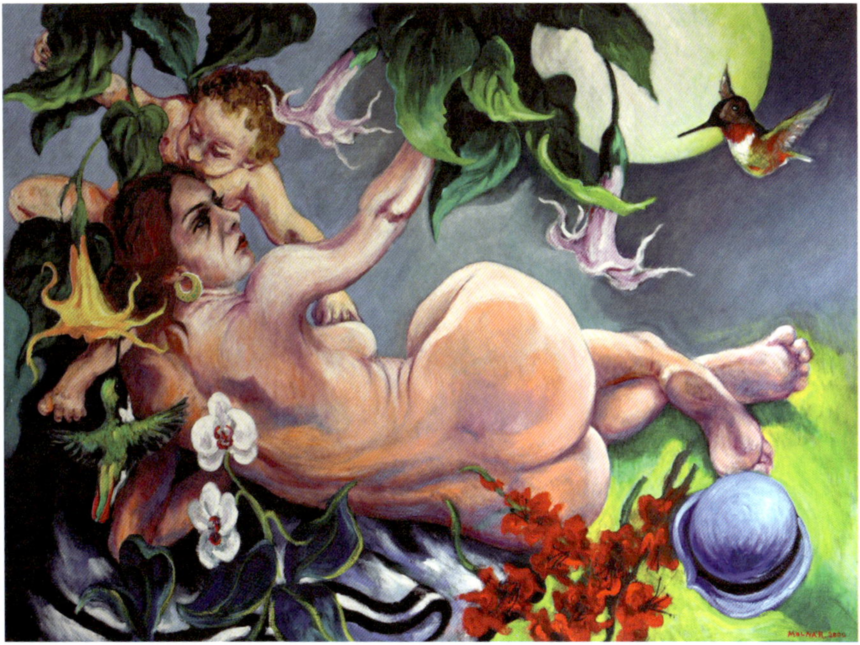

▲ Frank Molnar, *Valentine*, 2000, oil on canvas, 41" x 57"

PRIVATE COLLECTION
DAN FAIRCHILD PHOTOGRAPHY

◄ Frank Molnar, *Mulatto Nude with Yellow Flowers*, 1988, oil on canvas, 44" x 31"

PRIVATE COLLECTION
DAN FAIRCHILD PHOTOGRAPHY

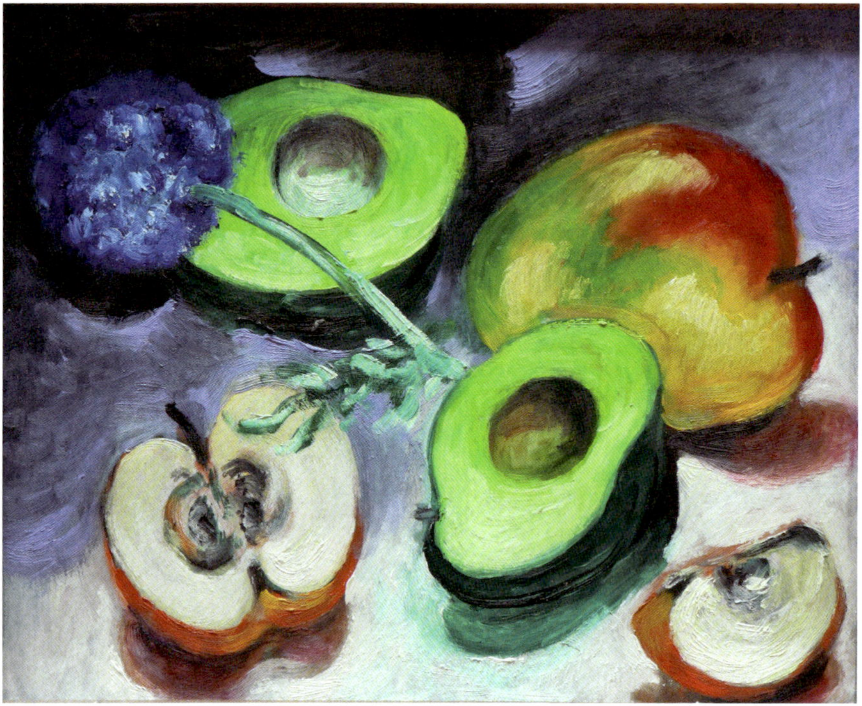

Frank Molnar, *Untitled*, 2005, oil on canvas, 11" x 14"

PRIVATE COLLECTION
DAN FAIRCHILD PHOTOGRAPHY

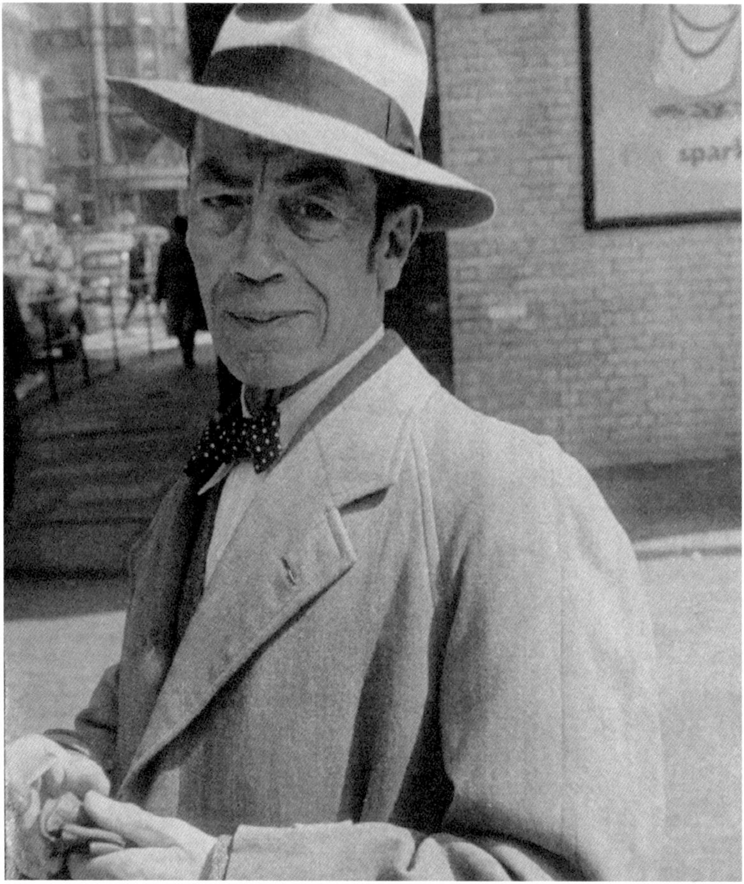

Arthur Pitts

1889–1972

"During an era when it was policy to purge our [First Nations] culture, Arthur Pitts quietly walked amongst us, as a friend, painting us as equals, respectfully capturing moments and people. Those who struggle with the concepts of 'cultural appropriation' and 'reconciliation' can learn from his example."

– CAREY NEWMAN, KWAKWAKA'WAKW/COAST SALISH ARTIST

Born 1889 in Bermondsey, a working class area of South East London, Arthur Pitts grew up poor, though his father worked steadily in the drapery and tailoring industry. While in school, he learned photography, but left at age fourteen to apprentice as a "learner designer" and then work as a stencil cutter with the Permanent Enamel Company. Later as a showcard writer with Clement Newbury and Company, he expanded his artistic skills, also taking some evening classes at the London City Centre School of Arts. By 1910 he was a certified showcard writer or commercial artist, eventually moving for higher wages to the firm of Tisdall and Wrikins, where he made enough money to buy himself a Kodak camera with a telescopic stand. Arthur avidly enjoyed walking and biking excursions into the countryside and kept journals of his trips, using his photographs as well as his drawing and painting skills to illustrate his adventures. He was a voracious reader and reflected the Edwardian interest in exploring the world.

SOUTH AFRICA, THE GREAT WAR, AND CANADA

Determined to see more of the world, Arthur saved his money and booked passage to Cape Town, South Africa, en route to Durban, Natal, where an aunt and uncle had already immigrated. Within weeks, he had a contract for twelve illustrations and secured a position as night clerk with the South Africa Railway at Malvern. After four months, he was promoted to station foreman at Naval Hill, Colenso. Arthur's passion for walking led to long daily strolls, photographing scenery and the Zulu people, homes, and ceremonies.

After returning home to England in 1914 to visit family, Arthur was ready for more travel and went by ship and then CPR train to Winnipeg, beginning a journal called "Illusions of a Wanderers Life." However, with World War I breaking out, he travelled to Vancouver to enlist with the 72nd Seaforth Highlanders, which landed him back in England for an enjoyable reunion with family and the purchase of a new camera before being sent to the trenches near Cassels, France. Always a keen learner, Arthur began teaching himself French, explored the culture and countryside when on leave and used his camera to document what he saw. After some close calls in the trenches, he was severely wounded by shrapnel when both arms were shredded and suffered compound fractures. Arthur was sent back to England for a slow recovery, discouraged that he might never be able to paint and photograph again. Eventually, the medical team recommended further treatments in Canada, and on New Year's Day, 1917, he arrived in Halifax and then travelled to Vancouver, where he purchased, with back pay, a new Kodak No. 1A camera, complete with attachments and case, as well as painting supplies.

Eventually transferred to Resthaven Hospital in Sidney, north of Victoria, Arthur felt isolated from the city, but he developed a routine of reading, strolling and sketching. He also started a military-sponsored course in bookkeeping (in case his dream of being a professional artist did not come true) as well as one in caricature and cartooning offered by the International Correspondence School (ICS) based in Toronto. In the spring, he met the love of his life—Peggy McKenzie, daughter of an upper-middle-class family, whose ancestors were farming pioneers near W̱SÁNEĆ First Nations land in the Mount Newton area of the Saanich Peninsula. Through this environment, he began a lifelong connection to Indigenous peoples of the province.

By the fall of 1917, with his rehabilitation deemed sufficient, Arthur was discharged and took a position as a clerk with the Leave and

Furlough section of the Medical Board. He increased his output of art work of local and First Nations people and scenes. On his next trip to the McKenzie property, he was anxious to visit the neighbouring Tsartlip Reserve.

> ....On arriving at the Reserve, a distance of 2 miles from Saanichton, I found very few of the inhabitants present, the majority being engaged fishing & in various other pursuits in the district. However, fortune aided me considerably & presented to my gaze a typical Indian family occupied on the adjacent shore mending nets & the like. On my enquiries for baskets they invited me into a large barn which I afterwards learned was often used for the purpose of dancing. An hour spent herein produced several baskets & a pair of hand-knitted socks made from the raw wool as taken from the sheep's back...Before leaving this interesting family I was fortunately able to secure a rough sketch of an old woman squatting around the fire & some smoking salmon hanging on the beams above.

Two years later, he began a job with the War Gratuity branch of the Army Pay Office and completed his coursework at the ICS, receiving a diploma with highest recommendations.

ART SCHOOLS AND VANCOUVER

Engaged to Peggy, who was finishing her nursing training, Arthur returned to England to establish himself as an artist, with the plan for her to join him. He enrolled in the Westminster School of Art and began producing work he hoped to sell to newspapers and magazines. Unsuccessful in launching a career as dreamed, Arthur returned to Victoria in the summer of 1921. Involved with the Victoria Sketch Club and the Island Arts and Crafts Society, he renewed his efforts to get paid for submissions of art to newspapers and magazines. But by 1923, with meagre income, he accepted the support of the McKenzie family who provided room and board in a summer cabin in exchange for chopping wood. Arthur reconnected with local First Nations people, who welcomed him to the Tsartlip Reserve, inviting him to ceremonies such as the Shwey Shwey dance. In 1924 he was able to get steady employment as a commercial artist at the Advertisers Engraving Company in Vancouver, and he and Peggy finally wed. With this secure job, Arthur actively painted and took evening classes at the Vancouver School of Decorative and Applied Arts, where his favourite instructor was Charles Scott. On Sundays, he and Peggy took excursions to Stanley Park, Capilano Canyon or other spots; Arthur would bring paper and pencils, or unpack his watercolours and card, which was his preferred media, while Peggy knit or read.

WEST COAST TRIPS AND PAINTING FIRST NATIONS

By 1926 Arthur began frequent day trips in the Vancouver area or caught the Union steamship up the coast. With his wife, he sketched intensely in the Saanichton area as well as travelling in an old Ford Roadster to the north of Vancouver Island. During the summer of 1929, they drove with friends through Southern B.C. to Cranbrook, returning by train to Vancouver from Golden. With the manager's job at Vancouver Engravers, the couple enjoyed buying antiques, a robust social life and a trip in the summer of 1930 to the west coast of Vancouver Island. However, due to the Depression, Arthur ended up at Zenith Engraving with longer hours and less pay. Still he was able to make a few sketching trips, one was to "an Indian village little known to Vancouver, south of Ladner."

Within his circle of friends were artists Max Maynard and Jock

Macdonald, and he was one of the first to become an annual charter member of the newly opened Vancouver Art Gallery. In addition to numerous commercial freelance jobs, Arthur joined Angel Engraving, and increased his work with portraiture. In order to keep finances under control during the Depression, Arthur and Peggy again returned to the Saanich Peninsula to live at the McKenzie home. Tommy Paul, Chief of the Tsartlip came to visit Arthur and see his picture collection. Soon after Arthur was completing the Chief's portrait, and began his practise of providing a duplicate picture for the sitter, building his "Indian Collection" of First Nations peoples in their traditional regalia. In 1933 the couple sailed from Seattle to Alaska, where Peggy's brother lived. Arthur found a wealth of subject matter in the Tlingit and Kaigani Haida cultures on Prince of Wales Island near Craig and the village of Taxican, where he used watercolours to depict villages, totem poles, community houses, canoes and gravesites. "We counted 45 totems with evidence of about 10 at least, rotting in the ground. Very little remains of their houses other than pillars. The foundations nevertheless could be easily traced in numerous community houses. A row or street extended from one end to the other. I lost no time [and] secured two pencil sketches."

SAANICHTON ARTIST

Residing on the Saanich Peninsula, Arthur continued to expand his collection of First Nations paintings, visiting nearby Tsawout Reserve as well as up the island to the Somenos and Quamichan Reserves. Through Peggy's sister, arrangements had been made for an exhibition of Arthur's work in Kimberley, so in 1934 the couple travelled to the Interior, which provided an opportunity to record life and people on the Kootenai (Ktunaxa) Reserve. After further work on the Songhees Reserve near Victoria and in the Cowichan area, Arthur had 74 paintings showing First Nations peoples and culture.

In 1935 he and Peggy embarked for England with the paintings and a collection of artifacts—baskets, adzes, a model pole and a Cowichan knit two-piece suit with pleated skirt, commissioned from Tsartlip knitters as a birthday present for Peggy. After travelling down the west coast and through the Caribbean, they arrived in London where Arthur searched for a gallery to show his collection. He also began sketching and photographing what he called his Vanishing London series, depicting its historic places. In 1936 he opened an exhibition of his Indian Collection at Whiteley's Gallery. Though he was able to eventually sell a few watercolours from Vanishing London, it was a hand-to-mouth existence until 1938 when he sold humorous sketches to various magazines. When World War II erupted, Arthur served in the Home Guard in Cornwall and painted from their home in Perranuthnoe. His first commercial success occurred in 1946 when 180 of his Vanishing London paintings were purchased outright by the dealers Puttick & Simpson Ltd., giving Arthur and Peggy the means to return to Vancouver Island. In 1954 he finally sold his Indian Collection—51 paintings went to the Provincial Archives of B.C., and the following year, 26 paintings of primarily Alaska subject matter went to the Glenbow Museum in Calgary. Arthur continued to travel and paint, exhibited his watercolours and added art instructor to his career by teaching at Norfolk School of Art, a sketch group of the Saanich Peninsula Arts and Crafts Society, and then the Saanich Peninsula Art Centre. In 1972 he passed away at age 82 in Resthaven Hospital, where he had first convalesced from his war wounds, and first met Peggy.

Arthur Pitts' work is held in the following public collections: in Canada, Royal British Columbia Museum, Sidney Museum, Burnaby Art Gallery, Glenbow Museum; in England, City of London, Guildhall Library (London).

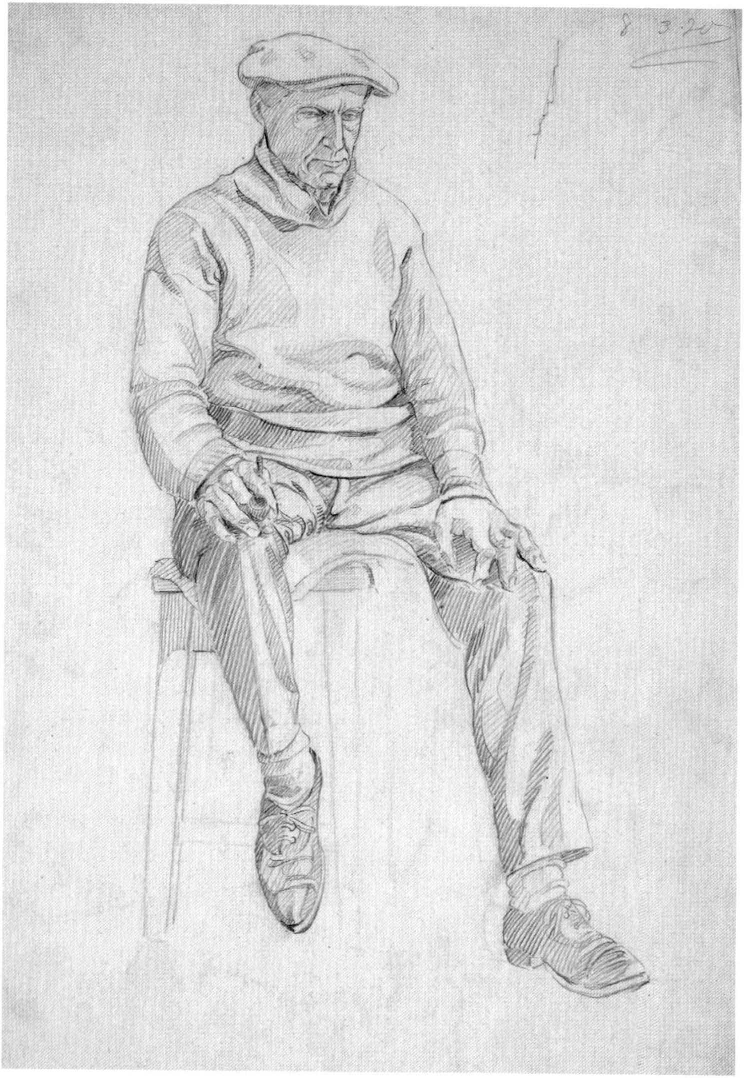

Arthur Pitts, *Figure, man*, 1920, graphite on paper, 15" x 11"

WESTMINISTER SCHOOL OF ART
K. MASON COLLECTION
PHOTO BY JANET DWYER

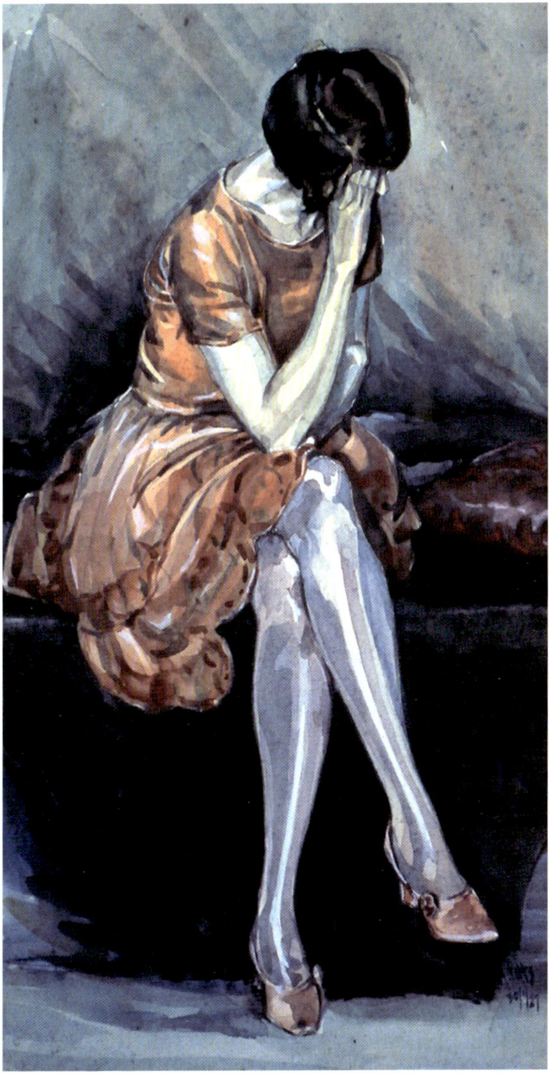

Arthur Pitts, *Peggy*, 1927, watercolour on paper, 11" x7"

PRIVATE COLLECTION

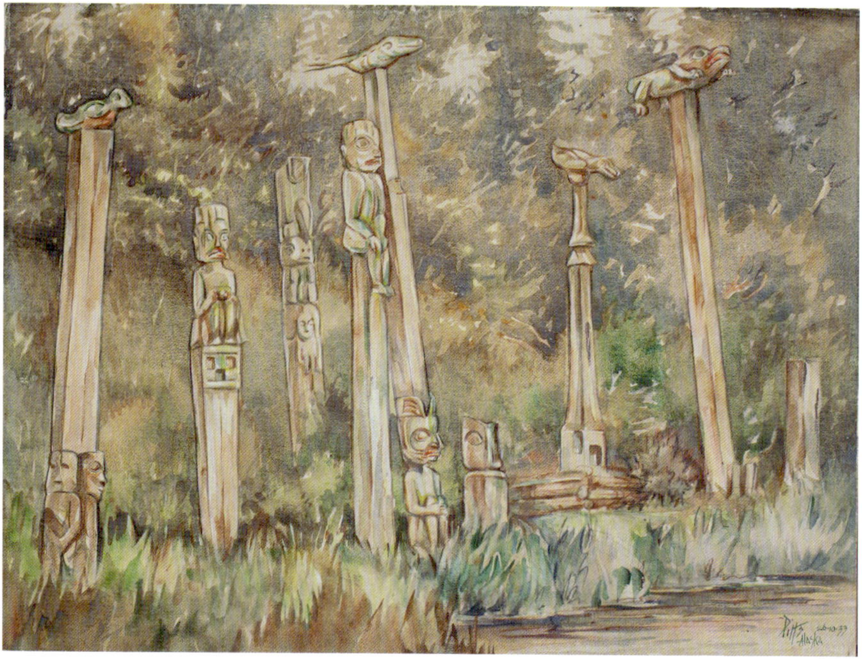

Arthur Pitts, *Mortuary Poles, Taxican II*, 1933,

watercolour on mat board, 19 1/2" x 13 3/4"

COLLECTION OF GLENBOW MUSEUM 55.10.27

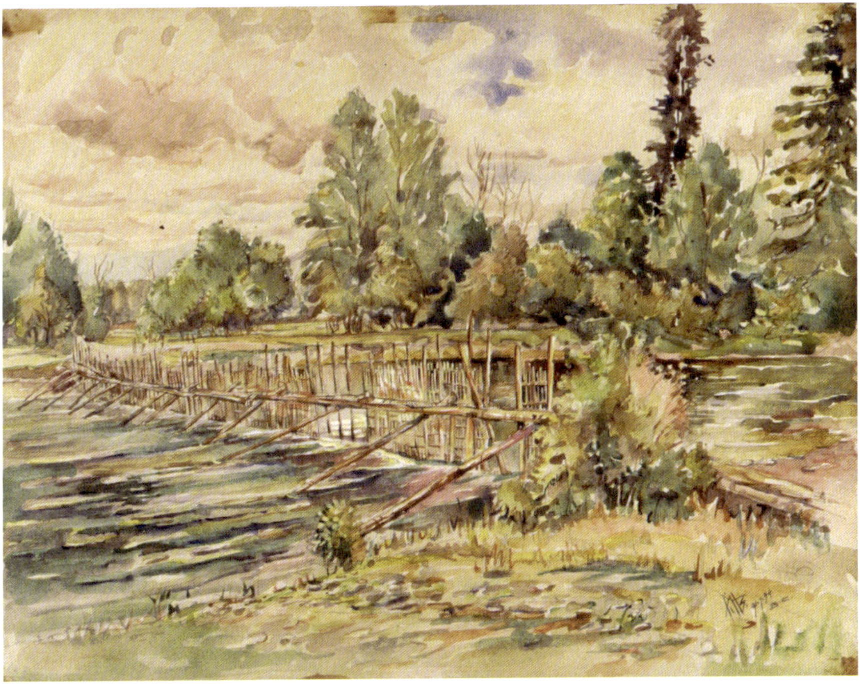

Arthur Pitts, *Fishing Weir on the Cowichan River, Koksilah Reserve*, 1934, watercolour on card, 14 7/8" x 19 7/8",

IMAGE PDP01482
COURTESY OF THE ROYAL BC MUSEUM AND ARCHIVES

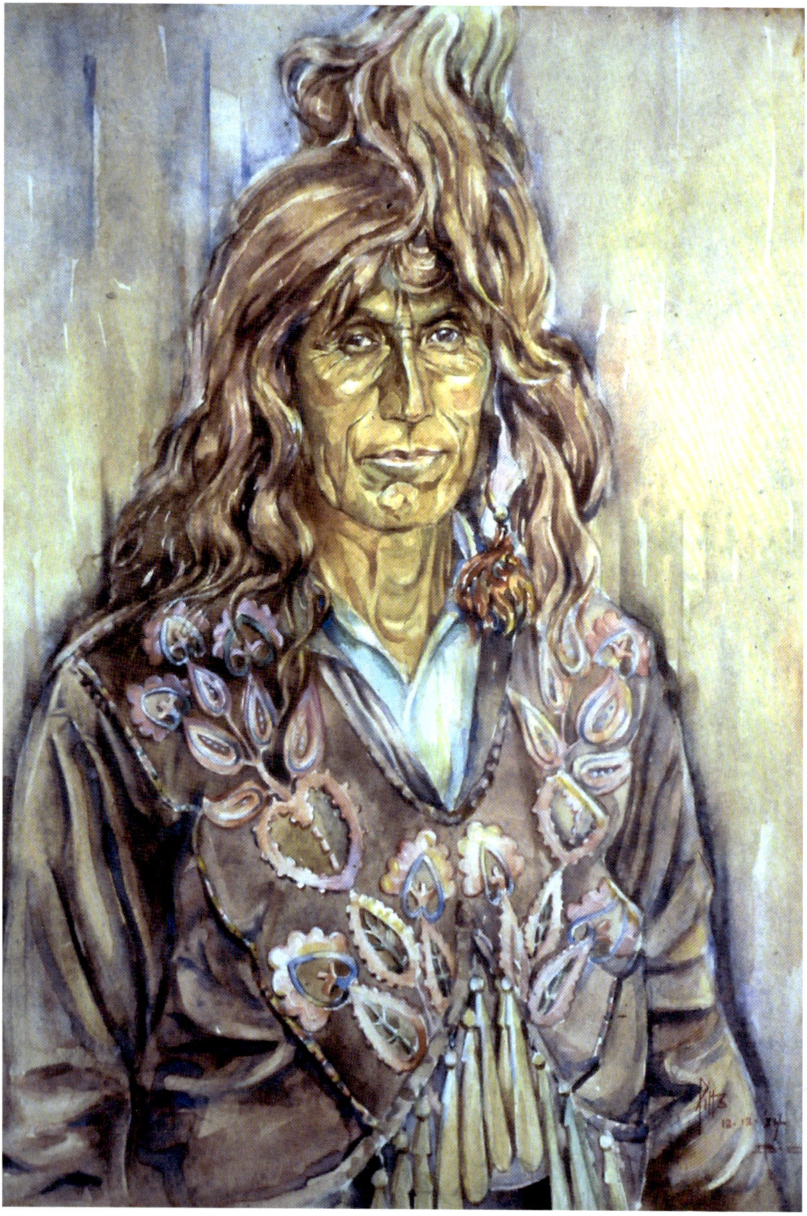

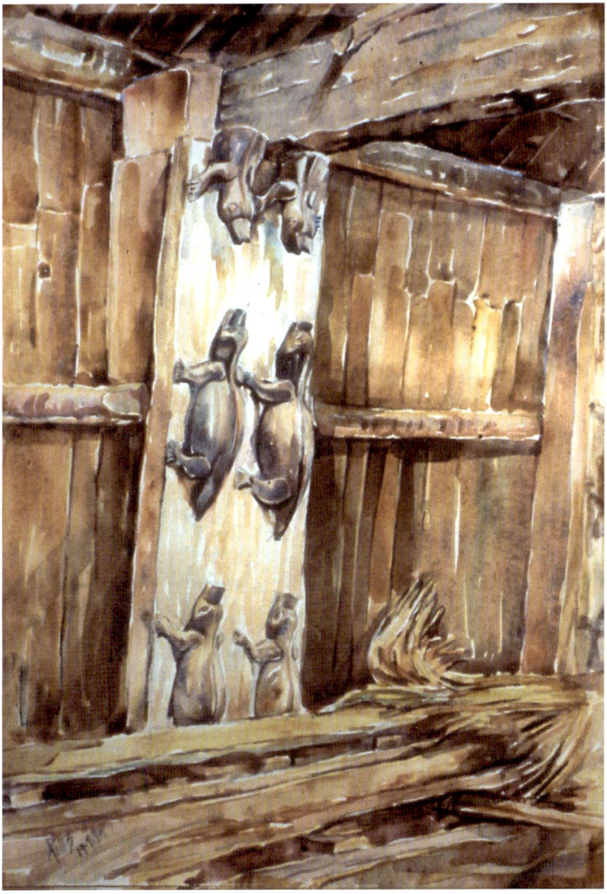

▲ Arthur Pitts, *Interior house Posts at Quamichan Reserve*, 1934, watercolour on card, 20 ¼" x 14 ⅞"

IMAGE PDP 01484
COURTESY OF THE ROYAL BC MUSEUM AND ARCHIVES

◄ Arthur Pitts, *Tommy Paul, Hereditary Chief of Saanich First Nations, Tsartlip, age 66*, 1934, watercolour on card, 20 ¼" x 15"

IMAGE PDP 01490
COURTESY OF THE ROYAL BC MUSEUM AND ARCHIVES

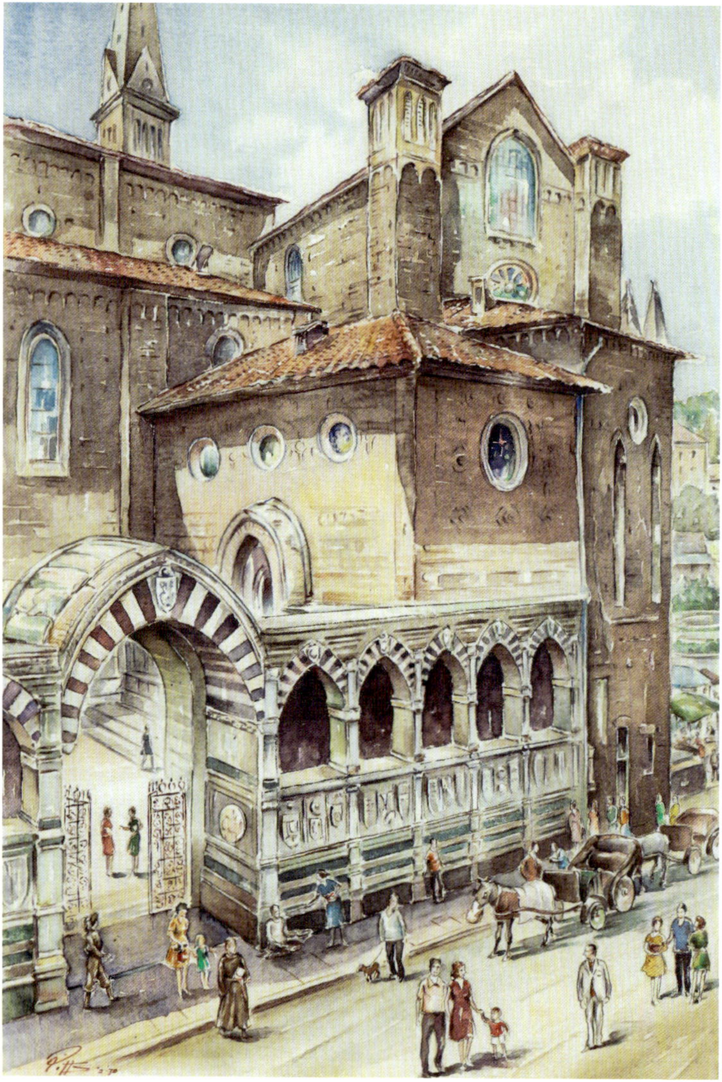

Arthur Pitts, *Santa Maria Novella, Florence*, 1970, watercolour on Arches paper, 24" x 12 ½"

AVIS RASMUSSEN COLLECTION
PHOTO BY JANET DWYER

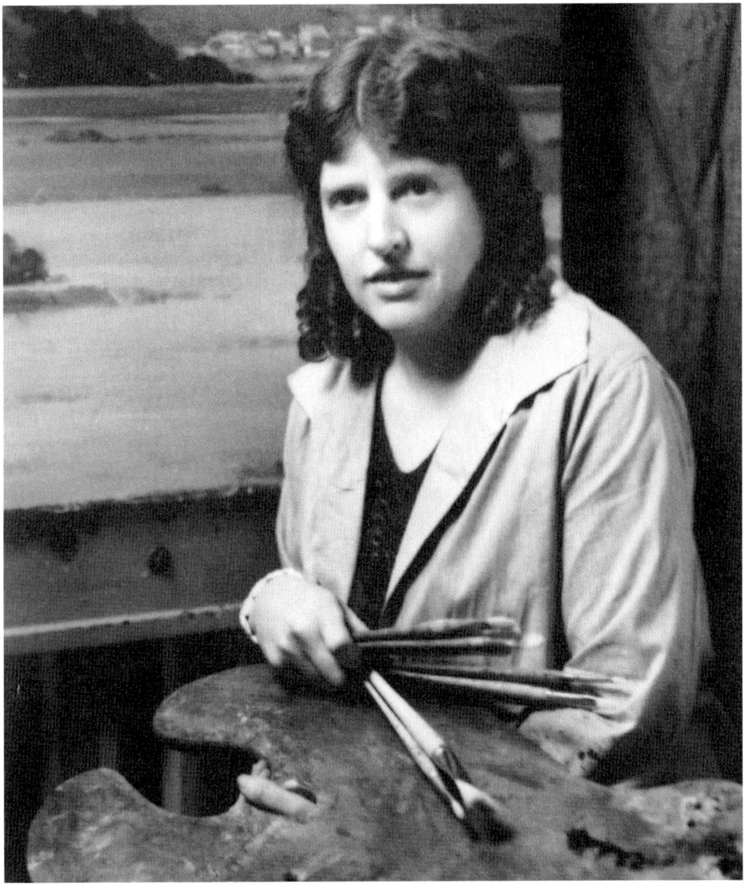

Mildred Valley Thornton

1890–1967

"Her work wasn't like a woman's [of the era]: by that I mean she did not make pretty pictures. She was gutsy. Her work reminds me a little of the freshness of Tom Thomson's. She was really, really good. I hope she gets some recognition now."

—GORDON SMITH, CANADIAN ARTIST

In 1890, Mildred Valley Thornton (nee Stinson) was born to a large farming family in the Rutherford area of southern Ontario. She grew up in the Chatham/Dresden region. When she was young, she developed lifelong interests in poetry, literature and art. In 1907, Mildred went to Olivet College, in Michigan, to study art. This Christian institute was open to all regardless of gender, race or social statue. Ethical principles and community service were emphasized, and for the rest of her life, Mildred was an advocate for social justice, equality, women's causes and racial minorities. She returned home, lived in Toronto for a few years and "briefly" attended the Ontario College of Art where she studied under George A. Reid and John William Beatty. She also greatly admired the work of Tom Thomson. Years later, Mildred spent one year at the Chicago Art Institute.

CAREER AND FAMILY

In 1913, adventurous Mildred, "with little more than her paint box" travelled alone on the Grand Trunk Pacific Railway as far as Regina, Saskatchewan. There she saw a berobed First Nations man standing on a railway platform, and considered him so dignified, she at once decided that here was the subject for her brush and Regina was where she would settle. After moving there Mildred supported herself by giving private painting lessons and selling landscapes and portrait studies. In the following two decades she joined several women's associations, taught at Regina College, became a noted Saskatchewan artist, married John Thornton and in 1926 gave birth to twin sons, Jack and Maitland.

Mildred was proficient with oils and watercolours, portraits and landscapes. She painted many distinctive prairie scenes, as well as portraits of eminent Saskatchewan citizens such as Arthur Meighan and Sir Frederick Haultain. She began travelling to stampedes and First Nations reserves across the prairies to paint Indigenous portraits.

Mildred showed her work in local venues, the CNE, the Ontario Society of Artists and the Montreal Museum of Arts. She was "the first resident Saskatchewan artist to be represented… in these organizations." In 1932, her landscape, *In the Touchwood Hills, Saskatchewan*, was exhibited with the Royal Canadian Academy of Arts; in 1934, the RCA showed two of her prairie landscapes, and in 1941, the portrait, *Dominic Jack, Okanagan Indian*.

VANCOUVER

The Depression ruined John Thornton's confectionery and restaurant businesses. In 1934, the family moved to Vancouver. There, Mildred became the art critic for the *Vancouver Sun* (1944 to 1959) and a journalist for the *Vancouver Sun* and the *Native Voice* (the first Aboriginal newspaper in Canada). In 1966, she published *Indian Lives and Legends*, which won the Canadian Authors' Association Award. Posthumously, *Potlatch People* and *Buffalo People* were published. She showed her work regularly in various venues and had two solo exhibitions at the Vancouver Art Gallery (1936, 1949).

Mildred became a community leader, joining numerous associations and often serving on the executives of those organizations. These included the Vancouver Poetry Society; the Canadian Authors' Association; the Women's Press Club; the Local Council of Women; the Vancouver Arts Council; the Totem-Land Society; the Art, Historical and Scientific Association (which later became the Vancouver Museum); the IODE and the Soroptimist Club.

ADVOCACY

Mildred became an advocate for the improved education and rights of females and Canada's Indigenous peoples. Her efforts were welcomed by many First Nations, and she was made a member of the Native Sisterhood. During the 1940s, Mildred spoke for Canada's Indigenous people in a series of provincial and national lectures. While her role as a spokesperson for First Nations is now considered problematic for various reasons, at the time many Indigenous people welcomed her advocacy. In fact, the wife of the Assiniboine chief Dan Kennedy-Ochankugahe made Mildred a buckskin dress to wear while lecturing. Chief Kennedy-Ochankugahe thanked Mildred for being "our ambassador of good will." Mildred appeared in regalia during her lectures not to pretend she was aboriginal but to honour First Nations customs and culture. She emphasized that the purpose of her lectures was to fulfill her "earnest desire" to create "more understanding and service toward these, your fellow Canadians."

PAINTING INDIGENOUS PEOPLE

Mildred was an adventurous, outgoing individual. She would leave home for a day, a week, a month or sometimes several months in search of subjects for her brushes. When her twins were younger, Mildred had to take them with her on painting trips. While the boys played, Jack recalls that their mother would be sitting on her collapsible stool, busily painting. Having small children along, Mildred said she "had to paint with one eye on my canvas and the other on the youngsters. This was good exercise for the eyes, but rough on the nerves." Later, Mildred's incredibly supportive husband cared for the boys while Mildred travelled throughout B.C., Alberta and Saskatchewan. Jack also remembered that his mother "was certainly not a cook or housekeeper. She spent most of her time in her studio painting, or away on trips; my father really raised my brother and me." Her sons grew accustomed to their mother's absences and she was supportive and encouraging when home.

Using a palette that was unusually vibrant for the era and large brushes, Mildred captured images of rugged terrain, totem poles, First Nations life, and portraits. Although images of the aged were not, and still are not, considered beautiful, Mildred found them intriguing. She saw the Elders as culture keepers, and her portraits made landscapes of their mature features while depicting a likeness as well as personality. Art specialist Uno Langmann says Mildred captured "the ultimate feeling that she saw in her sitters—their souls." Langman adds:

> Many of the early female painters used very light, pastel colours… She used pure colour, almost straight from the tube, and she was one of the first female Canadian painters to do so… Nobody painted the volume of portraits that Mildred did, and nobody painted portraits better than Mildred did, including Emily Carr. What strikes me about Mildred's work is its power. I didn't know the sitters, but I can feel Mildred's desire to demonstrate the character and history of the people she depicted.

Mildred painted her portraits with lightning speed: anywhere from twenty-five to sixty minutes was common for her. In some cases, her portraits are the only extant images of the individuals. Art consultant Anthony Westbridge describes Mildred's collection "as one of the most important historical documents of the twentieth century in Canada, particularly as it relates to the First Nations."

Mildred would travel by any method possible in her desire to document Indigenous individuals: on foot, or by bus, ferry, train, dugout canoe, and horseback. She wrote:

> The qualities of a good packhorse often seemed more important than intellectual equipment. Starting out on a trip with perhaps twenty or more boards to carry, as well as my heavy paint box, my suitcase, and in later years also a projector, slides and screen to show the Indians what I had done, required the limit of my strength.

Mildred's friendships with several First Nations Elders gave her access to sacred and secret ceremonies. Privileged to hear stories and myths of several tribes, Mildred respected the cultures she encountered, which only furthered her desire to document and preserve them as historical records. She became an amateur ethnologist, recording stories, songs and observations; in addition, she painted dances and rituals she was invited to.

Her whole life, Mildred was so driven, she said, "Sometimes the urge [to paint] was so strong it was as if someone were standing over me with a whip." That passion led her to complete a remarkable body of work: approximately 300 portraits of First Nations ancestors—an amazing feat that spanned nearly forty years. During that time, she also painted approximately fifty images that celebrate Indigenous life and customs and approximately forty paintings of totem poles.

THE COLLECTION

Mildred hoped that her Indigenous portrait collection would be housed by a Canadian museum or gallery as a legacy for all Canadians. She wanted part of the proceeds to support her during her widowed old age and part to be used for scholarships and bursaries for First Nations youth. One appraiser insightfully noted that the portraits "will have value for younger Indians, especially in years to come." But abstract and experimental art were more in vogue than representational work in the '50s and '60s, and some viewed Mildred's work as outdated. Finally, while the collection was large and costly, no reasonable negotiations occurred: consequently, the portraits were not purchased as a group.

On June 27, 1967, just prior to her death from a blood disorder, Mildred was distraught over the failure to house her life's work. She wrote a codicil to her will stating the collection should be sold in one large auction or burned at a dump. Luckily, the codicil was not properly witnessed, and her sons did not follow her wishes. After further unsuccessful attempts to sell the collection, the portraits were sold piecemeal. Today, some Indigenous communities are collecting Mildred's portraits. By 2011, the Squamish Nation had acquired seventeen portraits of their ancestors and hope to eventually own all twenty-four. Mildred's paintings are appreciated not "purely for art's sake, [but] because of the representation of the ancestors, …it is the actual image we value." The Squamish portraits are also part of a travelling education kit that has been shown at international conferences.

In 1993, twenty-six years after Mildred's death, Brooks Joyner, Director of the Vancouver Art Gallery, said, "I thought she was an important early-mid 20th century Canadian painter with a special contribution to the recording of the Native peoples and landscape of Canada and particularly British Columbia. Thornton's work resonated with me. It was crisp and robust and it had strong content."

Mildred Valley Thornton's work is held in the following public collections: Glenbow Museum, McMichael Canadian Art Collection, National Gallery of Canada, Royal BC Museum, Simon Fraser University and Vancouver Art Gallery.

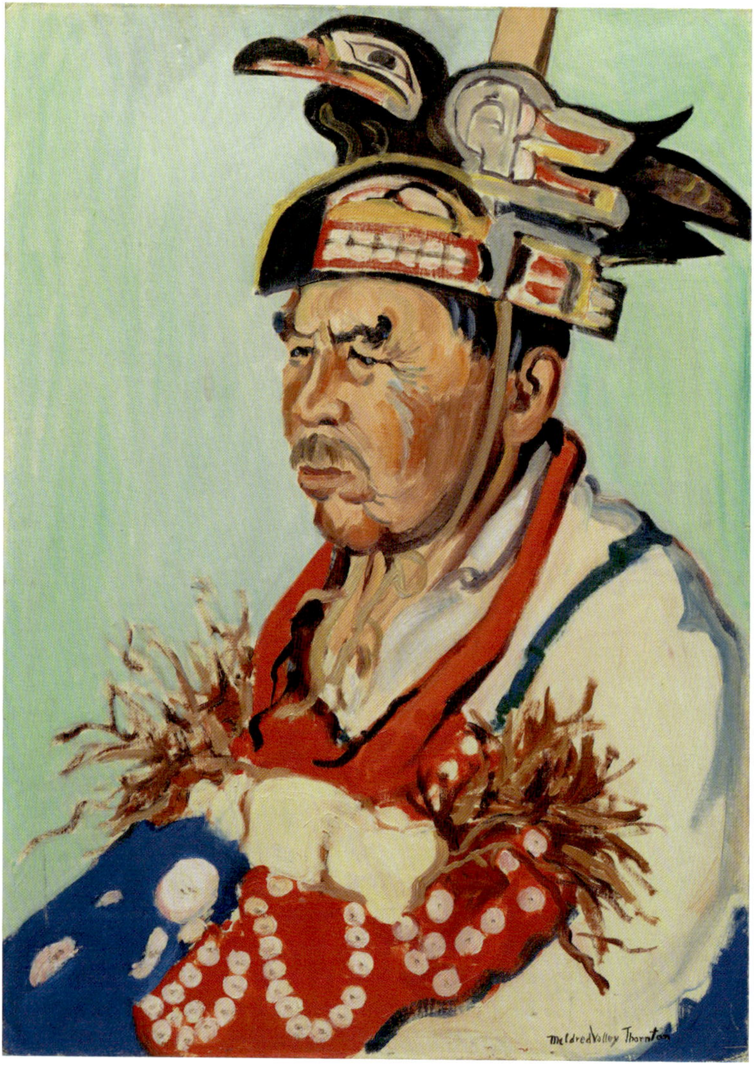
Mildred Valley Thornton

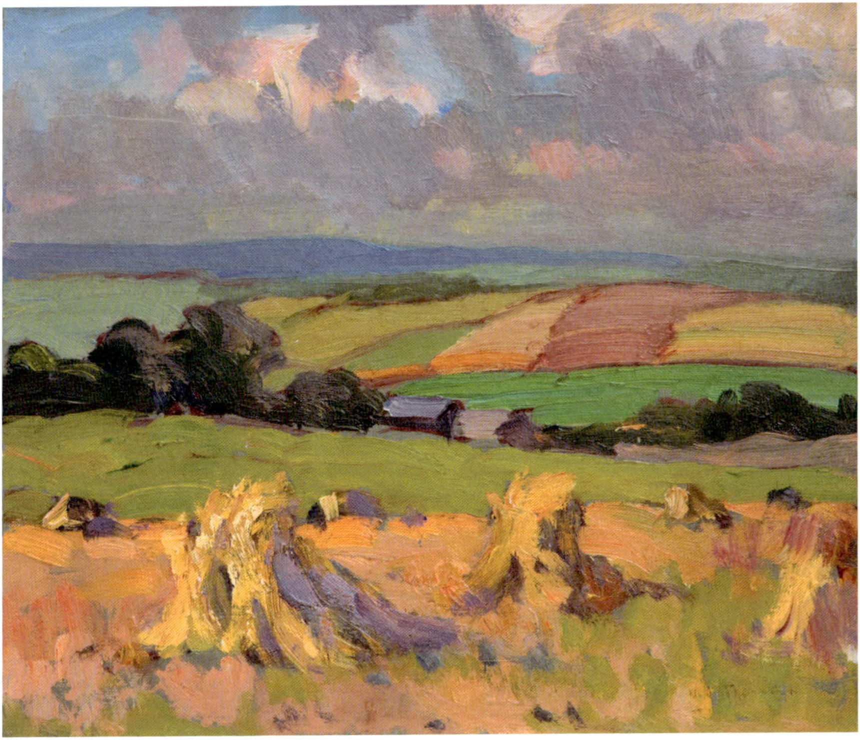

◄ Mildred Valley Thornton, *Willie Seaweed,* (Kwakwaka'wakw)
1946, oil on canvas board, 30" x 22"

COLLECTION OF THE VANCOUVER ART GALLERY, GIFT OF THE CANADIAN WOMEN'S PRESS CLUB, VANCOUVER BRANCH
PHOTO: RACHEL TOPHAM, VANCOUVER ART GALLERY

▲ Mildred Valley *Thornton, Sunlight and Shadows,* n.d., oil on board, 8 ½" x 10 ½"

PRIVATE COLLECTION
DAN FAIRCHILD PHOTOGRAPHY

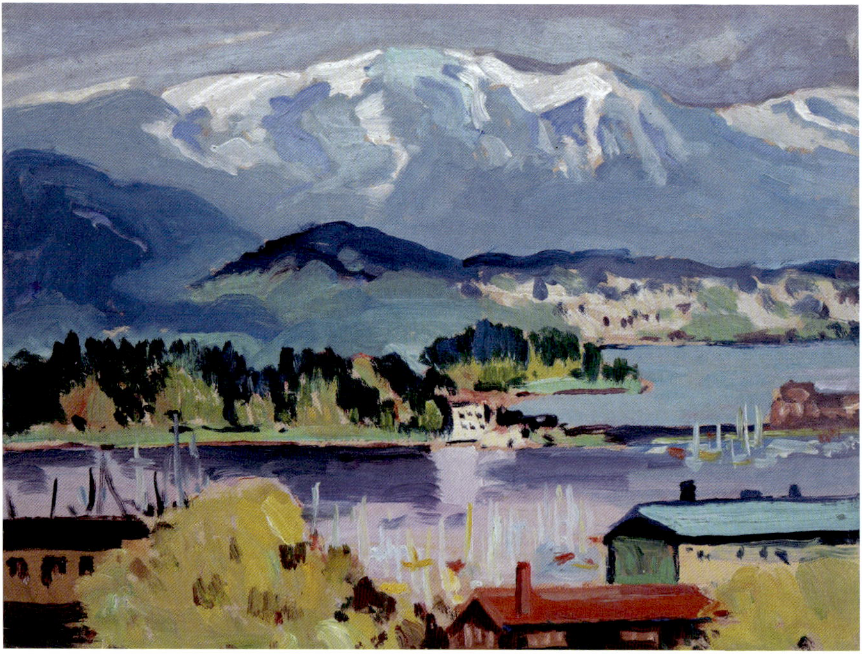

Mildred Valley Thornton, *Coal Harbour*, n.d.
oil on board, 9 1/2" x 13 1/2"

THORNTON FAMILY PRIVATE COLLECTION
PHOTO BY JANET DWYER

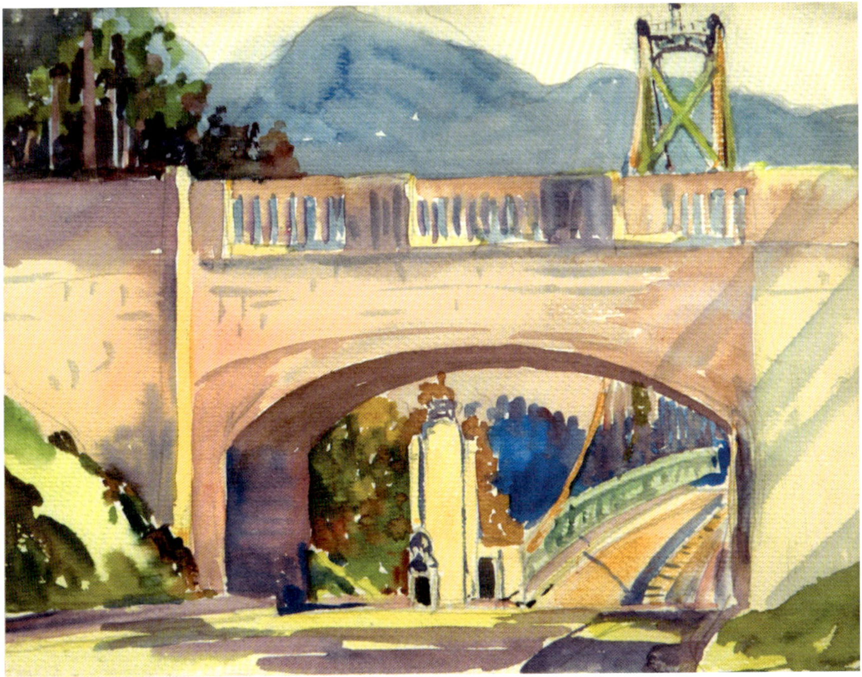

Mildred Valley Thornton, *Entrance to Lions Gate Bridge*, n.d., watercolour, 6 5/8" x 8 5/8"

PRIVATE COLLECTION
DAN FAIRCHILD PHOTOGRAPHY

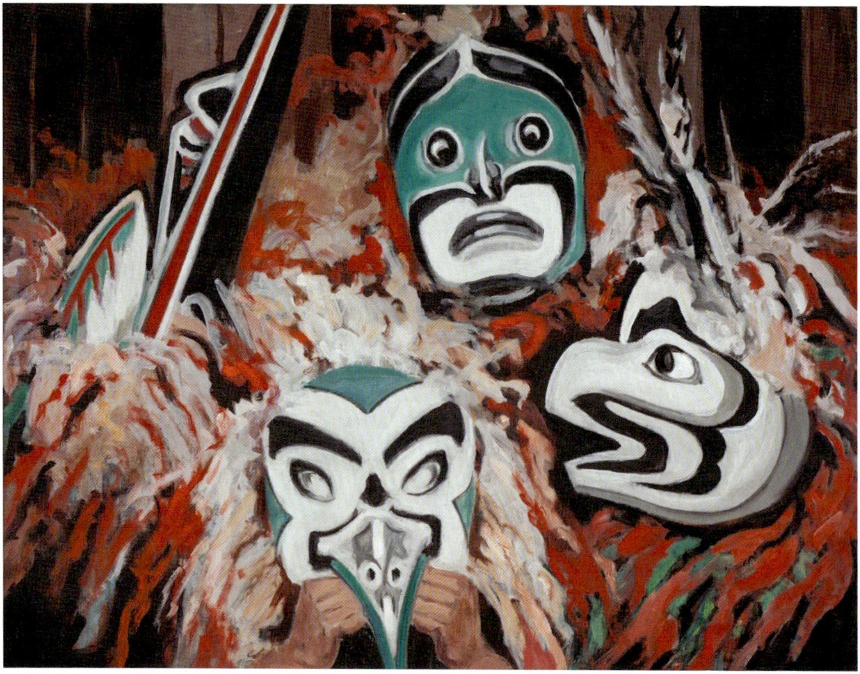

Mildred Valley Thornton, *Ceremonial Masks*, (Kwakwaka'wakw)
n.d., oil on canvas, 29 1/2" x 39 1/2"

PRIVATE COLLECTION
PHOTO BY JANET DWYER

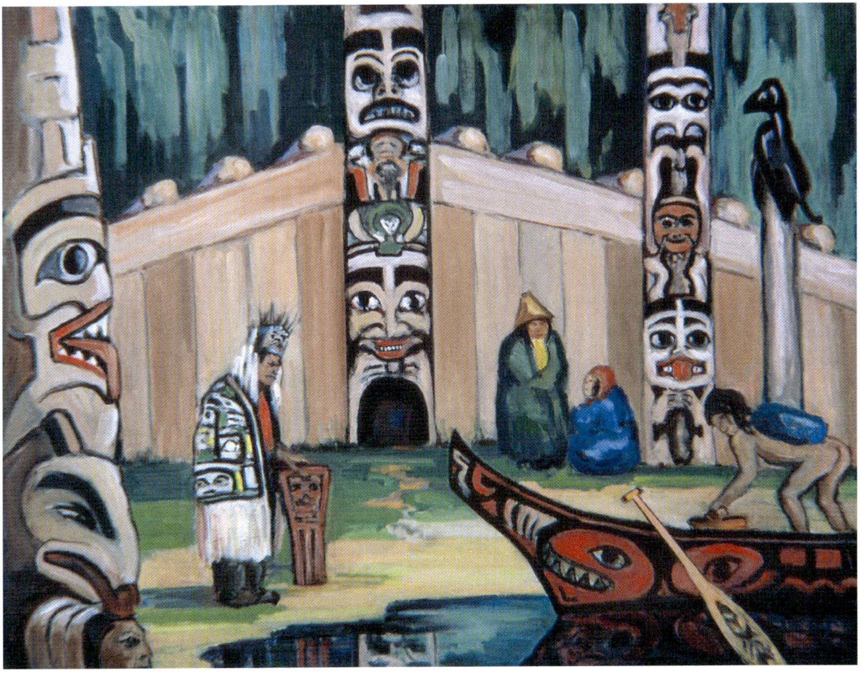

Mildred Valley Thornton, *Longhouse, Stanley Park,* (Squamish), 1945, oil on board, dimensions unknown

PRIVATE COLLECTION

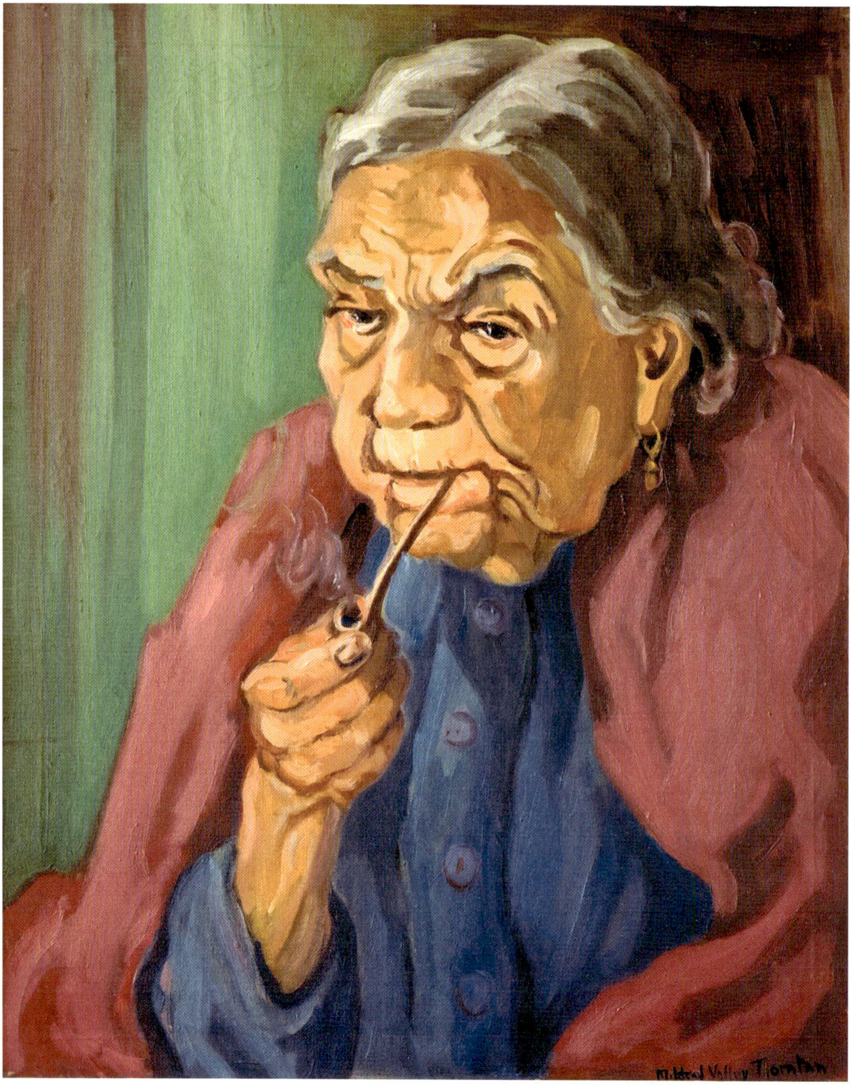

Mildred Valley Thornton, *Siyámlut* ("Aunt Polly") (Squamish), 1940, oil on board, 24" x 22"

UNO LANGMANN PRIVATE COLLECTION
DAN FAIRCHILD PHOTOGRAPHY

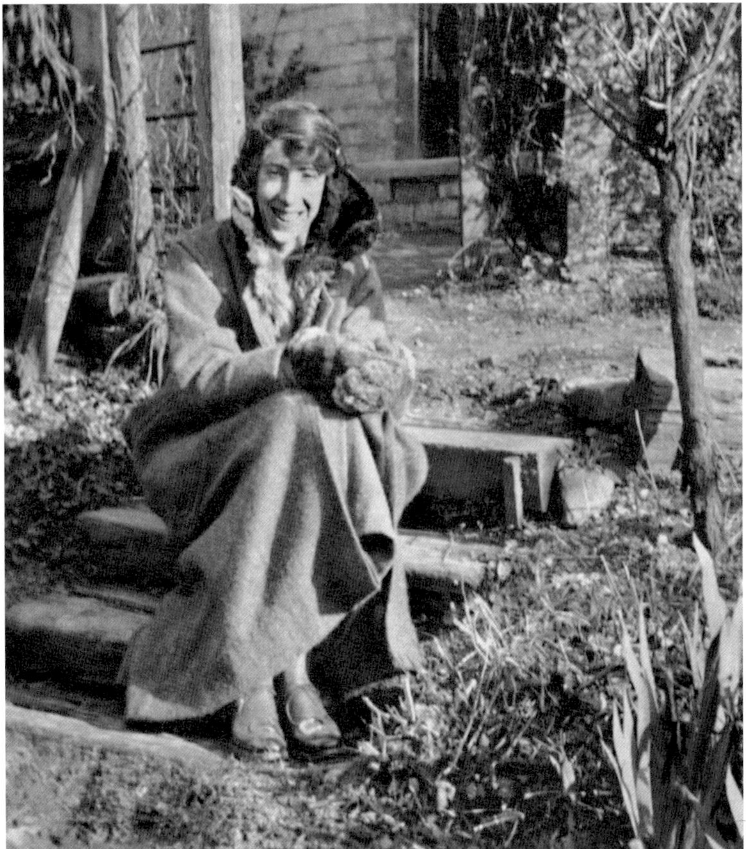

Ina D.D. Uhthoff

1889–1971

"Ina Uhthoff served the cause of the arts in Victoria with such self-disregarding dedication that few living in the city today are aware that hers was a major contribution. It was made over four decades beginning in the 1920's....Considering the demands made on her time and strength by her household, children, teaching, correspondence course and gallery, it is surprising that she left some 400 paintings and drawings....some of the finest portraiture yet produced in British Columbia and a long series of landscapes which testify to her deep involvement with the physical surroundings of Vancouver Island. What strikes one as remarkable, when one considers her lack of opportunity to travel abroad and the extreme conservativeness of the Victoria environment, is the open mind with which she received and endorsed, with enthusiasm, the various forms of abstract art that began to reach Victoria from the late 1940s onward."

–COLIN GRAHAM, FORMER DIRECTOR, ART GALLERY OF GREATER VICTORIA

Jemima (nicknamed Ina) Duncan Dewar Campbell was born in 1889 at Ericht Bank Villa, the family home near the mouth of the Clyde River, west of the large shipbuilding and trading city of Glasgow. Her well-to-do family provided a sheltered upbringing, which encouraged an appreciation of literature, the arts, natural sciences and a love of nature and the outdoors. Through her brother, she had lifelong skills and interest in fly-fishing. By 1905, her family was living in Glasgow, and she enrolled in the Glasgow School of Art, which was on an upswing with its new building designed by architect, designer and artist Charles Rennie Mackintosh. He and his artist wife Margaret were strong proponents of the Arts and Crafts and art nouveau movements. Painting was her emphasis, and she exhibited at the GSA from 1911 to 1913, as well as with the Royal Scottish Academy in 1912, the year she received her diploma.

ADVENTURE AND HOME IN THE KOOTENAYS

Sailing "deck cabin" on the *Empress of Britain*, then taking a train across Canada, a sternwheeler across Kootenay Lake to Crawford Bay, and a horse-drawn wagon, Ina ventured to Ledlanet Ranch, owned by friends from Scotland in the winter of 1913. Though she cried herself to sleep after "arriving at the end of the world in her fragile city shoes," she came to love the rural life and the stunning landscapes of B.C. It was here that she met her future husband, Edward (Ted) Uhthoff.

However, World War I intervened, and while Ted joined the 54th Kootenay Battalion CEF and saw action at Vimy Ridge and Passchendaele, Ina returned to Scotland to train under the Glasgow Provincial Committee for the Training of Teachers. She taught art in the public schools, and her recommendations described her as "a most competent and effective teacher of her subject." In addition to teaching, she continued her work as an artist, participating in group shows at the Royal Glasgow Institute of Fine Arts and the Royal Scottish Academy as well as a solo exhibition of Canadian scenes at the Ralph Pond Gallery.

In 1919, after the war ended, Ina and Ted married and returned to Canada, setting up their home, garden and apple orchards in Crawford Bay near the Purcell Mountains where they had two children. Ina described their life:

> The house was small but had charm and stood in magnificent surroundings. The life was a strenuous one consisting of early rising and long hours of physical labour, but there were many compensations. We grew our own food. I made my own bread and butter. We cured our own hams, preserved out own fruit and vegetables, caught fish in the nearby creek and lake, shot grouse in the season and canned them.

VICTORIA SCHOOL OF ART YEARS

By 1924, her husband became "incapacitated by wounds received in the Great War," so to support her family, Ina went to the capital city of Victoria to teach at the Summer School for Teachers. In 1925, she made quite an impression exhibiting with the Island Arts and Crafts Society Annual Exhibition of Paintings, Drawings, Designs, and Crafts, making contacts for teaching and selling her art. By 1926, Ina and the children had moved to Victoria where she was principal (and main teacher) of her own school, the Victoria School of Art, which offered a wide variety of classes for children and adults—Life Classes, Drawing and Painting from the Living Model, Illustration, Design, Landscape Painting, Etching, and Silversmithing. Until 1942, when World War II forced its closure, the school embraced the stance of fostering a variety of arts, many with commercial and practical applications, including taking over the Kingston School of Pottery in 1938. In addition, she taught again for the Summer School for Teachers, various independent schools, and for thirty years with the province's Secondary School Correspondence Course. Her school was described in 1939:

> There flourishes, right in Victoria's midst, one of the most successful adult education projects ever attempted in the West. Students, most of them wearing attractive workmanlike smocks, will be found nearly any morning or afternoon in an attitude of complete absorption at easel, potter's wheel, printer's block, drawing board, designing desk or potter's oven, their earnestness and enthusiasm a silent testimony to the popularity of the studies in which they are engaged.

Ina continued to create and exhibit her art (and the work of her students), often in the Island Arts and Crafts Society's annual show, as well as the B.C. Society of Artists Exhibitions at the Vancouver Art Gallery.

By 1931, Ina D.D. Uhthoff was listed in *Who's Who in British Columbia* and became a Fellow of the Royal Society of Arts, able then to add RSA (Royal Scottish Academy) to her credentials. Later, her name was included in the 1941 *Who's Who in Northwest Art.* She was well respected by a wide range of people. Ina was the illustrator for the conservative Women's Canadian Club's publication, *The Pioneer Women of Vancouver Island 1843-1866*, yet in partnership with Emily Carr, she hosted the abstract expressionist artist Mark Tobey for a master class in her studio. Ina Uhthoff was the only artist who exhibited in both the Modern Room and the main exhibition at the Island Arts and Crafts Society's 1932 show.

ARTIST, GALLERY FOUNDER AND COLUMNIST

By 1944, Ina D.D. Uhthoff was listed for the first time in the B.C. and Yukon Phone Directory as an artist. She maintained a studio where she taught and painted in a variety of media—oils, watercolours, gouache, pastels, pen and ink. Along with portraits and still lifes, she worked *en plein air*. The war years did not dull her output nor energy. She obtained a pass to sketch in the West Coast shipyards, and her *Girl Welder at Work* appeared in the British Columbia at Work series at the Vancouver Art Gallery, organized by the Labour Arts Council. She bought her first home, overlooking the sea in Esquimalt and, as always, used the community—woods, sea, boats, a rainy street in downtown Victoria, the local Esquimalt fair—as subjects for her paintings. She continued with B.C. Artists exhibitions in Vancouver and became a member of the B.C. Society of Fine Arts in 1945.

One of her most lasting gifts to the art world was her stalwart effort to establish a civic art gallery in Victoria. The art gallery movement was officially founded in 1944 with artists under the banner Vancouver Island Region of the Federation of Canadian Artists. Ina was on the board of directors and the display committee when the Little Centre opened July 1946 in an automobile showroom. The group survived even when this space was lost, and in 1949, the gallery relocated on Broughton Street under the name Arts Centre of Greater Victoria, with Ina heading the exhibition committee. By 1950, the gallery announced the start of a permanent collection, with the first acquisition being Ina's *Sunflowers.* One year later, Sara Spencer donated her family residence on Moss Street as a permanent home for the gallery. The board of directors, including Ina, aimed to establish a gallery beyond regionalism, believing its mission was to educate the people of Victoria about modernism, allowing the city to take part in the living culture of its time, rather than merely revering the past. Key to its success was Ina persuading Colin Graham to be the first professional curator or director of the gallery. With his Vancouver roots, professional education and experience from the University of British Columbia, Cambridge University, Stanford University and the University of California (Berkeley), he proved to be an exceptional leader for what has become the Art Gallery of Greater Victoria.

To her work on the board and exhibition committee, Ina added instructor for gallery art classes and reviewer for the *Victoria Daily Colonist.* Art classes began almost immediately after Colin Graham's arrival. In 1952, Ina closed her downtown studio and began teaching at the AGGV. The long lines outside the mansion on registration day revealed the interest in learning how to create art. Classes took place upstairs; with the students working on the floor of the old Spencer bedrooms until furniture was purchased. Of special interest was the "businessman's art course," under Ina's direction. The Gallery was responding to "paint to relax," a "wave that [had] been sweeping Britain and [North America]." It was believed that busy city executives, who doodled during meetings and long-distance phone calls, were seeking an outlet for their artistic souls. Physicians were indicating that a healthy hobby could add years to the life of a harried career man. The class was to be diversified with oils, watercolours, composition, design, landscape, portrait and drawing. The male executive was certainly a lucrative demographic for the Gallery. The many student exhibits over the years built up a viewing public through families, creating ever greater support for the Gallery.

Ina always gave attention to student art from the Gallery and the schools and described her observations about child art and reflected why she valued it. "Drawing is a spontaneous activity in young children. Their mental "images" are extraordinarily clear; they express in line and color what interests them; their concepts are fresh and amusing. Statements are made in untrammeled color and bold line with an authority that many an adult artist might envy." She noted that a child could complete a large painting in 15 to 20 minutes and rarely overworked it.

THE LAST DECADE

By the 1960s, the gallery was well-established, due in large part to Ina's devotion to its activities. In 1962, she had a solo exhibition at the gallery, and a reviewer noted that it showed Ina's firm belief that an artist should start from nature, allowing it to express itself. Ina continued to teach with the provincial correspondence course in art and to write reviews as an art critic.

As she got older and could not keep up her usual pace, she resigned from her gallery responsibilities. The gallery responded by appointing her a member of the honourary advisory board, calling her the "doyen of Victoria painters." After she passed away in 1971, the gallery organized a memorial exhibition.

Ina D.D. Uhhoff's work is held in the following public collections: Art Gallery of Greater Victoria, Burnaby Art Gallery, B.C. Archives, Glenbow Museum, University of Victoria Legacy Art Gallery, Vancouver Art Gallery.

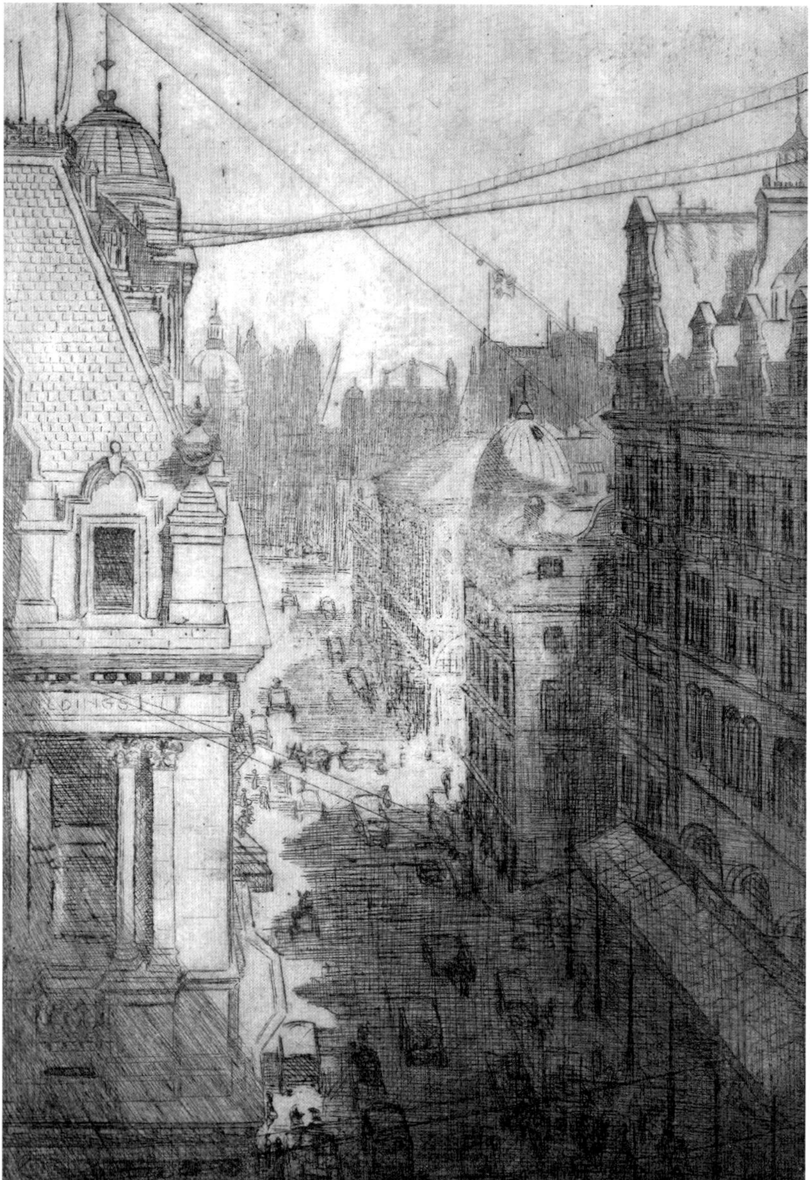

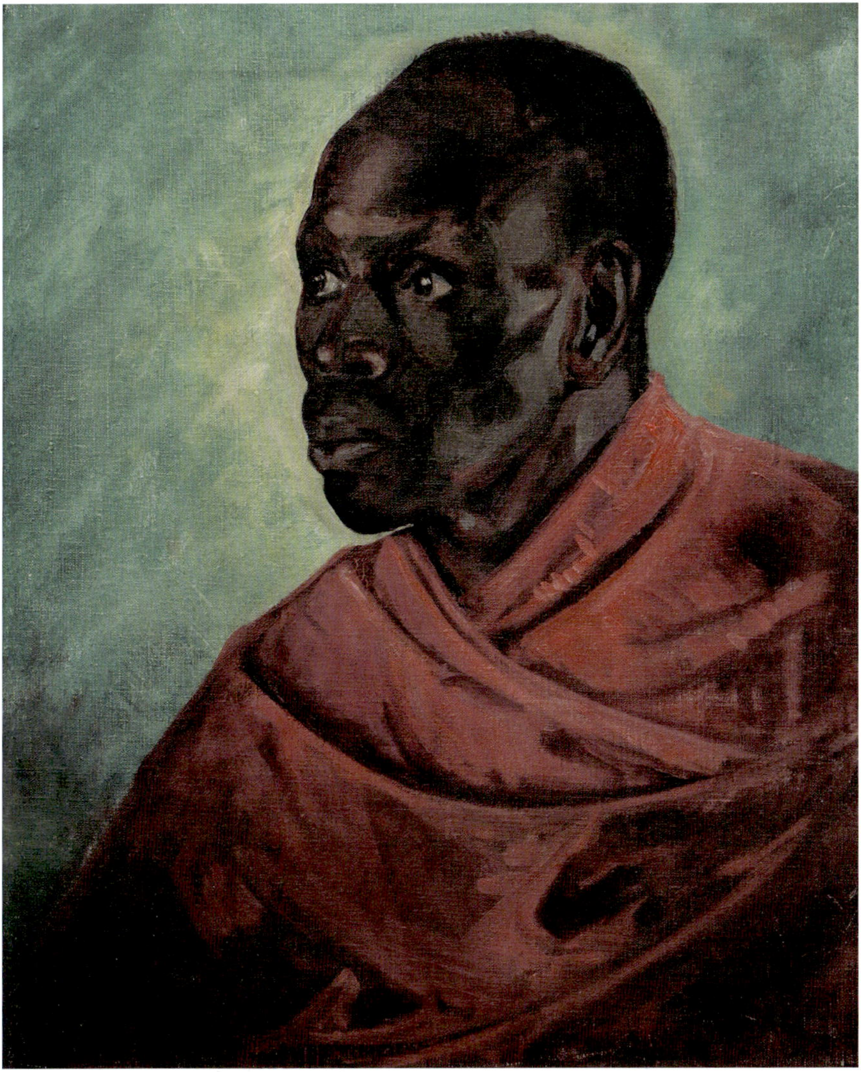

◄ Ina D.D. Uhthoff, *Gordon Street, Glasgow*, n.d., etching, 14" x 9 ½"

JOY UHTHOFF/NANCY WHITE COLLECTION
PHOTO BY NANCY WHITE

▲ Ina D.D. Uhthoff, *Jamaican*, circa early 1930, oil on canvas, 19 ½" x 16"

PRIVATE COLLECTION
PHOTO BY JANET DWYER

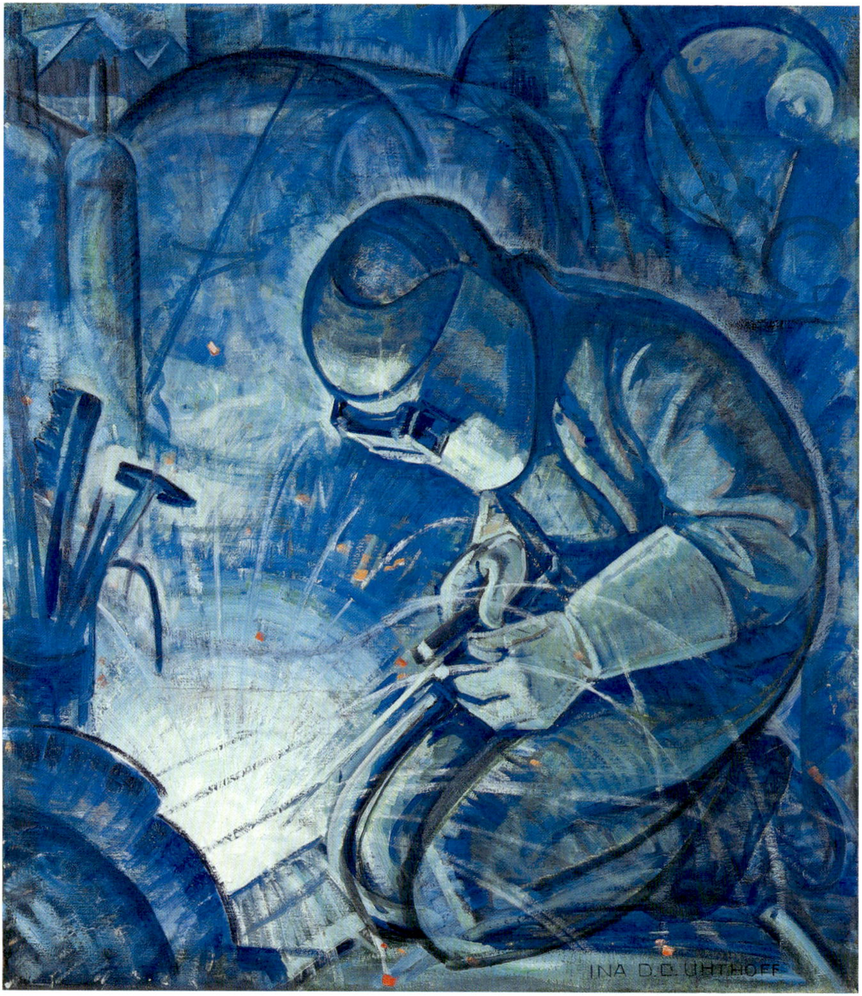

Ina D.D. Uhthoff, *Girl Welder at Work*, 1943, oil on canvas, 30 " x 27 ¼"

FROM THE ART GALLERY OF GREATER VICTORIA COLLECTION

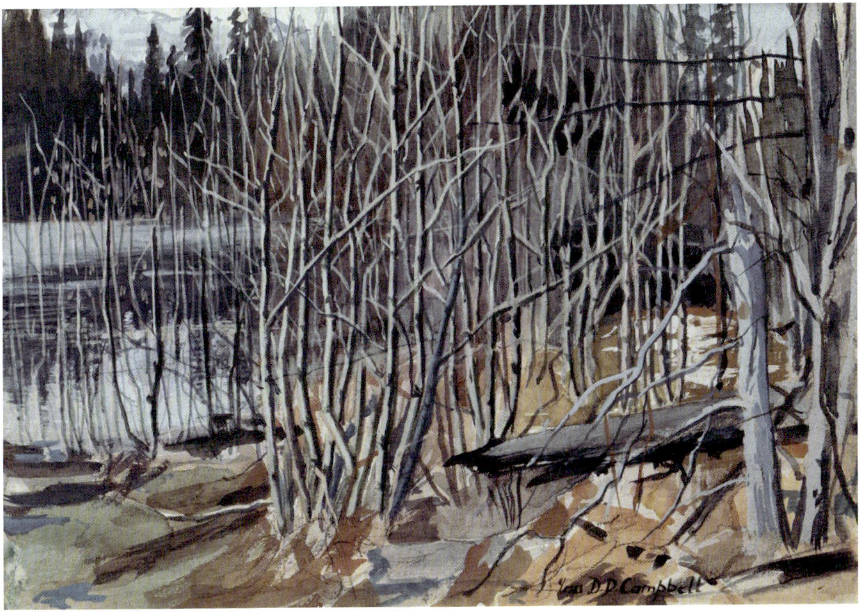

Ina D.D. Uhthoff, *Untitled,* n.d. watercolour, 6 ¾" x 10"

MICHAEL UHTHOFF COLLECTION
PHOTO BY JANET DWYER

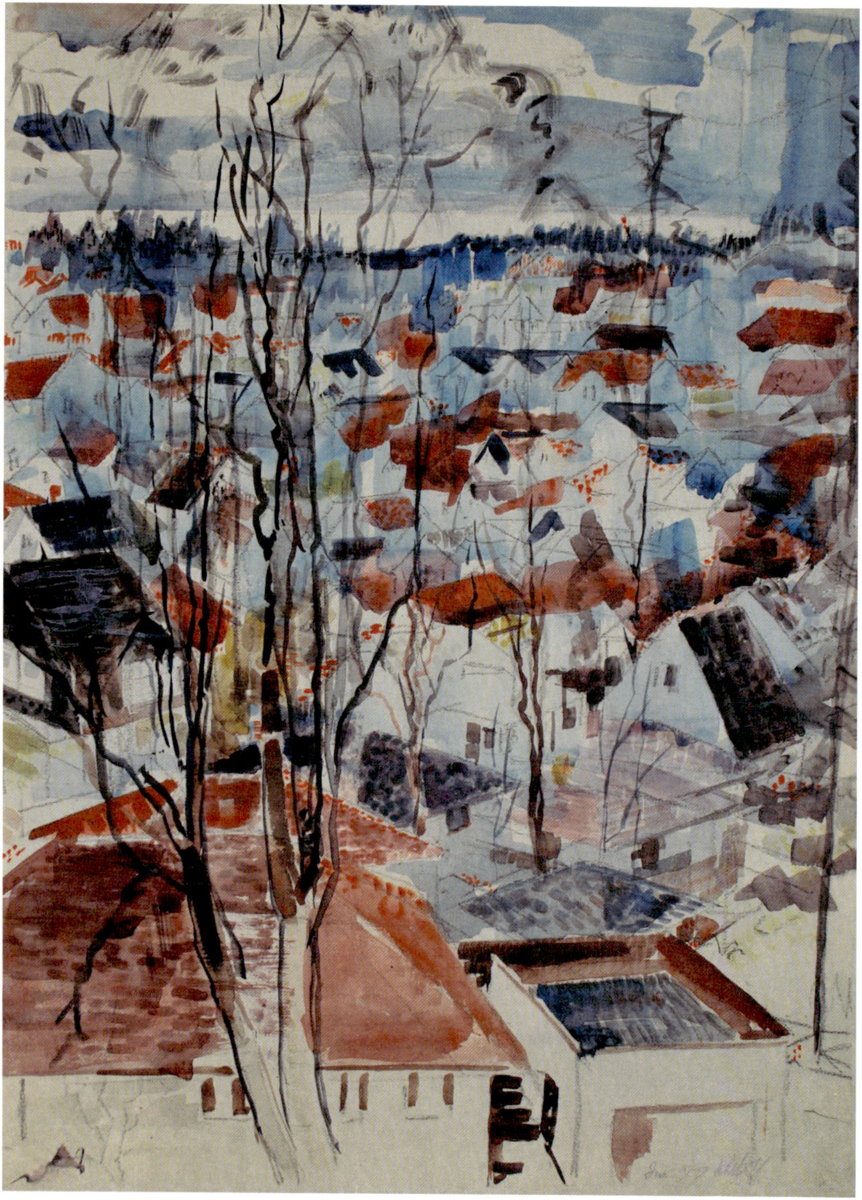

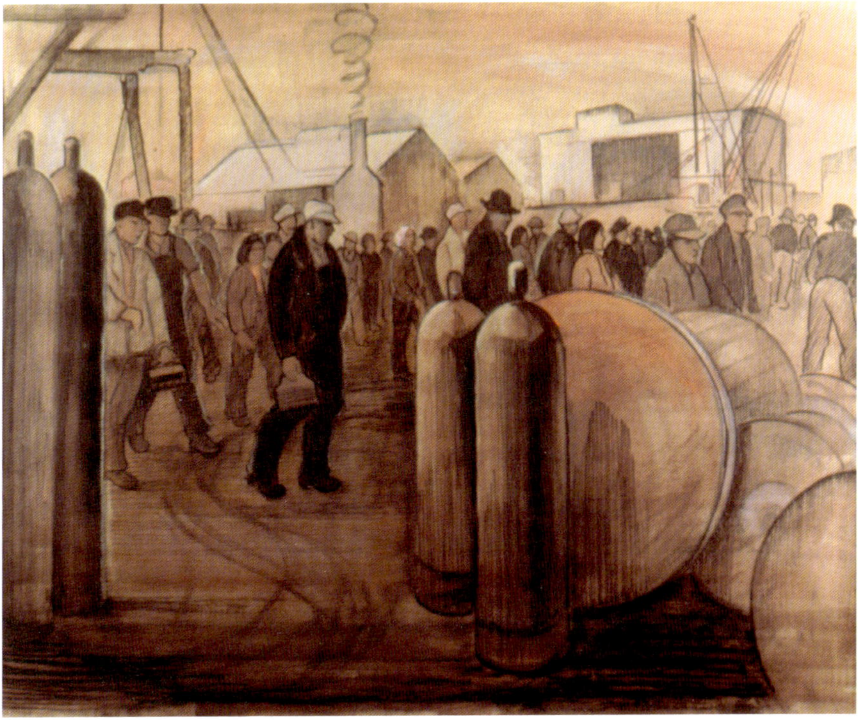

▲ Ina D.D. Uhthoff, *Factory Scene*, circa 1944, watercolour/pastel, 22 ½" x 28 ½"

IMAGE #PDP05543 COURTESY OF THE ROYAL BC MUSEUM AND ARCHIVES

◄ Ina D.D. Uhthoff, *Untitled*, n.d. watercolour on paper 23 ½" x 18"

NANCY WHITE COLLECTION
PHOTO BY NANCY WHITE

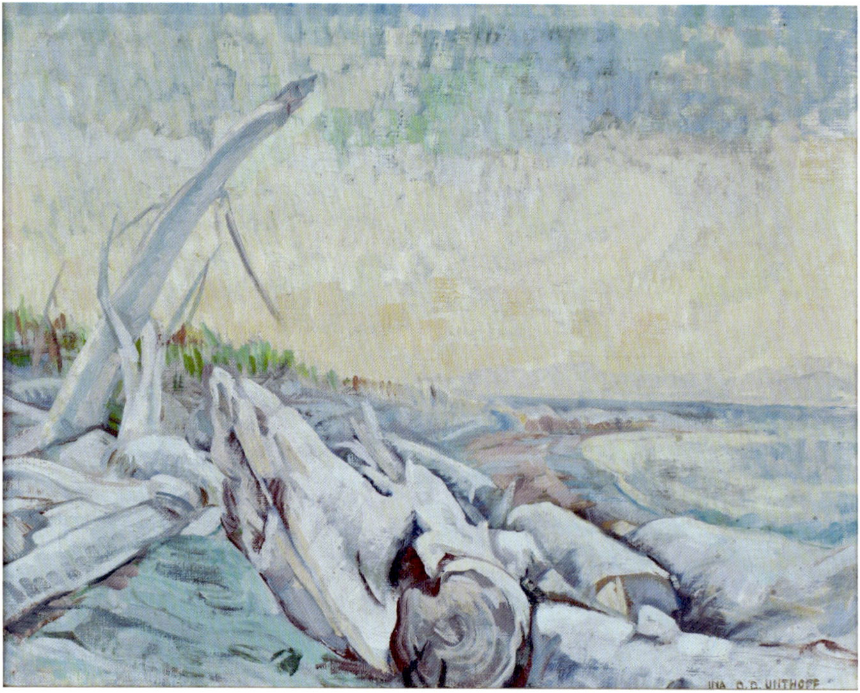

Ina D.D. Uhthoff, *Untitled*, n.d. oil on canvas, 22 ½" x 17 ½"

FIONA HERT COLLECTION
PHOTO BY MICHAEL A. COOK

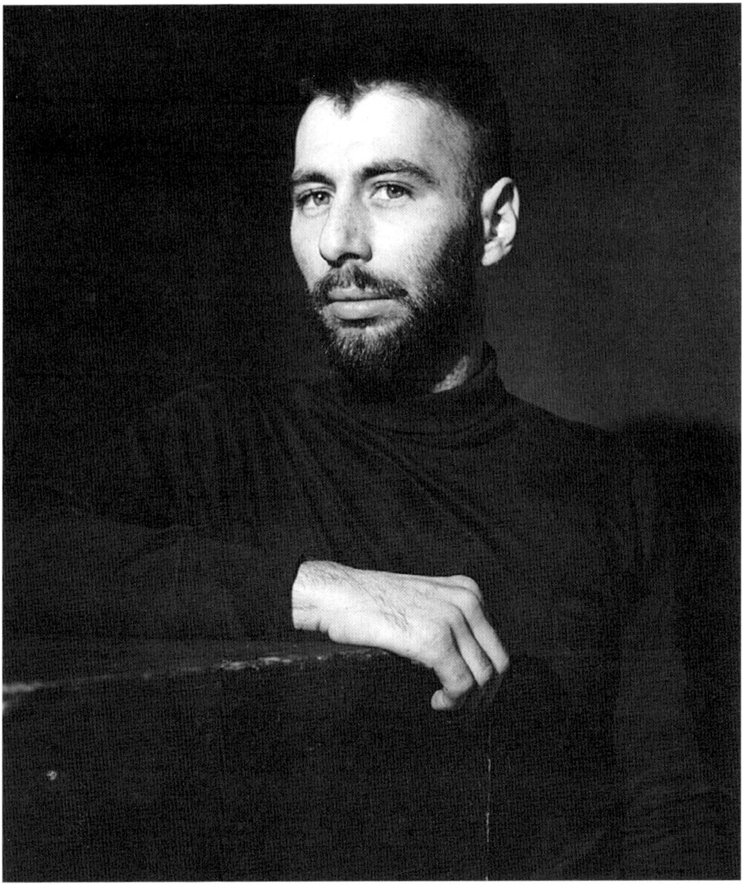

Harry Webb

1927–1995

Harry [and Jessie Webb's] work, a blending of abstraction with landscape, still life or figurative elements, is playful, yet very solid in composition. They echo Matisse and Picasso, who riffed off each other for decades. Their art also parallels that of other pioneering modern painters in Vancouver such as John Koerner, B.C. Binning, Don Jarvis and Lionel Thomas."

—GREGG SIMPSON, BRITISH COLUMBIA ARTIST AND MUSICIAN

Harry James Webb, born in Toronto on March 7, 1927, grew up as an only child in a close community of aunts, uncles and cousins. He loved to draw, beginning early by sketching bicycles and cars. After he completed two years at Danforth Technical High School, his parents sent him to St. Margaret's Sea Training School in Nova Scotia. He served in the Canadian Merchant Marine during the final months of WW II, before relocating to British Columbia.

EARLY YEARS IN VANCOUVER

In 1946, Harry, a newly minted veteran, joined his father and stepmother on the West Coast, eager to enroll in the Vancouver School of Art (VSA) with funding from Veterans Affairs. Instructors included Jack Shadbolt, Lionel Thomas, Peter Aspell and Bruno Bobak. A year later, he met Jessie Hetherington in painting class, and they spent most of their time together, often in the Georgia or Devonshire Hotel beer parlour sketching the patrons. While working part-time in the Vancouver Post Office at Granville and Hastings, Harry became friends with jazz pianist Al Neil, which led to his participation in the founding of the Cellar Jazz Club a decade later. Harry graduated in 1950 and married Jessie that summer. The next ten years, they moved from one apartment to another, often after only a couple of months, while Harry worked night shifts at the post office so he could concentrate on painting and printmaking.

Their circle of friends included artists and designers who were all beginning their careers, such as Bob Reid in typography, John Grinnell in interior design, George and Arlyn Kuthan in illustration, Jack Long in photography and Joy Long in painting. Harry's more restrained geometric arrangements in linocuts gave way to bright colours and dancing forms that celebrate intricate jazz melodies. Images of trios began to appear, and he used them to explore relationships between the characters and the space between them. Boundaries between life and art began to blur and everyday objects such as fridges and walls became canvasses. Harry also produced a series of paintings he called "brush drawings" through which spontaneous brushstrokes defined the negative space, while simultaneously revealing figurative elements, similar to the "automatic" procedure of Dada and surrealistic artists. This would prove valuable when he began to design gardens.

Part of the beat generation, the Webbs were not driven to accumulate wealth, but they recognized the importance of good-quality tools: engraving tools, pigment, Chinese brushes, onionskin, gelatin brayers and thick brown "battleship" linoleum.

LANDSCAPE ARCHITECTURE

In 1955, Harry met architectural photographer Graham Warrington at Bob Reid's printing shop, who in turn introduced him to Desmond Muirhead, a British town planner who soon asked him to join his firm. Specializing in landscape and garden planning for single-family homes in Shaughnessy, Point Grey and West Vancouver's British Properties, they needed an artist to do perspective renderings. At first Harry was worried about "selling-out" to a middle class he had tried hard to escape after the war and saw himself becoming "a square." But as an apprentice landscape architect, he met contractors, engineers and architects; used felt pens, coloured pencils, drawing templates and display boards and adapted his drawing techniques to the work. He realized that he could retain his free spirit and even a degree of anarchy in this new field. Over the next ten years, Harry brought a natural understanding of rhythm and proportion to projects as varied as the Bayshore Inn, Victoria's Centennial Square, the Finning Tractor offices and to dozens of residential gardens in and around Vancouver.

JAZZ AND THEATRE

In 1956, the Musicians and Artists Society opened near Main and Broadway. The club was called the Cellar, and Harry contributed a large mural (enamelled linocut) of a jazz trio, as well as posters for the one-act plays Barry Cramer produced. One night, Harry Redl, a photographer friend, arranged for Kenneth Patchen, the American beat poet, to read at the Cellar. These sessions, released as an LP on the Folkways Label in 1959, have since become a classic recording. Afterwards Harry and Jessie were delighted when Redl brought Patchen to their apartment for tea. The Webbs loved to listen to recordings of poetry, wrote poems themselves and invested in a high-fidelity Heathkit sound system, playing Dave Brubeck, Charlie Parker, Gerry Mulligan and Lennie Tristano. During this period, Harry also created a *Long Playing Painting*, an abstract picture designed to roll past a television camera to be accompanied by live music. An experimental piece, it explored the relationship between visual art, music and time. Harry and Jessie took part in the landmark 1958 exhibit, 100 Years of B.C. Art, at the Vancouver Art Gallery. In 1959, Harry and Jessie moved to the first of what would be a series of rented beach cottages in West Vancouver, with their daughter, Adrienne, age two.

THE 1960S

In 1964, Harry heard that Al Neil wanted to take a break from the music scene and invited him and his new wife, Marguerite, to move into the Dundarave beach house. That same year, Harry received his most significant commission. Park & Tilford Distillery executives initially asked him to design a small garden, where staff could eat lunch at their North Vancouver office. They were also intrigued by the Amazonian-style paradise that Anheuser-Busch had created in Los Angeles and wanted to consider building a public garden. Therefore, they asked Harry to design a two-acre garden on Cotton Road, across from the CN railway line. The master plan, which featured seven gardens resembling a series of interconnected wheels or cogs, was just what the executives were looking for, so he started five years of detailed design and construction. Meanwhile, Harry was involved in founding the British Columbia Society of Landscape Architects (BCSLA), and Justice & Webb had become one of the city's largest firms. Over the next two decades, it provided a training ground for many young designers. Fred Brooks remembers him:

> [He was] a true artist, and it was very important at that time how he represented the profession and helped to incubate the BCSLA. An additional legacy is that everyone who has their BCSLA certificate proudly hanging on their wall owes both its existence *and its design* to Harry.

For many years Harry and his daughter would visit Duthie's Books on Robson Street on the weekends. In the mid-1960s, he was reading Marshall McLuhan and R. Buckminister Fuller and was so enthused about McLuhan's ideas that he wrote a letter to McLuhan on a scroll, some twenty-five feet long, hand-lettered text within a serpentine "river" down the centre. While he was working on it the letter ran across the floor, out the door, through the hallway and into the kitchen. After he developed rheumatoid arthritis Harry Webb rarely produced linocuts; the cityscape he completed in 1964 turned out to be his last print. The wick pen and later felt pens were more comfortable tools to use, so he embarked on an extensive series of sketches of futuristic sheet metal sculptures he called *The Human Head as Architecture,* based on Buckminister Fuller's exploration of the geometry of human thought.

In 1966, McGavin Toastmaster commissioned Harry to design a unique one-piece fiberglass bus stop for their building at Broadway and Arbutus. When the prototype was installed, an industry newsletter reported that civic authorities were not keen on the idea of having flagrant advertising on the shelter but did not seem too opposed to some fragrant advertising. The idea of injecting the baking smell sprang from a desire to pipe heat into the structure, and the closest source just happened to be the bakery.

Park & Tilford Gardens opened on January 25, 1969, the first of seven themed gardens. Vancouver sculptor Jack Harman created bronze busts of plant explorers, and there were two aviaries: one with cockatoos and ring-necked parrots and the other with songbirds. The project provided Harry with the chance to design dozens of elements, comprising pergolas, bridges, screens, brackets and finials. These included Christmas display plantings, covered with plexiglass domes and heated by the distillery operations. The gardens were a great success and have since become a cherished public amenity in North Vancouver.

When Harry and Jessie divorced in 1972, he was at the peak of his career and Jessie was at a low point in her own. He remained in the West Vancouver house with their daughter, now fifteen years old, and Jessie moved in with her parents nearby.

In landscape architecture, a great deal of work occurs after the drawings are completed. Harry enjoyed working with neighbourhood residents on the programming and construction of public parks, for example, the redevelopment of McLean Park in Strathcona, where locals collaborated with city planners, landscape architects and contractors to construct a bandstand and putting green. At the same time, he defended the value of the design drawing as artwork in its own right, given its value "as an ordering system, a score (as in music) that energizes and involves people."

In 1974, Harry met Carmen Cote, a Montreal landscape architect, and the next year, after she moved to B.C., they began a comfortable life together that would last two decades.

In the early 1980s, he was more confident than ever as a designer, providing cedar suppliers and local precast concrete fence fabricators with portfolios of ideas for their promotional efforts. Harry designed the interior of the Avant Gardener store in Kitsilano some thirty years after working on the interior design and signage with Jessie for the Pick-a-Pocket Book Shop in Dundarave.

RETIREMENT

Having four granddaughters in common, Harry and Jessie saw each other at birthday parties and other family gatherings. He used alcohol to dull his pain from years of rheumatoid arthritis, and realizing this would compromise his health, he quit drinking several times. Meanwhile, he continued to design gardens and prepare site development plans for residential and commercial projects. This abruptly ended in January 1991 when Harry was struck with an acute case of Wernicke's disease; within weeks, it was clear he would never walk without support, drive a car or draw again. Having lost both physical and emotional stability, he spent the next few years reading the paper and discussing the news. Harry suffered a fatal heart attack in the spring of 1995, age sixty-eight.

Harry Webb's work is held in private collections and at the Vancouver Art Gallery.

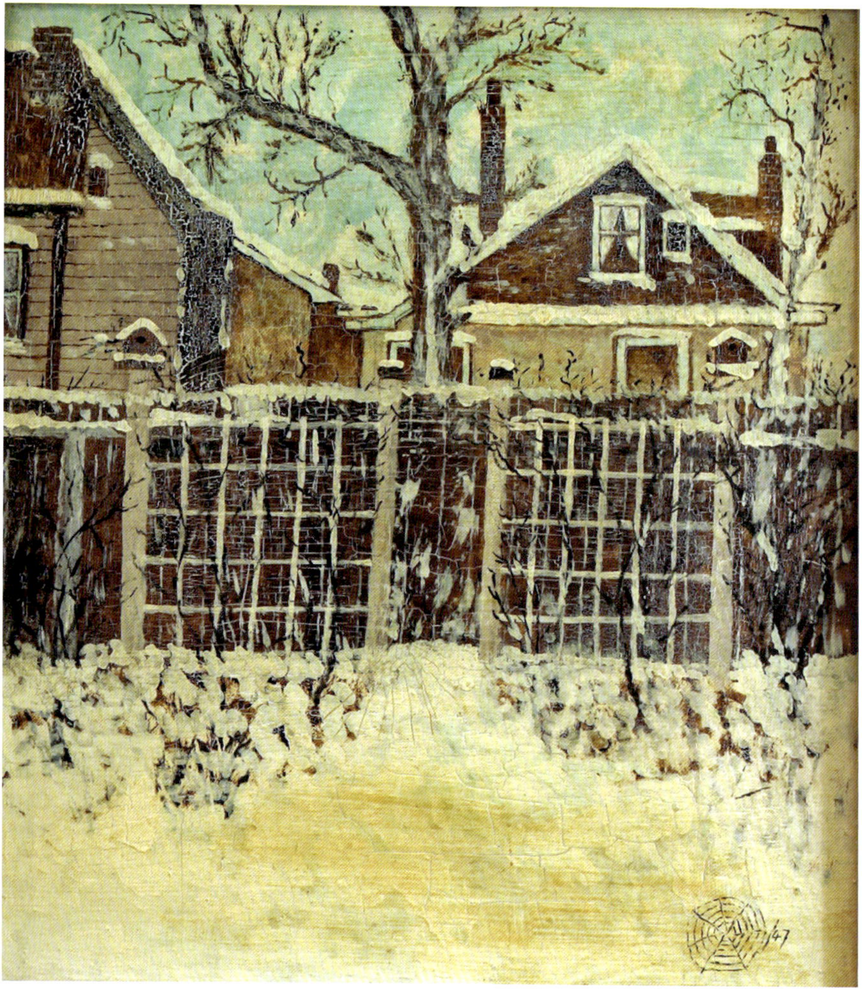

Harry Webb, *Backyard, Kenilworth Avenue, Toronto*, circa 1947, oil on board, 16" x 14"

PRIVATE COLLECTION
DAN FAIRCHILD PHOTOGRAPHY

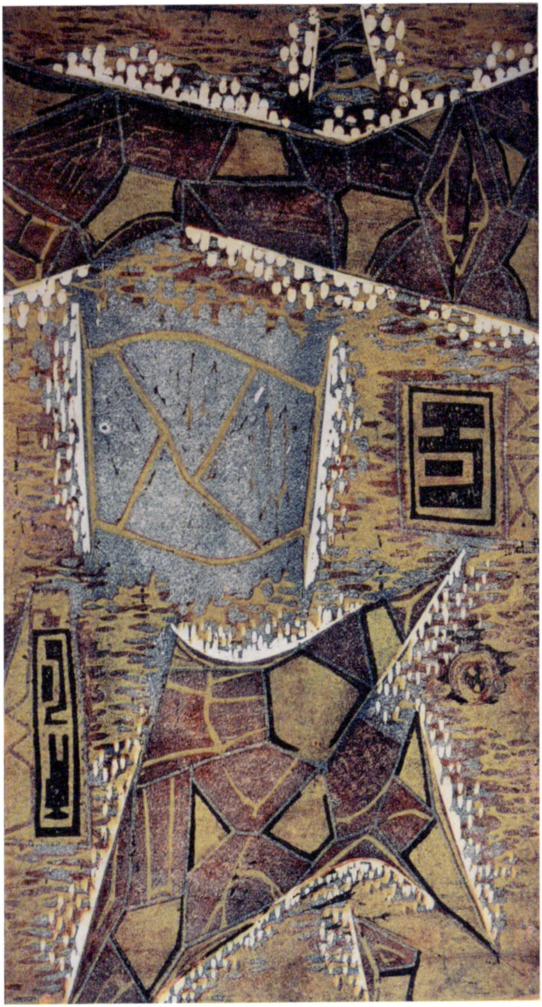

Harry Webb, *No Left Turn*, 1950, progressive linocut, 15 ½" x 8 ½"

PRIVATE COLLECTION

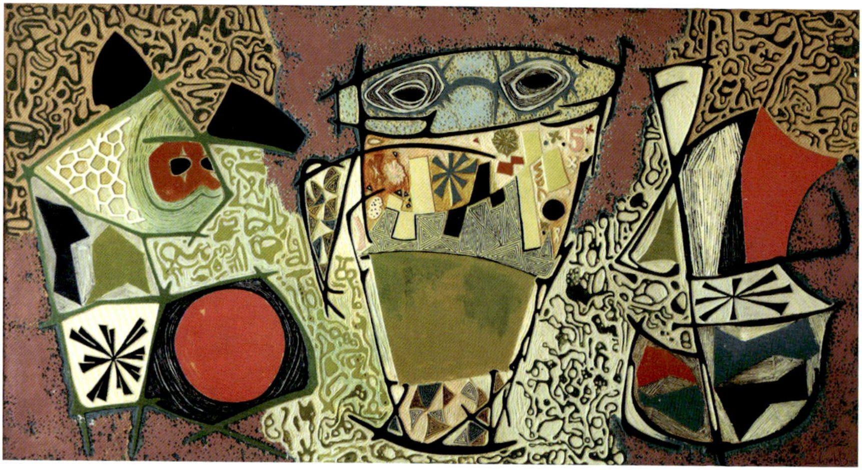

▲ Harry Webb, *The Trio*, 1954, enameled linocut, 38 ½" x 73"

PRIVATE COLLECTION
DAN FAIRCHILD PHOTOGRAPHY

➤ Harry Webb, *Untitled*, 1956, progressive linocut, 8" x 7"

PRIVATE COLLECTION
PHOTO BY JOHN SEALE

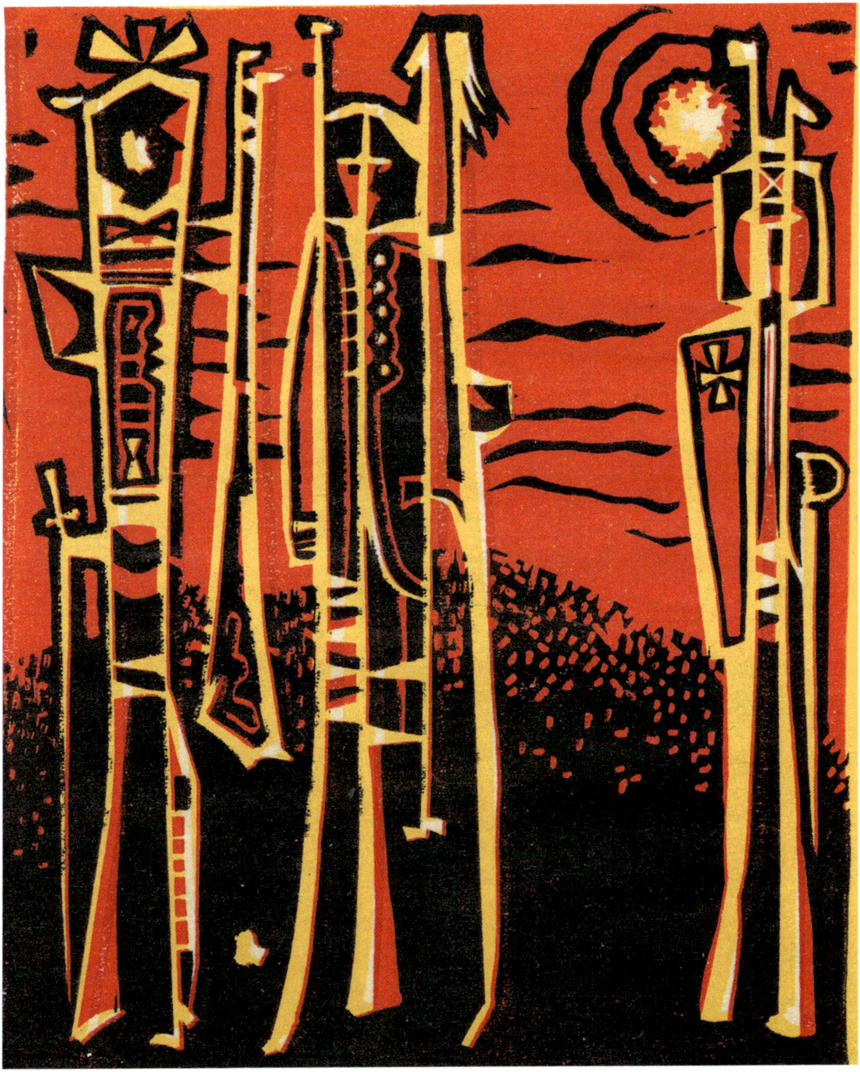

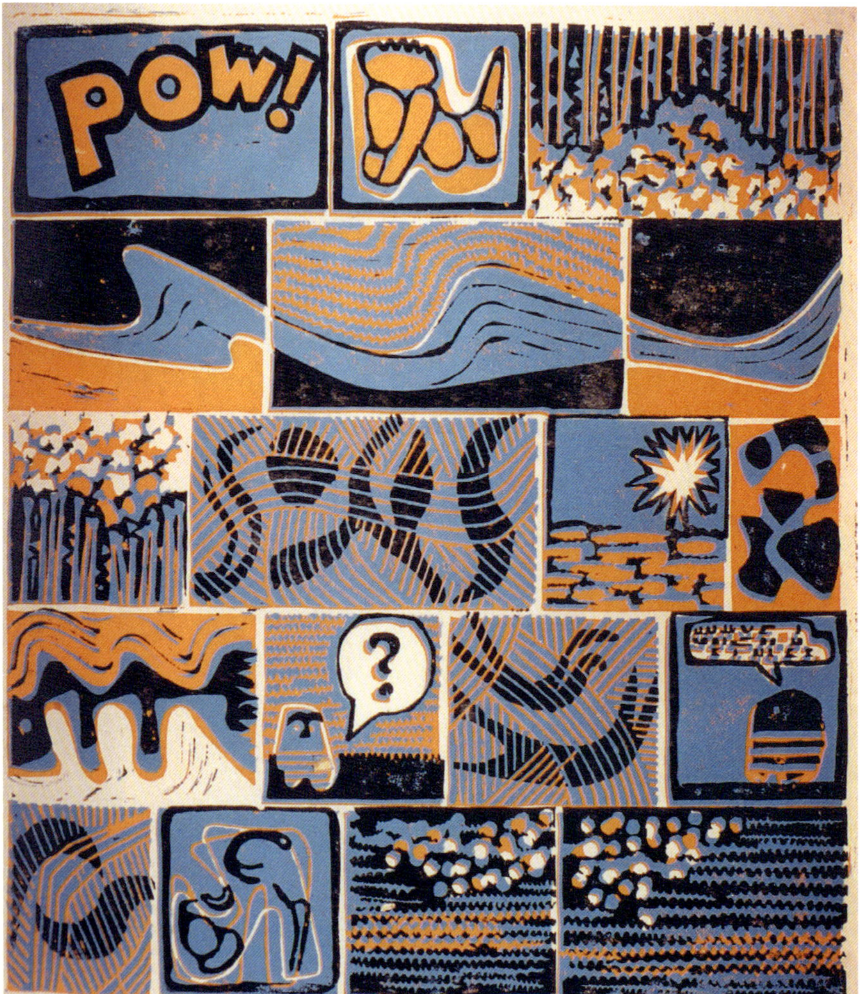
POW!
?

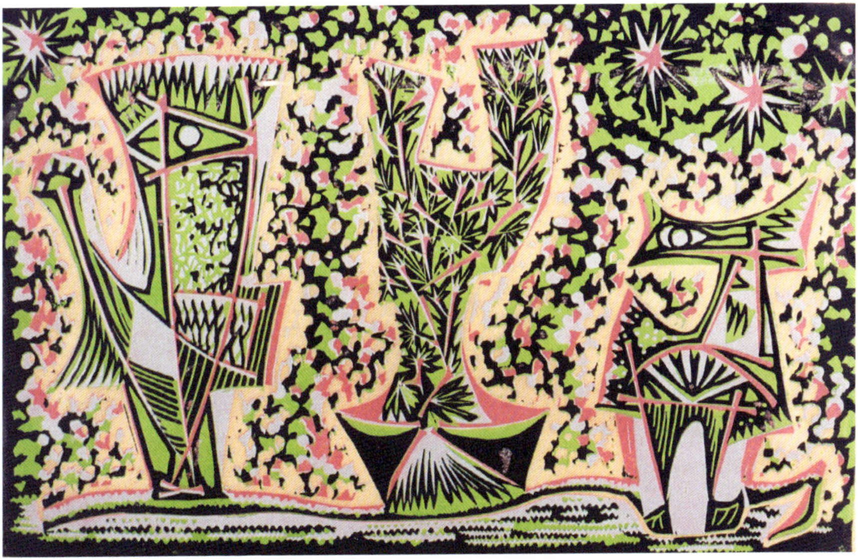

▲ Harry Webb, *The Purchase of a Potted Pine by a Rare Bird*, 1957, progressive linocut, 9 ½" x 15"

PRIVATE COLLECTION
PHOTO BY JOHN SEALE

◄ Harry Webb, *"Pow!"*, n.d., progressive linocut, 15 ½" x 13 ½"

PRIVATE COLLECTION
PHOTO BY JOHN SEALE

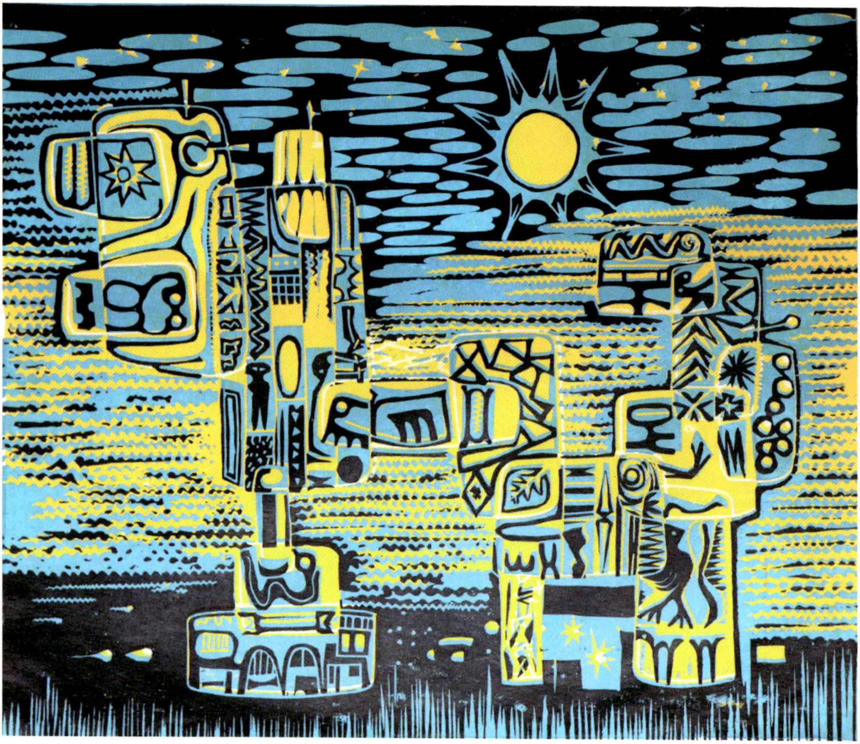

Harry Webb, *Untitled* (Cityscape), 1964, progressive linocut, 14 ½" x 17 ½"

PRIVATE COLLECTION
DAN FAIRCHILD PHOTOGRAPHY

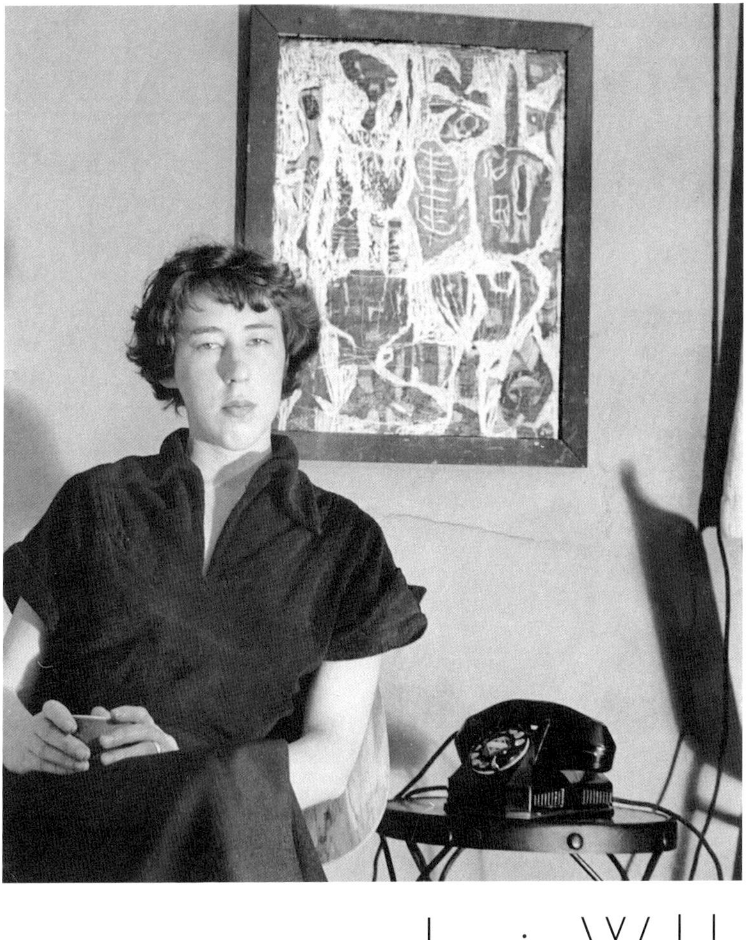

Jessie Webb

1930–2011

> *"The progressive prints, as well as the water colors and wood engravings by Jessie Webb, have apparently a connection with reality. Titles such as* Left Turn *and* Neon Night *suggest city streets with traffic and other signs and block divisions as might be seen from above. In all instances the exhibits have a richly decorative aspect, an aesthetic charm."*
>
> —PALETTE, VANCOUVER SUN

Born in Vancouver on October 16, 1930, Jessie Marion Hetherington grew up in Grandview spending her early years mostly with her mother while her father, Percy, a marine engineer was away "on the boats." After suffering a serious mastoid infection at the age of six, she slowly recovered and began to demonstrate what would be a lifelong commitment to art.

THE VANCOUVER SCHOOL OF ART

In 1939, her teachers recognized her talent and recommended she attend the Saturday Morning Junior Classes as the Vancouver School of Art (VSA). The instructors there included Jock McDonald, B.C. Binning and Fred Amess. In 1947, Jessie began post-secondary courses at the VSA while completing grade 12. Her paintings and pastels from then include views of Stanley Park and Coal Harbour that capture the dark postwar mood in Vancouver. One of her high school friends was Arnold Belkin, the future great Canadian-Mexican muralist. He left for Mexico soon after he graduated, writing excitedly to Jessie in 1948: "Really Jess, you can't beat Mexico for studying art and meeting artists. All schools are free, even for foreigners… I have a studio penthouse with a tile floor and all the conveniences and I pay 25 pesos monthly… Why don't you come down here?..."

After school she worked part-time in the Fine Arts & Music Department in the Vancouver Public Library at Main and Hastings.

In 1949, Jessie met Harry Webb in painting class. They were both greatly influenced by VSA teachers Lionel Thomas and Peter Aspell, as well as the art of Wassily Kandinsky, Paul Klee, Joan Miro and Arshile Gorky and books including *Vision in Motion* by Lazlo Moholy-Nagy, *Language of Vision* by Gyorgy Kepes and *The Dada Painters and Poets*. The couple soon became inseparable, and on a hot afternoon in July 1950, they married at the Registrar's office.

Jessie's paintings depicted Vancouver with its many neon signs dissolving light onto the dark wet streets. Harry supported her need to question the established social imperatives by combining a commitment to making art with domestic life.

PAINTINGS AND LINOCUTS

In the fall of 1951, Jessie became art editor of *pm*, a short-lived arts magazine that borrowed production concepts from the American magazine *Flair*, featuring die-cut pages, foldouts and tipped-in plates. The art was so well-received that readers encouraged the team to create original silkscreen prints and linocuts to pull out of the magazine and use as Christmas cards. Writers Phyllis Webb, Marya Fiamengo and Al Neil and artists, including Jack Shadbolt, Don Jarvis and Patricia Thomas, contributed to the publication. With about sixty pages, *pm* was a little bigger than a pocket book. Meanwhile, VSA instructors Fred Amess and B.C. Binning were developing the Art in Living Group, which had been founded in 1943 to promote good design as morally and spiritually uplifting and the advantages of planning your own environment. Jessie and Harry designed their own coffee table and a series of fiberglass pendant lamps decorated with linocuts. At that time, they were reading the San Francisco poets and making their own shoes with latex and leather.

In 1952, Jessie and Harry participated in the exhibition of prints that coincided with the opening of the new Vancouver Art Gallery on

West Georgia Street. Concluding that painting and printmaking suited their goals, and with few opportunities to use a mechanical press, Jessie created most of her multicolour progressive linocuts by hand.

In 1956, Jessie was disappointed, but not surprised, when she was laid off from her job halfway through her pregnancy. Feeling healthy and energetic, she created hats and baby outfits and their daughter, Adrienne, was born on March 8, 1957. The following year, Jessie continuing printmaking and painting while designing and fabricating murals for Muirhead & Justice's designed gardens and creating the decor for the Lougheed Hotel dining room in Burnaby. In 1961, her friend Bob Reid was producing a catalogue for the inaugural Burnaby National Print Show, and he arranged for Jessie to create a full-colour graphic for the cover. Her work appeared in the show, as well as in a solo exhibition at the Arti Domo Gallery and at the Mary Frazee Gallery in 1963 and 1970. After settling in a West Vancouver beach cottage, Jessie and Harry created a store interior for Stephen and Elsa Franklin. Preparing to open the Pick-a-Pocket Bookshop, the young writers and editors commissioned them to design and fabricate the furnishings and exterior signage. The cash desk was done up as a carousel, complete with a blue and green oilcloth canopy.

WEST VANCOUVER

Soon after moving to Ambleside, Jessie became interested in documenting the old cottages and historical scenes depicting the local community. Having learned traditional oil painting techniques from Lionel Thomas, including rabbit skin glue for sizing the canvas before applying the paint, she used these techniques for representational and historical works. However, despite her talents, ambition and dedication to art, Jessie was wracked with self-doubt, which led to her destroying her art. She wanted to be respected as a serious artist but had grown up to accept a domestic value system that was at odds with this ideal.

In 1965, after renting various beach homes near Dundarave for nearly a decade, Harry and Jessie bought a small WW II bungalow in the area, and Jessie learned yoga, discovered health food and sewed everything from patio pajamas to floor-length tablecloths. Over these years, Harry was building his career as a landscape architect, while Jessie became increasingly isolated and dispirited. With many of their friends experiencing separations and divorces, she wrote: "Marriage on rocks. Divorced 1972. I moved in with retired parents—father's home 15th and Inglewood. Adrienne stayed with Harry. We were all close friends with six couples during previous 20 years—all had fine children & all successful in their careers. ALL had split up."

SINGLE AGAIN

After a year or so with her parents, Jessie found an apartment and began working at the Lions Gate Times newspaper. She sold classified advertising and enjoyed visiting the presses, which reminded her of collaborations with commercial printers. However, as she recalled, "the newspaper job wasn't going to pay enough to keep up with inflation," so in 1977, she began waitressing at the White Spot Coffee Shop. Pragmatic enough to ignore the social stigma associated with this work, she may have viewed it as a period of redemption, or possibly a penance for past failures.

Years later, Jessie returned to painting, experimenting with acrylics. She realized her goal of creating depth and luminosity, and the resulting series of still lifes, indicated a return to her roots as an artist driven to master technical challenges. Jessie created a series of interactive paintings "with curved surfaces and moveable parts that blurred the line between painting and sculpture," including a spherical piece depicting the interior of an American tavern.

The notion of moving beyond prototypes was at odds with Jessie's need for autonomy.

EXPERIMENTATION AND PROTOTYPES

Through the late 1980s, Jessie painted corner grocery stores. She liked them because they represented a surviving artifact from a world that had disappeared. She produced a series of linocuts based on the Fraser Grocery, which stood at 58th Avenue.

The Record Store (JW, 2007)
Please ask the engineer to play that riff again–
I do believe I heard it first when I was ten
Was that when most of us were into Zen?
No–long before–down at the store–
You must remember that fantastic store
It's there no more–the record store–
That sold the cactus needles!

Jessie also painted strippers dancing in local pubs, exhibiting in 1982 at the Marion Scott Gallery in Vancouver. Intrigued by the social normalization of a naked woman cavorting while fully dressed men drink beer, she found it remarkable that the woman's nudity remained so unremarkable in today's society, viewing it as a counterpoint to *Le déjeuner sur l'herbe* by Edouard Manet in how it raises questions about the objectification of women. Through this period, she focused on babysitting her four granddaughters, all the while making dolls, painting the girls' portraits and producing an original illustrated poem for each and every birthday.

In the early 1990s, Jessie completed a series of impressionist landscapes with oil pastels and paper collages depicting Stanley Park and Lost Lagoon. Her subject matter had come full circle back to the park after fifty years. Now the images were comprised of *Western Living* magazines and Nabob Tradition coffee bags enriching the landscapes with a layer of calligraphy.

During her 70s, Jessie produced light-hearted poems that featured arguments between bowling trophies and glue spoons, as well as a dialogue between sperm and an egg in a petri dish while a rubber glove enters to perform in vitro fertilization. In the early 2000s, a *Lux Knitting Book* pattern from WWII inspired Jessie's last major creative endeavor. Adapting a design of knitted hexagons, she created a series of shawls, treating each one as a separate exploration of colour and texture on themes that included *Jasper Johns, Bollywood, Queen Charlotte, Kind of Blue, Nights in Tunisia, Polka Dots & Moonbeams and M&M's.*

She continued to see old friends occasionally, including artist Joy Long whom she had known since art school, but the demons that contributed to her marriage breakdown continued to haunt her. Her daughter became increasingly aware that Jessie was a hoarder, filling up the apartment with canvases, framing supplies, brushes, wool, tools, dress material, books, compact disks. By the time Jessie broke her leg in 2009, there was little room for a wheelchair or a walker.

For nearly eighty years, Jessie Webb led a self-directed life that revolved around art. She produced work that was every bit as substantive and avant-garde as that of the men around her, during a period when few women were regarded as fully-fledged players. She retained a genuine curiosity about culture and society and brought a uniquely creative point of view to everything. She continued to work until four months before her death, and facing her final illness with some disbelief, she exclaimed, "But I have four projects on the go!" Jessie Webb died of lung cancer in North Vancouver on April 21, 2011.

Jesse Webb's work is held in private collections and at the Vancouver Art Gallery.

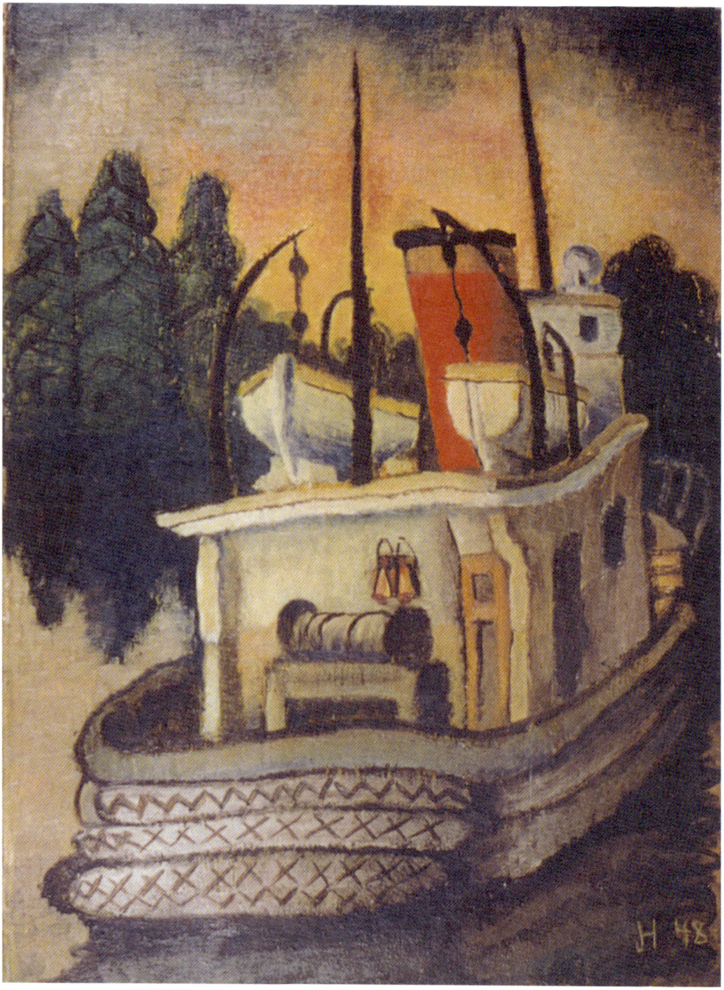

▲ Jessie Webb, *The Lorraine in Coal Harbour*, 1948, oil on canvas, 23 ½" x 18"

PRIVATE COLLECTION
PHOTO BY JOHN SEALE

➤ Jessie Webb, *Chinese Rain*, 1950, watercolour, 12" x 9"

PRIVATE COLLECTION
PHOTO BY INGEBORG HARDMAN

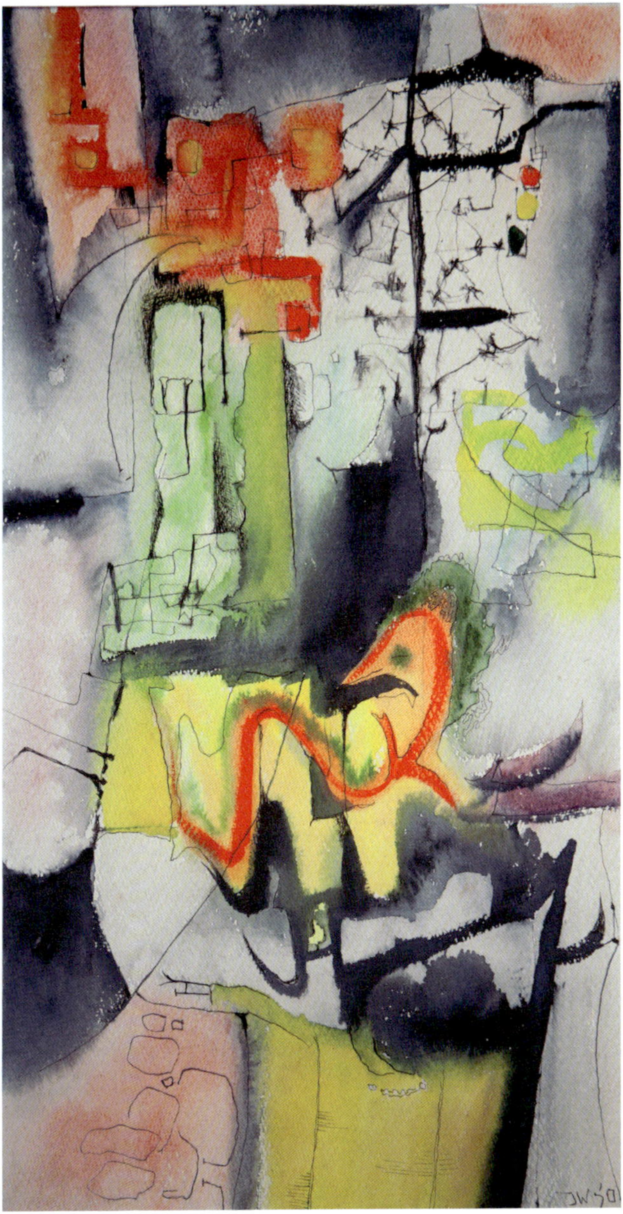

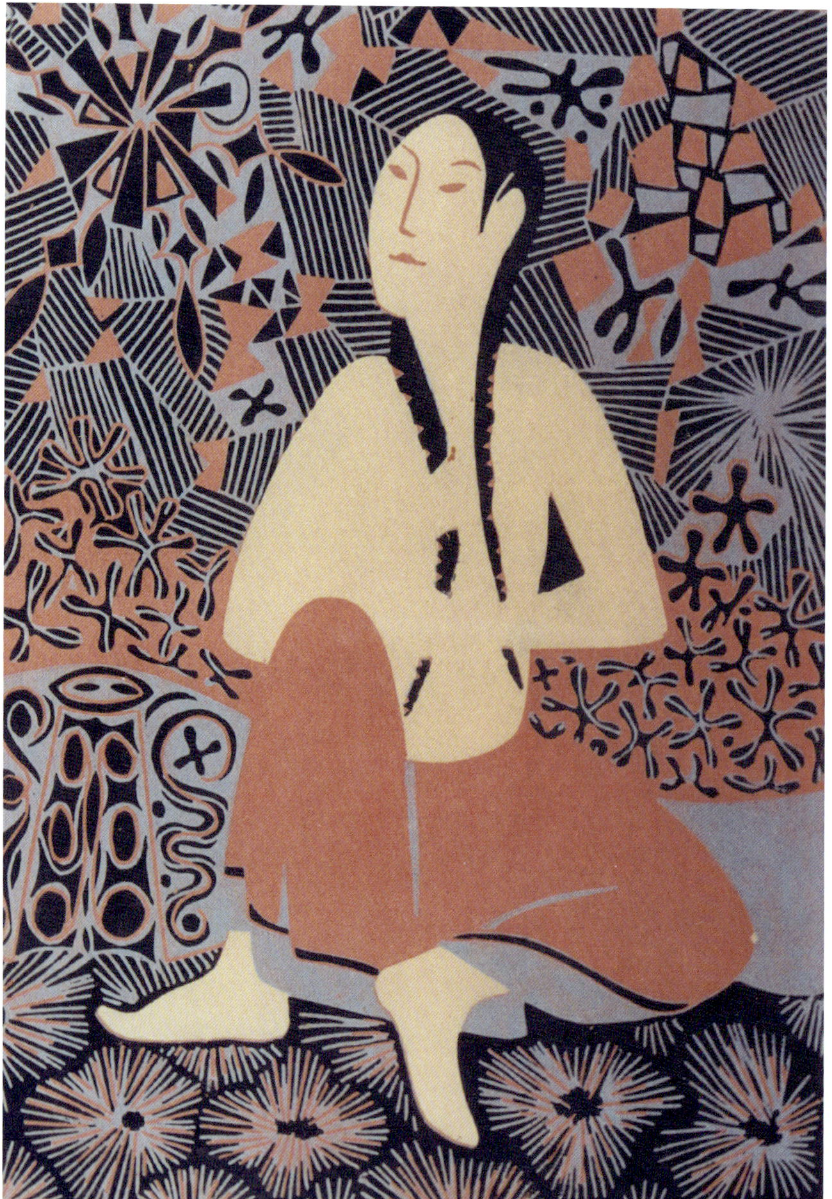

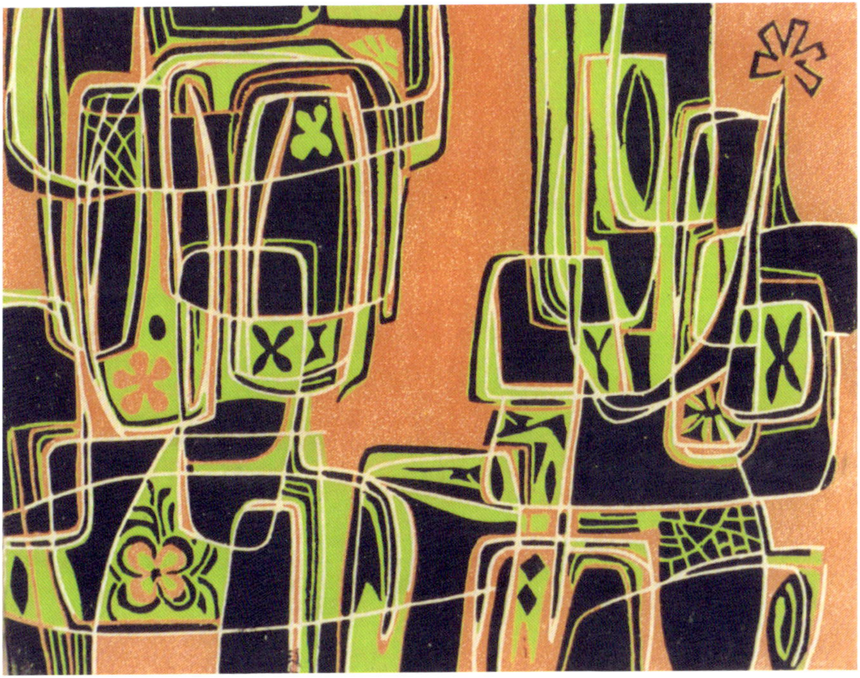

▲ Jessie Webb, *Untitled*, 1961, progressive linocut, 12 3/4" x 17 1/2"

PRIVATE COLLECTION
PHOTO BY DAVID BROWN

◄ Jessie Webb, *Untitled*, 1958, progressive linocut, 15" x 10"

PRIVATE COLLECTION
PHOTO BY DAVID BROWN

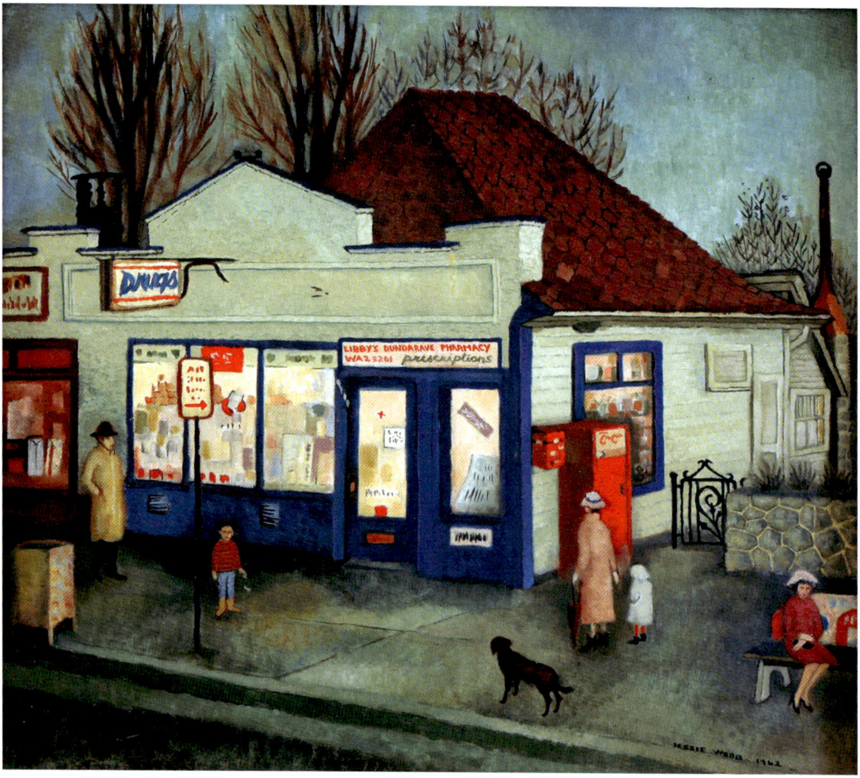

Jessie Webb, *Libby's Drugstore*, 1962, oil on canvas, 27 ½" x 31 ½"

PRIVATE COLLECTION

DAN FAIRCHILD PHOTOGRAPHY

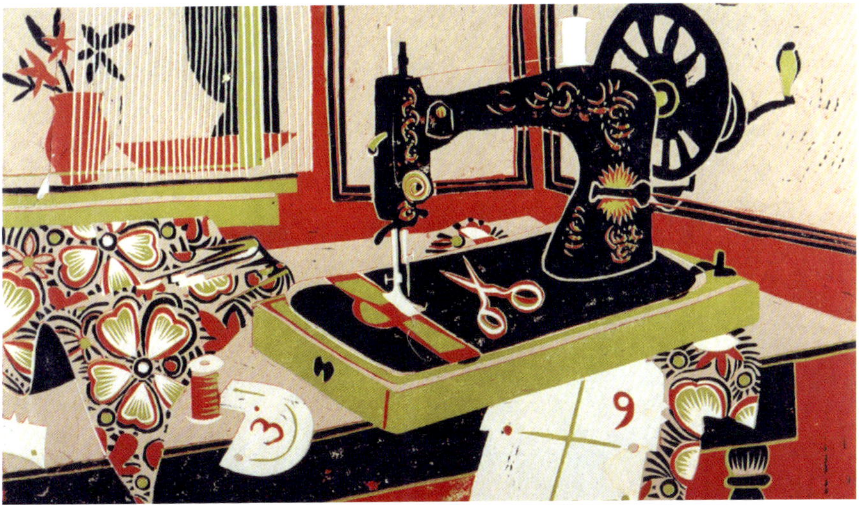

Jessie Webb, *Joy's Sewing Machine*, 1964, progressive linocut, 11 1/2" x 19"

PRIVATE COLLECTION
PHOTO BY JOHN SEALE

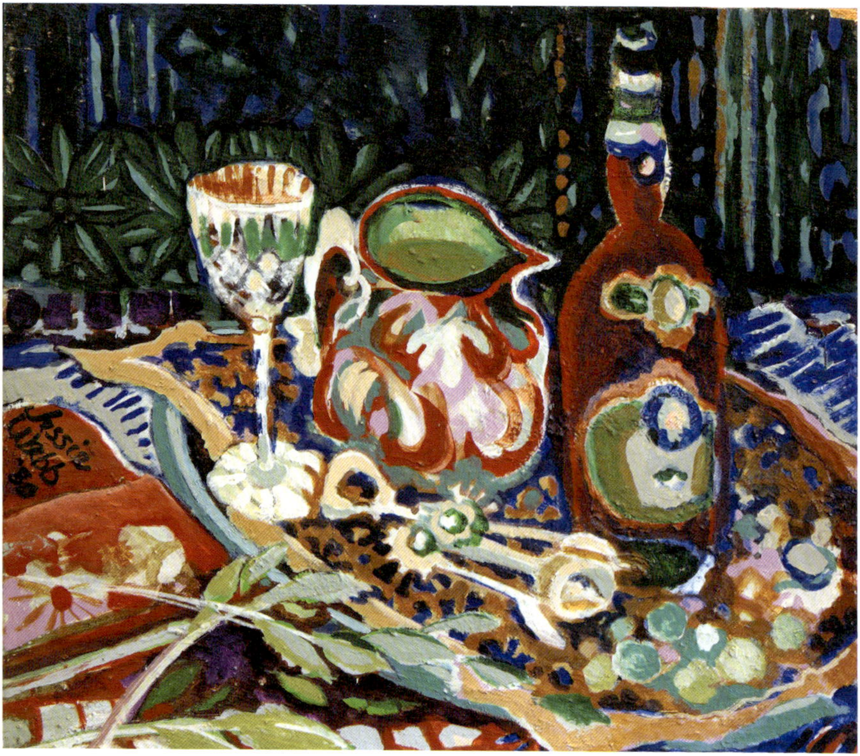

Jessie Webb, *Still Life*, 1980, acrylic, 18" x 20"

PRIVATE COLLECTION
DAN FAIRCHILD PHOTOGRAPHY

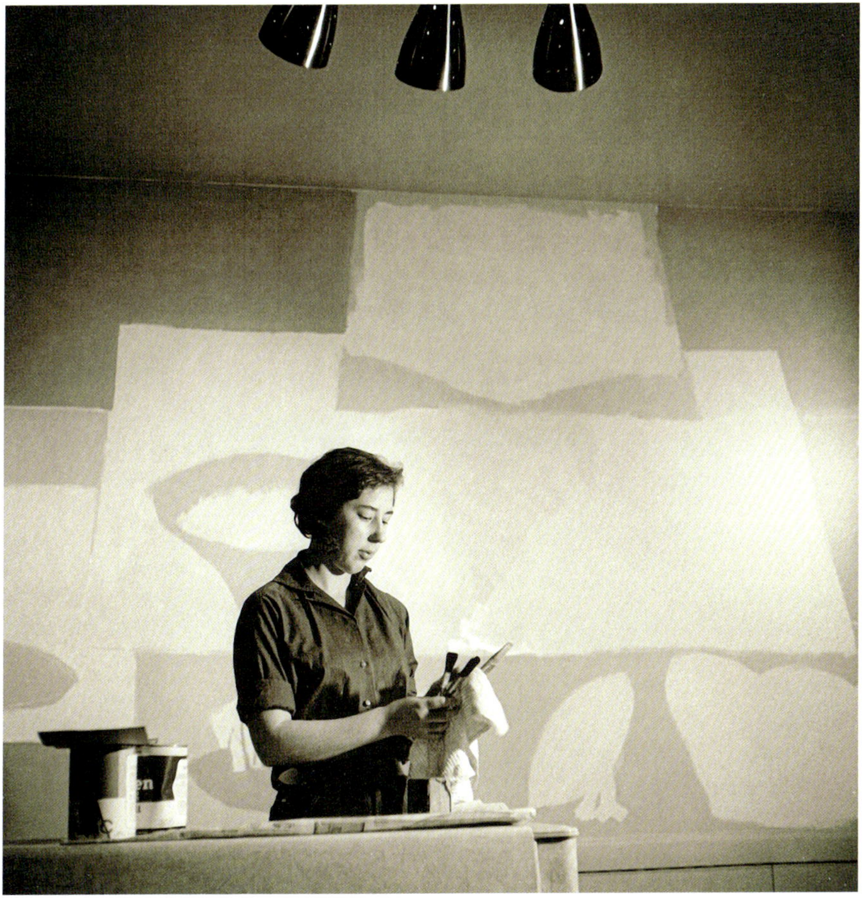

Jessie Webb painting mural in Vancouver, circa 1959

PHOTO BY JACK V. LONG

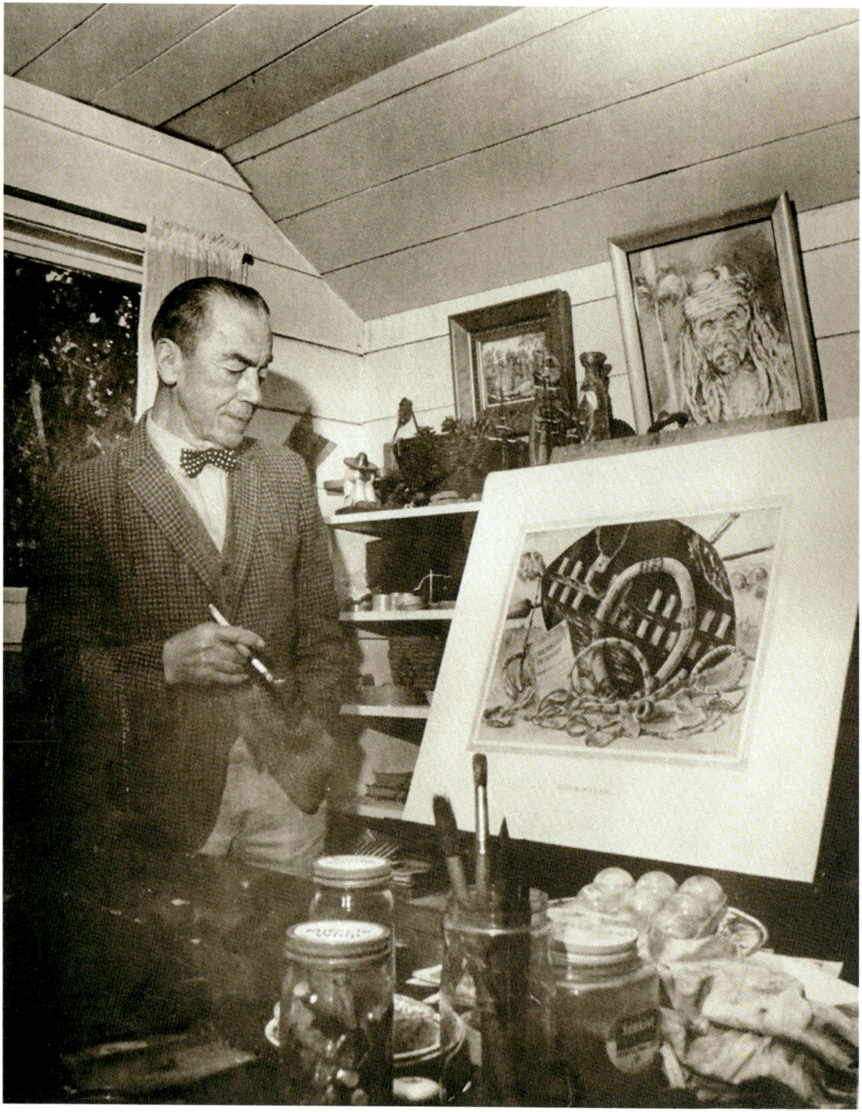

Arthur Pitts in his studio, Erin Cottage, Saanich Penninsula, circa 1963

PHOTO COURTESY OF THE SIDNEY MUSEUM

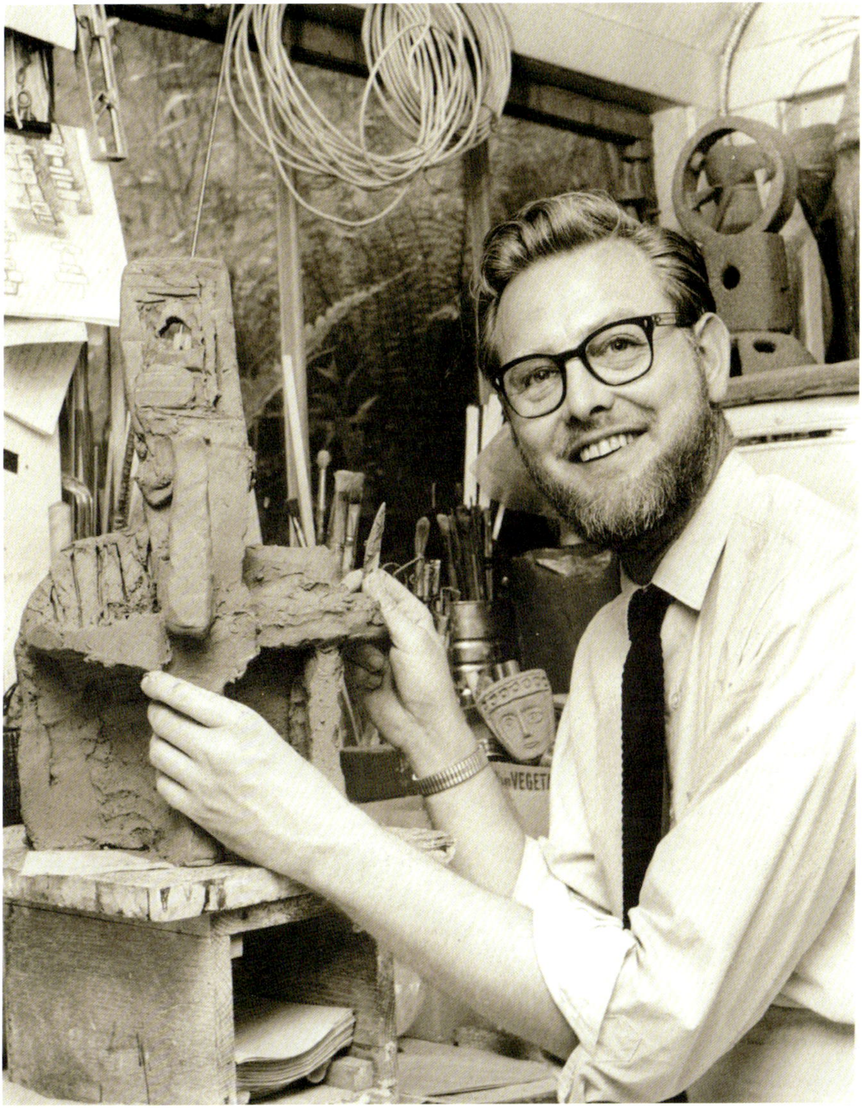

Jack Hardman in his Burnaby studio, 1964

PHOTO BY BASIL KING

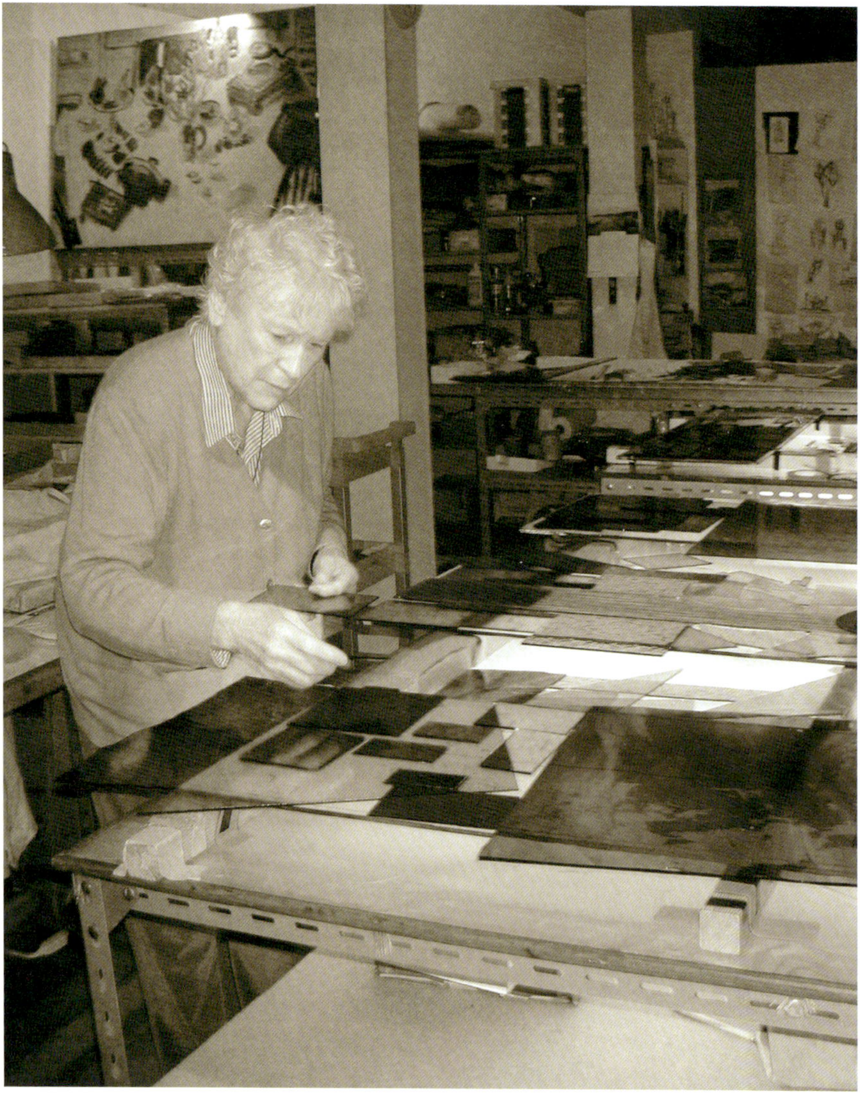

Mary Filer in her Vancouver studio, 2007

PHOTOGRAPHY BY M.E. LINARDIC

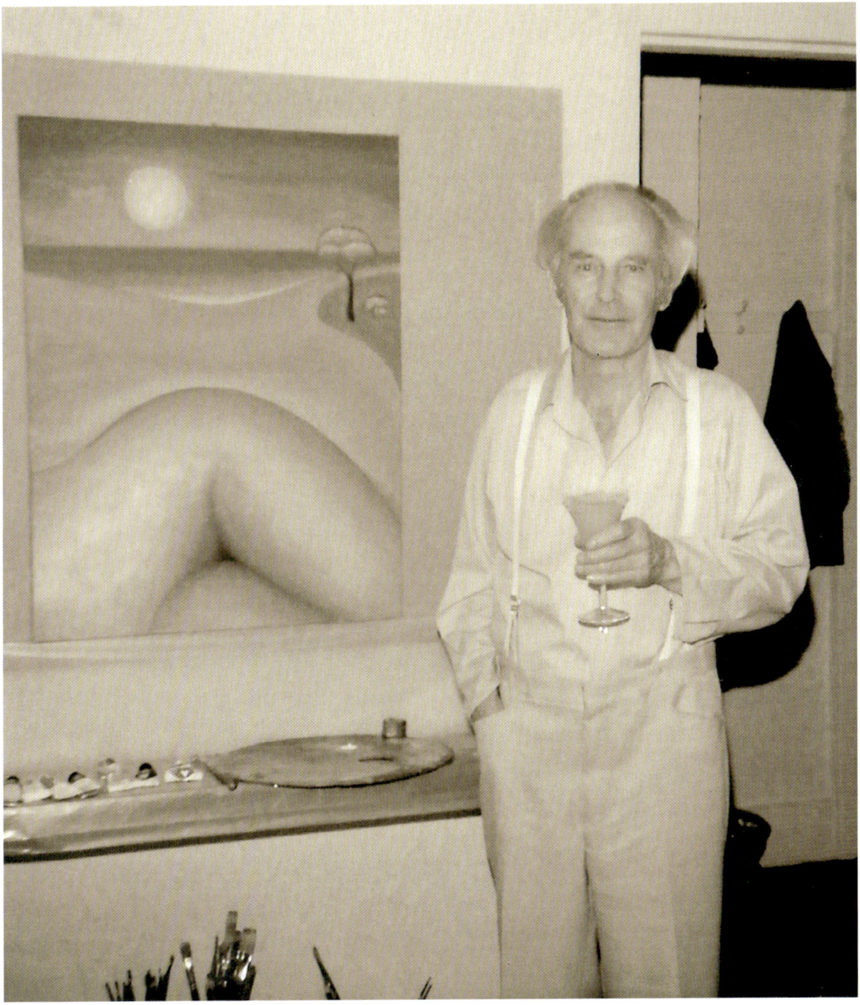

George Fertig in his livingroom in Vancouver, 1981

PHOTO BY EVELYN FERTIG

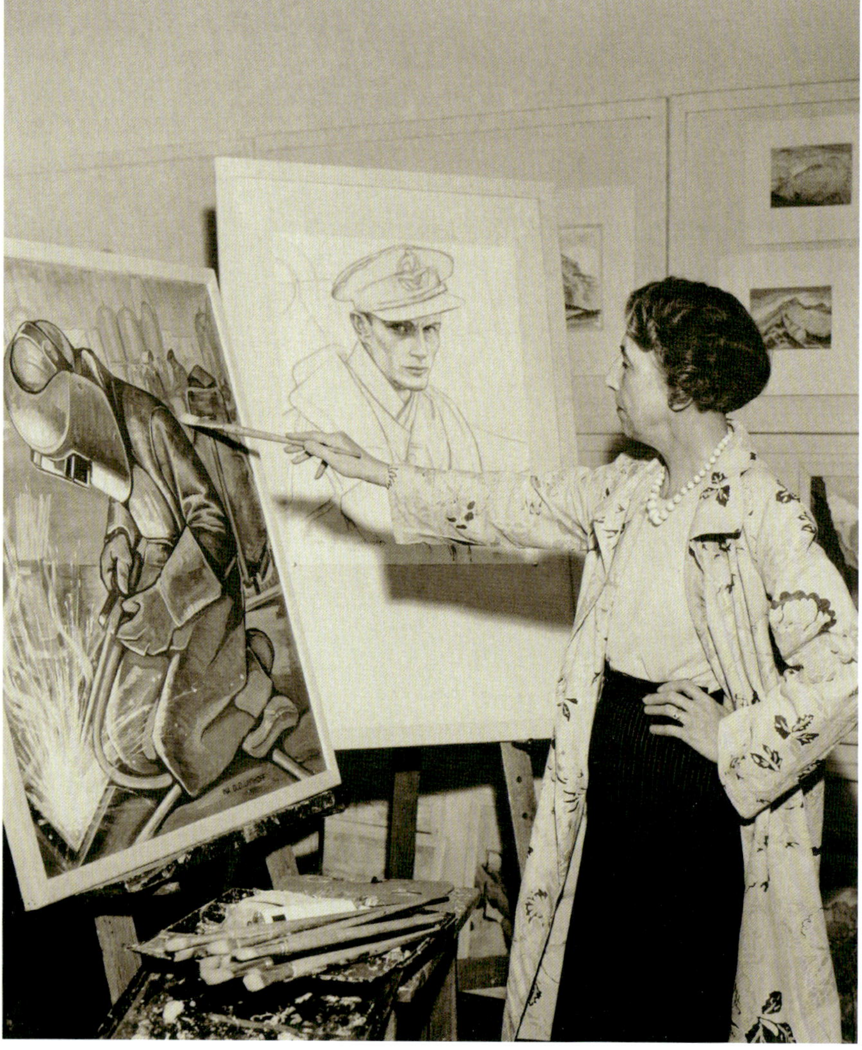

Ina D.D. Uhthoff in her Victoria studio, 1944

UHTHOFF FAMILY COLLECTION. PHOTOGRAPHER UNKNOWN